Gallipoli
The Ottoman Campaign

Edward J. Erickson

Pen & Sword
MILITARY

First published in Great Britain in 2010 by
Pen & Sword Military
an imprint of
Pen & Sword Books Ltd
47 Church Street
Barnsley
South Yorkshire
S70 2AS

A CIP catalogue record for this book is available from the British
Library

Printed and bound in England by CPI Antony Rowe

Pen & Sword Books Ltd incorporates the imprints of Pen & Sword
Aviation, Pen & Sword Maritime, Pen & Sword Military,
Wharncliffe Local History, Pen & Sword Select, Pen & Sword
Military Classics and Leo Cooper.

For a complete list of Pen & Sword titles please contact
PEN & SWORD BOOKS LIMITED
47 Church Street, Barnsley, South Yorkshire, S70 2AS, England
E-mail: enquiries@pen-and-sword.co.uk
Website: www.pen-and-sword.co.uk

Contents

Dedicated to my very good friends
Stephen P. Dawkins, US Foreign Service (retired)
The Revd Dr Wayne D. Pokorny
Professor Yigal Sheffy, Tel Aviv University
Professor John Gooch, University of Leeds
Professor Keith Wilson, University of Leeds
Ms Jennifer Collins
who all encouraged me to write

List of Plates

List of Maps

The maps in this book are copied from the 3-volume Turkish official history of the Gallipoli campaign, which contains an astonishing total of 124 colour maps. These maps are packed with graphic information, which significantly adds to our knowledge of these events. This is particularly true in comprehending which Ottoman units were involved in the fighting and where they were located. The maps also aid in the development of coherent understandings of Ottoman orders of battle. The maps, themselves, are based on Ottoman tactical maps, war diaries and situation reports from the campaign that are located in the Turkish military archives. While there are occasional errors and misprints, the maps in general are accurate. The twenty-four Turkish maps found in this study are used with the gracious permission of the Turkish General Staff's Military History and Strategic Institute in Ankara, Turkey.

Key to Maps

⊠   Infantry

☐   Artillery

☐   Engineer

◩   Cavalry

☐   Medical

☐   Logistics Trains

◩   Communications

   Artillery Piece: Gun

   Artillery Piece: Howitzer

   Search Light

   Automatic Weapon

☐   Machine Gun

☐   Headquarters Locations

List of Tables

Introduction

The Gallipoli campaign continues to generate interest around the world. Historian George H. Cassar claims that 'there are more books written about Gallipoli in the English-speaking world than on any other campaign in World War I.'[1] The Gallipoli campaign was unique among First World War battles as it combined modern amphibious joint operations with multinational combined operations. It took place on a landscape pockmarked with classical and romantic sites and memories, just across the Dardanelles from the ruins of Homer's Troy. The name Gallipoli itself evokes controversy and the campaign is, perhaps, the greatest 'what if' of the war for two reasons. First, the concept behind it was grand strategy of the first order that might have led to conditions ending the war two years early on allied terms. This might have avoided the bloodletting of 1916–1918, saved Czarist Russia from revolution, and side-stepped the disastrous Treaty of Versailles – in effect, altering the course of the entire twentieth century. Secondly, the campaign appeared to be a near miss for Britain on at least three occasions (18 March, 25 April and 6 August 1915) and, moreover, a battle that might easily have been won. For Britain the Gallipoli campaign was a disaster. For the Australians and New Zealanders the campaign was a coming of age as these peoples entered the mainstream of the twentieth century. But, for the Turks, the Gallipoli campaign was monumentally important. For the Turks, Gallipoli marked the first time since the seventeenth century in which they were able to defeat a great European power making the campaign a threshold event in the re-emergence of a new national identity and pride.

The English-language historiography of the campaign and its battles has been constructed over the past ninety years using mostly western sources.[2] These include, for example, such familiar works as C.F. Aspinall-Oglander, *Military Operations Gallipoli*, vols 1 and 2 (1924–1930), C.E.W. Bean, *Official History of*

Australia in the War of 1914–1918: The Story of ANZAC, vol. 1–2
(1942), Alan Moorehead, *Gallipoli* (1956), Robert Rhodes James,
Gallipoli, The History of a Noble Blunder (1965), Nigel Steel and
Peter Hart, *Defeat at Gallipoli* (1994), Philip J. Haythornthwaite,
Gallipoli 1915, Frontal Assault on Turkey (n.d.) and Michael Hickey,
Gallipoli (1995). Much of the information contained in these works
about the Ottoman side came from German participant memoirs
and sources, such as Hans Kannengiesser, *The Campaign in
Gallipoli* (n.d.), Carl Mühlmann, *Der Kampf um die Dardanellen
1915* (1927) and Otto Liman von Sanders, *Five Years in Turkey*
(1928). Moreover, such additional information as was included in
the English-language histories on Ottoman participation came
mostly from partial Turkish participant memoirs or from
Maurice Larcher's influential *La Guerre Turque Dans La Guerre
Mondiale* (1926), which cited only 12 percent of its sources as
Ottoman and the remaining 88 percent of sources as European.
The result of all this is an architecture of 'history' that is built on
a bed of incomplete information and understandings.

   This body of Eurocentric received wisdom has led to a number
of generalized beliefs about the Gallipoli campaign that are
incorrect. The most commonly held western notion about the
Ottoman victory is that the Turks stubbornly held on long
enough for a series of allied mistakes to disable the allied plan.[3]
A recent history of the tactical battles blames British command
failures, friction between the army and navy and inexperienced
troops and commanders as reasons for failure.[4] At the operational
level, a 1995 history noted that 'the Turks always managed to
concentrate more troops at the crucial points for the simple
reason that they had more troops readily available on the peninsula.'[5] A third history published in 2003 found that the campaign
itself, at the strategic level, was ill conceived and incompetently
executed.[6] The older histories, including the Australian and
British official histories, all contain variants of these themes,
which are essentially apologia to explain why the allies lost
the campaign.[7] Collectively, the English-language campaign
historiography treats the Ottoman victory as passive rather than
active.[8] As supplementary reasons explaining why the Turks
won, the western histories basically advance two ideas. The first
is that the Turks won because of the generalship of Liman von

Sanders and Mustafa Kemal and, secondly, because their fighting men were incredibly tough and resilient soldiers.[9]

It is only recently that western historians have begun to reassess the battles from the Ottoman perspective and it is becoming clearer that bravery and German command assistance, although important, were only components of a larger mosaic of Ottoman combat effectiveness.[10] Of note, the recent work of Tim Travers, *Gallipoli 1915* (2001), Edward Erickson, *Ottoman Combat Effective in World War I: A Comparative Study* (2007) and Robin Prior, *Gallipoli, The End of the Myth* (2009) have all sought to use the Turkish official histories and military archives more fully to achieve more nuanced understandings of the Ottoman campaign. Unfortunately, in Turkey itself, few military historians have emerged to engage the west with counterpoint analysis and arguments regarding the conduct of the campaign. There is, however, a growing interest in Ottoman military history in Turkey, which has helped open the military archives and make possible the publication of a number of diaries and memoirs from participants in the campaign. This awakening of interest has provided a deeper field of material than previously available and greatly assisted the present author in understanding what happened.

This book, *Gallipoli, The Ottoman Campaign*, presents the events of this famous First World War campaign from the Turkish 'side of the hill'. It is not designed to be a comprehensive history that tells the entire story from both sides and all perspectives in a balanced narrative. Rather, this is the campaign as the Turks understand it and it tells their story. Readers wanting the complete details of each battle from the allied side must conduct parallel readings from the exhaustive western historiography. *Gallipoli, The Ottoman Campaign* is based largely on original source documents from the Ottoman Fifth Army residing today in the Turkish general staff's archives in Ankara and from documents contained in the modern Turkish official histories of the campaign (the 3-volume basic set on the Gallipoli campaign contains 1,429 pages, 124 colour maps, 42 order of battle diagrams, 23 organizational charts, dozens of photographs and many reprinted original documents). Supplementing this are memoirs and diaries from Ottoman and German officers, who held command and staff positions from army level down to battalion level. The author has made a concerted effort to maintain the integrity of the factual basis of this book based on materials contemporary with the campaign.

The Ottoman campaign for Gallipoli is divided into four phases based on the strategic posture of the Ottoman Fifth Army and its predecessors. These are presented as separate chapters in the book. The first phase, 'Ottoman Preparations', begins in 1912 with the fortification of the peninsula in the Balkan Wars and runs through 24 April 1915. The Ottoman army's posture in this phase is constructive and forward leaning. The chapter details the on-going planning, fortification and garrisoning of the peninsula to repel an amphibious invasion. Particular attention is paid to the command structure, defensive planning efforts and the training of Ottoman army units sent to the peninsula. The second phase, 'the Landings', starts on 25 April and ends on 1 May 1915. This phase details the deployment of the Fifth Army and its operations in response to amphibious invasion. In this phase, the Fifth Army posture is defensive and reactive and involved divisional level battles. The third phase is titled 'Stalemate', 2 May–6 August 1915, and presents the Ottoman Fifth Army in an offensive posture and actively trying to crush the allied beachheads. This phase is characterized by the formation of group-level head-quarters to control the ever growing army on the peninsula and by large-scale Ottoman counteroffensives. The fourth and final phase of the campaign is called 'Anafarta' by the Turks them-selves (and 'Suvla' by the British) and ran from 7 August until 8 January 1916. In this phase the Fifth Army returned to a defensive and reactive posture as it responded successfully to Hamilton's second amphibious invasion. The book concludes with a fifth chapter titled 'the Fifth Army Rear Area' which presents an in-depth look at the administration and logistics of the Ottoman Fifth Army.

The current author maintains that the Turks won the Gallipoli campaign because, in many ways, their army was more combat effective than the allied armies in 1915. Combat effectiveness is defined as the relative relationship between combatants in their ability to accomplish desired objectives. This is not the same as military effectiveness or military efficiency, which are terms associated with the waging of war by nations and the extent to which resources are employed. In truth, the Turks fielded a very well-trained, well-led and highly motivated army on the Gallipoli Peninsula that met the Australians, British and French man-to-man on very even terms. Unlike the Western Front, neither side enjoyed nearly unlimited resources nor were the battles on the peninsula ones of *Materialschlacht*, as were occurring in France in the same year. Instead, the Gallipoli campaign seems to highlight the art of command as well as the criticality of effective staff work to a greater extent than other contemporary operations.

What emerges from this study of the Ottoman army at war on the Gallipoli Peninsula in 1915 are the following points about Ottoman army combat effectiveness:

- Ottoman officers led aggressively from the front and were able to operate effectively with or without German advice and assistance;
- Ottoman planning systems, for both deliberate and hasty operations, were effective;
- The Ottoman army possessed well-developed levels of mobility that enabled it to concentrate and mass at points of its choosing;
- The Ottoman reporting system enabled their army to anticipate and operate consistently inside the British decision cycle;
- The Ottoman army's triangular divisional/regimental architecture enabled it to tailor and task organize its forces effectively;
- The Ottoman army's standardized doctrines and tactics, based on the German 'way of war', enhanced inter-operability between German and Ottoman officers;
- The Ottoman command structure, particularly at corps and army level, operated at much higher levels of effectiveness than the allied command structure, especially regarding its situational and spatial awareness.

Likewise, there were dysfunctions and weaknesses in the Ottoman army during the Gallipoli campaign which reduced its capability, such as

- An over reliance on poorly supported massed night attacks leading to excessive casualties;
- An inability to mass troops without being discovered leading to a loss of surprise;
- A tendency to launch attacks without adequate preparations and without giving the troops involved enough time to ready themselves;
- Informal channels of information, both Ottoman and German, which bypassed the formal chain of command;
- Failure to reinforce the Fifth Army decisively in phase two of the campaign (a strategic mistake by Enver Pasha and the general staff rather than an operational mistake by the Fifth Army).

Finally, this work is a campaign history and focuses on the operational level of war primarily at field army and army corps level. Tactics, human-interest vignettes and cultural affairs are only briefly mentioned to support the overall narrative. The framework of *Gallipoli, The Ottoman Campaign* is designed to show how the Turks planned their operations, how they occasionally executed their plans successfully and how they adapted when their planning and execution failed. The focus is on command and control as these factors affected the conduct and course of operations. The author's purpose is to illuminate how the Ottoman Fifth Army fought a successful and prolonged campaign against an enemy that possessed greater resources, advanced technologies and command of the sea and air.

Chapter 1
Ottoman Preparations, 1912–24 April 1915

Introduction

The first phase of the Ottoman campaign for the defense of the Gallipoli Peninsula begins in 1912 with the efforts to fortify the Dardanelles strait against threats to the peninsula from the Bulgarian army and Greek navy in the Balkan Wars of 1912/13. The Dardanelles defenses consisted of fortifications dating back to the seventeenth century. Serious construction of the modern fortifications began in the late nineteenth century and consisted of a number of concrete and earth embrasured gun positions on both sides of the strait. Before 1912, these installations fell under the command of the Çanakkale Strait Forces and Fortification Command, one of a number of Ottoman fortresses defending strategic points.[1] In the winter of 1912–1913 the command was actively engaged in combat operations during the First Balkan War. In the post-war reorganization of the Ottoman army in 1913–1914, the Strait command was renamed the Çanakkale Fortified Area Command, but continued to maintain its artillery brigades and command of all of the forts on both sides of the Dardanelles. The place name Çanakkale (known to the British as Chanak in 1915) is used throughout this book as an exception to the general usage of English place names because of its significance as the Turkish name of the campaign (*Çanakkale Cephesi*)

When the Ottoman army mobilized in August 1914, its tactical units began to prepare for war under the dynamic training guidance of a revived military machine. Soon thereafter the army deployed mobile tactical ground forces to the strait and the peninsula. These units were continually reinforced after a brief Royal Navy bombardment in November and vigorously prepared the defenses to repel an allied amphibious invasion. As the Empire

1

entered the First World War defensive planning was modified
using the plans developed in 1912, to include a larger defensive
area and the reinforcement of the command by the Ottoman
army's III Corps.[2] After very heavy naval attacks on the strait in
February and March 1915, the Ottoman high command activated
the Fifth Army on the peninsula and a new XV Corps in Asia.
When the allied amphibious assault occurred on 25 April it was
met by well-trained, well-led, and well-prepared infantry divisions of the Ottoman army. This came as a shock and a surprise
to the allies, who had expected an easy victory over what they
had perceived to be a rag-tag poorly led army. This phase ended
on 25 April 1915, when the allies invaded the beaches of the
Gallipoli Peninsula and Kum Kale in Asia.

The Dardanelles in the Balkan Wars[3]

The Dardanelles strait was the most heavily fortified point in the
Ottoman Empire and its defensive works dated back hundreds of
years. During the 1880s work began, under mostly German direction, to modernize the fortifications against a naval attack on the
strait.[4] The defenses until the Balkan Wars of 1912/13 were
composed entirely of coastal defense guns, underwater minefields and searchlights oriented on the strait itself and presented
a thin ribbon of forts along the water's edge. In the fall of 1912 the
strategic situation changed and, against the threat of a Greek
amphibious invasion, the Ottoman general staff ordered a more
comprehensive fortification of the entire Gallipoli Peninsula
itself. Moreover, a corps-level command was created on the
peninsula to construct and occupy the defensive works that
would guard the strait's fortifications against an enemy landing
in their rear.[5]

   The Gallipoli historiography largely ignores the fact that the
Dardanelles defenses were given a thorough workout during
the First Balkan War (1912–1913). In fact, it was during this war
that the Ottomans put together the basic defensive plans and
concepts used subsequently to defend the peninsula in 1915
against the British. Prior to the Balkan Wars the peninsula was a
sleepy garrison backwater for the Ottoman army's 5th Infantry
Division and Çanakkale Fortress Command. However, in the
Balkan Wars the Ottomans deployed a greatly reinforced army to

defend the Gallipoli Peninsula. This was brought about when the victorious Bulgarian army reached the Sea of Marmara and cut off the peninsula on 12 October 1912. The Ottomans reorganized their forces by placing the Dardanelles strait and the peninsula under the independent command of the Çanakkale Strait Forces and Fortification Command.[6] The general staff rushed the regular 27th Infantry Division, a provisional infantry division, and the Afyon, Çanakkale, and Edremit Reserve Infantry Divisions to the peninsula. The newly organized headquarters also commanded the Menderes Detachment (*Menderes Mufrezesi*), a provisional cavalry brigade, and three independent batteries of artillery. The preexisting fortress command of three heavy coastal artillery regiments was absorbed into the new force. Altogether for the defense of the peninsula in 1912, the Ottomans had 40,000 men armed with 27,000 rifles, 38 machine-guns, and 102 cannon (not counting coastal artillery).[7]

Command of the Çanakkale Strait Forces and Fortification Command was given to Brigadier General Fahri Pasha, who quickly created the basic defensive plan and layout for the peninsula by establishing four primary defensive groups: one guarding the beaches of the lower peninsula, one guarding the narrow neck of the peninsula (at Bulair), one guarding the Asian beaches, while one remained in immediate reserve. Fahri stationed two of the three reserve infantry divisions in beach defense roles on the peninsula, placed the 27th Division at Bulair and the Menderes Detachment along the Asiatic shore. He kept his third reserve division as a general army reserve at Maidos (modern Eceabat). Thus, by the end of the year, the general configuration of the Ottoman defense was established (this general layout would be repeated in 1915). Map 1.1 shows this deployment.

Fahri assigned the Çanakkale Reserve Division, composed of men from Gallipoli, Çanakkale (Chanak) and the villages of the peninsula itself, to the southernmost tip of the peninsula (the area later known as the Cape Helles front). He stationed the Edremit Reserve Division on its right flank (covering the area later known as Anzac and Suvla Bay). The Ottoman reserve infantry divisions were much weaker than its regular infantry divisions and together were approximately same strength as the Ottoman 9th Infantry Division, which later defended the peninsula in 1915.

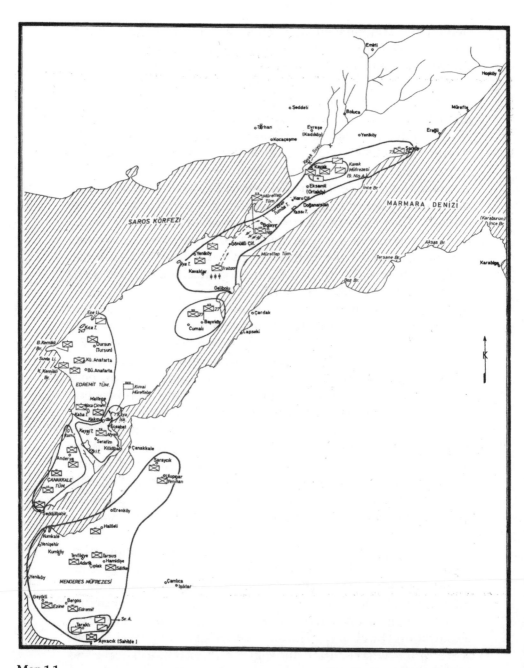

Map 1.1
Gallipoli defenses, 1912. The general operational configuration into a Saros Bay/isthmus group, a peninsula group and an Asian group is clearly apparent, as is the central positioning of an operational reserve at Eceabat (Maidos). In 1915, Mustafa Kemal's 19th Division would occupy the positions that the Afyon Division occupied in 1912.

These two divisions constructed battalion-sized strong points on the key terrain features overlooking the beaches. The beaches themselves were covered by company sized elements and the divisional artilleries were positioned centrally to support the divisional sectors. In reserve the Afyon Reserve Division lay in garrison at Maidos and was prepared to support either the Çanakkale or the Edremit divisions. The reserve soldiers began to dig trenches and gun pits and developed a road and communications network, and rehearsed counterattack plans. The Australians would later discover what they called 'the Balkan Pits'[8] in their sector in 1915, which were the remnants of these defensive preparations. Across the strait near the ruins of Troy in Asia, the Menderes Detachment had grown to divisional strength and began similar defensive preparations at Kum Kale and the adjacent coastlines. In the peninsula's neck the 27th Infantry Division faced the Bulgarians, who had closed on the Ottoman Bulair lines in early February 1915. Although defending the peninsula from the north, the 27th Division fulfilled a similar mission in the area, which would be defended by the 7th Infantry Division in 1915.[9] Serving on the Bulair lines as chief of operations (*1nci Şube Müdürü*) was Staff Major Mustafa Kemal (later and more famously known as Atatürk).[10] Finally, Fahri established a provisional army corps headquarters at Maidos to command and control the mobile divisions on the peninsula and the Menderes Detachment in Asia. This command arrangement was formalized as the Provisional Forces Command during the armistice that brought combat operations to a halt in December 1912. Although the anticipated amphibious invasion by the Greeks never materialized, there was a pitched battle on the neck of the peninsula during the First Balkan War.

In early 1913, the Bulgarian high command massed their Fourth Army, composed of about 92,000 officers and men, north of the Bulair lines.[11] The armistice expired at 7 pm on 3 February 1913 and the Bulgarian 7th Infantry Division moved forward the next morning closing on the Bulair lines on 6 February. The Bulgarians did not know that the Ottomans were, themselves, planning to conduct an amphibious invasion of their own in the Sea of Marmara with the objective of encircling the Fourth Army. Fahri's Gallipoli forces were ordered to conduct a supporting attack, which would serve to distract the Bulgarians from the coast. He planned a simple and direct attack out of the Bulair lines using the 27th Division on the right and a provisional infantry division on the left. Releasing the Afyon Reserve Division from its role as the operational reserve, Fahri intended to use it as his second echelon in the attack. Altogether he could mass over 20,000 men for the attack. Planning was meticulous and Ottoman commanders down to regimental level had ample time to organize their operations. The Ottomans estimated that they would face two enemy infantry regiments supported by four artillery batteries. To better control operations Fahri positioned himself immediately behind his attacking divisions. The attacking Ottoman regiments began moving forward at 5.30 am on 8 February and the attack was launched as scheduled at 8 am.

Unfortunately the Turks faced the 2 infantry regiments of the recently arrived 1st Brigade of the Bulgarian 7th Division supported by not just 4 but 14 artillery batteries (78 guns) with 6 more batteries in general support. This was a notable intelligence failure and when 15,000 Ottoman soldiers charged across the open terrain of the narrow peninsula neck on an attack frontage of only 2,600m there were met by rifle and machine-gun fire and a terrible barrage of artillery shells. They were slaughtered in the thousands and perhaps as many as 6,000 died in the doomed attack.[12] Although some Ottomans actually punched through and reached the Bulgarian artillery batteries, the attack was both hopeless and pointless. By noon the catastrophic assault was finished as were Fahri's offensive operations for the remainder of the First Balkan War. However, in the Second Balkan War, Fahri's force, now refitted and designated as the Gallipoli Field Army broke out of the peninsula to assist in the recapture of the city of Edirne (Adrianople). Major Mustafa Kemal was active in the successful planning of these operations. After the Treaty of London ended the Second Balkan War in 1913, the troops remaining on the peninsula were sent home and it returned to its normal peacetime routines.

The Çanakkale Fortified Area Command, 1914[13]

After the Balkan Wars, the defense of the Dardanelles returned to the hands of the commander of the Çanakkale Fortified Area

Command. This was a fortress command that had control over the string of elderly forts and command of a brigade of three heavy artillery regiments. The forts and guns were clustered at the mouth of the Dardanelles and at the narrows and, in times of peace, were manned at very low levels. This would change in the summer of 1914 and, although the Ottoman Empire would not enter the war until November 1914, the army on the Gallipoli Peninsula was active much earlier.

In the spring of 1913, great tension existed between the Ottoman Empire and Greece over the status of the residual Muslim population living in newly Greek-occupied western Thrace. War seemed probable and the Ottoman III Corps was ordered to plan for movement to the peninsula while the Ottoman V Corps was ordered to occupy the famous Çatalca lines. The actual reactivation of the defensive plans for the peninsula began as early as 31 July 1914, when operations conducted by Greek warships and aircraft near the mouth of the Dardanelles alarmed the Ottoman general staff.[14] The War Ministry issued a special limited mobilization order at 11.45 am on that day that alerted the fortress commander to begin preparations for war and to expect reinforcements.[15] The III Corps chief of staff, German Lieutenant Colonel Perrinet von Thauvenay, arrived on the night of 8/9 August and began to update the defensive plans the next day. The plans called for the Ottoman III Corps to reinforce the fortress and to provide the troops to defend the peninsula.[16] They were based on the 1913 defensive plan for the peninsula but with a significant change. The northern limit of the 1913 plan was the narrow peninsula neck at Bulair (simply because of the presence of the Bulgarian army). In truth the best landing beaches in the region lay just to the north of Bulair in Saros Bay (a fact that would bedevil Liman von Sanders during the entire campaign). This vulnerability caused the Ottoman general staff to assign the entire Saros Bay coastline to the fortress command for defensive planning purposes. In early August 1914, the fortress command revised its war plan so that three major operational groups would defend the Gallipoli Peninsula: one in Asia (unchanged from 1913), one on the peninsula south of Bulair (unchanged from 1913) and one in the new Saros Bay sector.[17] On 12 August, Enver Pasha alerted the fortress that, although the Empire had purchased the *Yavuz Sultan Selim* (ex-SMS *Goeben*) and *Midilli* (ex-SMS *Breslau*), the British might attack through the strait to get at the ships.[18]

Neither the fortress nor the III Corps was ready for war in early August 1914. Nevertheless, as a result of the July crisis but separate from their concerns about Greece, the Ottoman general staff decided to conduct national military mobilization as a precautionary measure, even though the Empire was not yet at war. At 1 am on 2 August 1914, the Ottoman General Staff sent mobilization orders to the commander of the III Corps in Rodosto (modern Tekirdağ).[19] The following day, which was the first numbered day of mobilization (3 August), the III Corps began its preparations for war.[20] However, its initial strength returns of about 15,000 officers and men reflected the low condition of peacetime readiness that the Ottoman army operated under.[21] Nevertheless, by 21 August the corps was at full strength with 12,937 men in the 7th Division, 13,061 men in the 8th Division and 2,907 men assigned to the corps troop units. In fact, the III Corps was the only corps of thirteen Ottoman army corps to mobilize within its time requirement of twenty days. On 22 August the regiments and battalions of the corps began to move from home garrisons to staging areas surrounding Rodosto for training and shaking out.

Upon mobilization, the plans called for the III Corps to detach the 9th Division to the Çanakkale Fortified Area Command for beach defense and mobile reserve operations. Technically, it still remained under the command of III Corps, but for all intents and purposes, the division fell under the operational control of the fortress commander. On 27 August, the 9th Infantry Division commander began conversations with the commander of the fortress concerning the deployment of his division to the Gallipoli Peninsula and by mid-September 1914, the division was moving into observation positions overlooking the peninsula's beaches. This effectively removed the division from III Corps control. After the training regime associated with mobilization the corps began to move into the peninsula. The 7th Division began to deploy there on 29 October and the III Corps headquarters moved from Rodosto to the town of Gallipoli (modern Gelibolu) itself on 4 November. The 8th Division remained, for the moment, in its staging areas outside Rodosto. Thus, when the Empire actually entered the war and by the time of the first Royal Navy bombardment (3 November), the Ottomans had three full months of preparation time to position substantial forces for the defense of both the peninsula and the strait (a mobile army corps of two divisions).

In spite of these preparations, the defense of the Dardanelles remained weak due to the poor condition of the fortifications, the antiquity of many of the cannon, the scarcity of ammunition and supplies and the lack of good coordination between the Fortress Command and the corps headquarters. To rectify the technical deficiencies of the coastal defenses, the Germans dispatched Vice Admiral Guido von Usedom, who had expertise in coastal artillery and gunnery, to advise the Turks. Accompanying the admiral were about 500 Germans who were coastal defense experts specializing in coastal artillery, communications, military engineering and underwater mines. None of these men were assigned to the mobile Ottoman III Corps. The Germans likewise dispatched limited quanities of war material to Turkey through the neutral countries of Romania and Bulgaria. On 3 November the Royal Navy briefly bombarded the Ottoman forts at the entrance of the Dardanelles. This attack achieved no objective of military value, and indeed, only served notice on the Ottomans regarding the vulnerability of the strait. In fact, the British attack so thoroughly alarmed the Ottoman general staff that it accelerated the program of fortification and defensive improvements. However, because of an emerging plan to invade Egypt the general staff decided to detach the 8th Infantry Division from III Corps alerting it for service on the Sinai front and began preparations for its departure in late November 1914. This caused Esat Pasha, the III Corps commander, to dispatch a long report to the First Army outlining the case for more forces to defend the peninsula.[22] As a result the 19th Infantry Division was activated on 1 January 1915 to take the place of the 8th Division and assigned to the III Corps.[23]

Defensive planning and training, particularly anti-invasion drills, now began in earnest, and the troops began to improve the seaward defenses and also worked to construct additional roads and interior communications. By February 1915, the Fortress

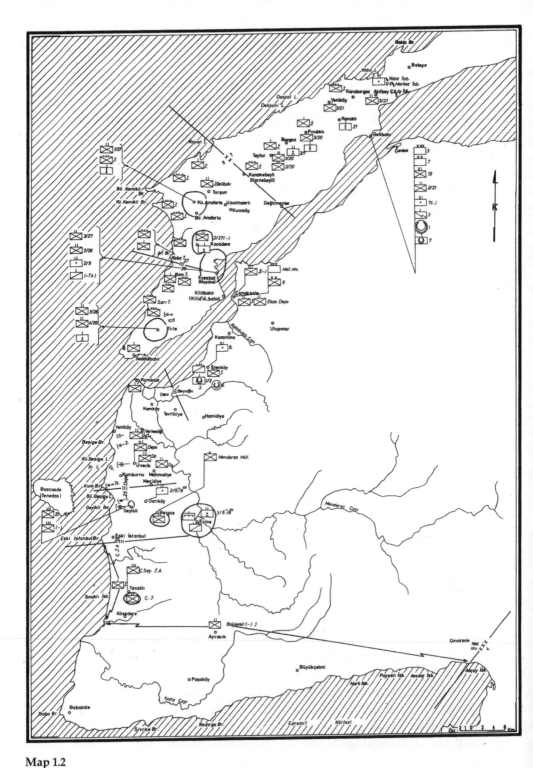

Map 1.2
7th and 9th Infantry Division situation, 18 February 1915. The general similarities with the 1912 plan are apparent, especially the positioning of the 19th Division near Eceabat. In both cases, the defensive planning hinged on the proper positioning of reserves decisively to counterattack the invaders.

Command had (including the 9th Infantry Division) over 34,500 soldiers, armed with 25,000 rifles, 8 machine-guns and 263 cannon, on the peninsula. Moreover, the mobile III Corps (now consisting mainly of the 7th Infantry Division) had 15,000 soldiers in position, armed with 9,448 rifles, 8 machine-guns, and 50 cannon.[24] The unready 19th Infantry Division remained off the peninsula in the Rodosto garrison where it was undergoing intensive training under its new commander, the young and aggressive Lieutenant Colonel Mustafa Kemal Bey. Map 1.2 shows the peninsula defenses on 18 February 1915.

The power of the Çanakkale Fortified Area Command lay in its heavy coastal artillery, which was organized into the 2nd Artillery Brigade and concentrated in fourteen permanent forts lining the strait. There were three regiments assigned to the brigade, the 3rd, 4th and 5th Heavy Artillery Regiments (3, 4 and 5 Heavy Arty Regts).[25] The 2nd Battalion, 4th Heavy Artillery Regiment (2/4 Heavy Arty Regt) garrisoned the fortifications on the European side of the narrows around Maidos and Kalid Bahr. The 1st and 2nd Battalions, 3rd Heavy Artillery Regiment (1/3 and 2/3 Heavy Arty Regt) garrisoned the Asiatic narrows forts around Çanakkale. The 5th Heavy Artillery Regiment garrisoned the outer forts at the mouth of the Dardanelles with its 1st Battalion at Sedd el Bahr (1/5 Heavy Arty Regt) in Europe and its 2nd Battalion at Kum Kale in Asia (2/5 Heavy Arty Regts). These formations were armed with coastal defense cannon ranging in size from 87mm up to 355mm, however most of the more powerful heavy ship-killing guns were with 3 and 4 Heavy Arty Regts in the narrows. Peacetime ammunition supplies were maintained in magazines within the forts and the quantities on hand were reported to the fortress commander by type of gun (Table A.1 in Appendix A shows the quantities on hand on 14 August 1914). On mobilization the brigade's regiments stocked over 8,000 round of heavy caliber ammunition (8in up to 14in) in magazines adjacent to its guns and maintained several thousand more in its depot facilities.

The eighty-two guns in the three regiments were, by themselves, insufficient to defend the strait under full wartime conditions against a force such as Britain's Royal Navy and required heavy augmentation, therefore the Ottoman general staff began to deploy additional cannon to the strait from less threatened areas. Throughout August 1914, a variety of cannon arrived at the Çanakkale fortress from the fortresses of Edirne (Adrianople) and Çatalca (Chatalja), as well as from the ships of the Ottoman fleet in Constantinople.[26] The first minefield was laid in the narrows on 4 August 1914. On 17 August a battery of 75mm ship's guns were sent to the peninsula and on 23 August the first six 120mm howitzers arrived. Alert to the increased dangers posed by the allies, the Ottoman general staff ordered further artillery reinforcements to the area from the Bosphorus fortresses area on 19 September 1914, in the form of the 8th Heavy Artillery Regiment (8 Heavy Arty Regt). [27] This formation was armed with twenty-two 150mm howitzers (later this would rise to a total of thirty-two) and was later augmented by fourteen 120mm howitzers. The regiment began to arrive on 25 September and was assigned kill zones to augment the intermediate defenses in an anti-ship role. Lieutenant Colonel Mehmet Zekerriya commanded the 8 Heavy Arty Regt. On 4 and 7 November six heavy 210mm mortars made their way to the rapidly growing defenses. So many howitzers arrived that Lieutenant Colonel Mehmet Zekerriya was able to form a third battalion (the standard in the Ottoman army at that time was two battalions in artillery regiments). A variety of smaller field and mountain artillery batteries were also added to the defenses.

Additional Ottoman artillery officers and NCOs were assigned from Constantinople to the staff of the fortress commander. On 1 September, German Admiral Schack arrived to assess the defenses and render a report to the general staff. His report noted deficiencies in ammunition quantities, the deteriorated condition of the fortifications, and an absence of funds for repair parts and upgrades. He was especially concerned with the torpedo batteries and he judged the fortress unready for combat.[28] Schack's report along with the increasingly complex problems involving integrating the tactical deployment of the incoming mobile artillery battalions with the static heavy artillery regiments caused concern in Constantinople. The Ottoman general staff sent a directive to the fortress on 22 October 1914 to develop a new plan for the defense of the strait.[29] To assist the fortress staff, Enver sent German Lieutenant General Merten as his personal delegate, who with German Lieutenant Colonel Wasillo and fortress chief of staff Lieutenant Colonel Salahattin formed a planning group to study the problem. On 8 November, the group issued its revised plan, which became the basis for the defense of the strait against enemy ships.[30] The plan organized the fortress into four defensive areas, the first or entry area (the outer defenses), the second area (the howitzer zone), the third area (the intermediate defenses: Kepez–Soganlı) and the fourth area (the inner defenses: Çanakkale–Kilid Bahr). The new howitzer zone was a major change in the defensive plan and was to be responsible for the delivery of plunging fires on the enemy ships, which had relatively thin horizontal deck armor compared to their vertical side armor. The incoming 8 Heavy Arty Regt was ordered to provide forces, command and control for the howitzer zone, which was put under the overall command of German artillery specialist Lieutenant Colonel Wehrle. The creation of the howitzer zone allowed the Turks to integrate effectively the reinforcing artillery with the fortress artillery as well as coordinate procedures for the centralized delivery of fires. Crew training for the men manning the coastal artillery pieces had been ongoing since mobilization but a high percentage of the men were newly conscripted and untrained. To rectify this Merten assigned German noncommissioned officers directly into the Ottoman gun crews.

Additional guns arrived throughout December and January, including more 120mm howitzers; 37mm anti-aircraft guns; and 47mm and 75mm ship's guns. By 18 February 1915, there were a total of 235 cannon operational in the 4 artillery regiments assigned to defend the Dardanelles.[31] The outer defenses were in the hands of 5 Heavy Arty Regt, the mobile 8 Heavy Arty Regt lay in the howitzer zone, and 3 and 4 Heavy Arty Regts manned the guns assigned to the intermediate and inner defenses. Ammunition for most of the newly arriving howitzers and guns was fairly plentiful. The artillery situation report of 26 February 1915 shows 8 Heavy Arty Regt was particularly well stocked with 8,229 shells for its howitzers (see Appendix A, Table A.2). Map 1.3 shows the coastal defences for the strait on 18 March 1915.

Altogether, by the time of the allied naval attack of 18 March 1915, the Ottomans had 82 guns operational in fixed positions

Map 1.3
Çanakkale Fortress artillery positions, 18 March 1915. The positioning of the howitzer battalions to deliver plunging fires in the waters below the narrows is apparent. These weapons played a key role in the allied defeat on 18 March.

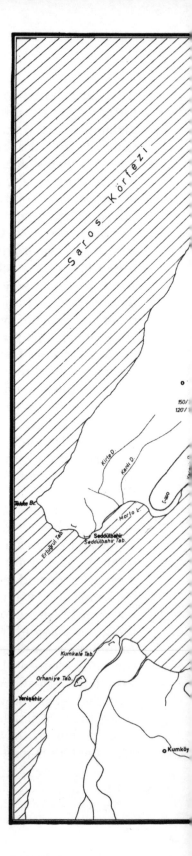

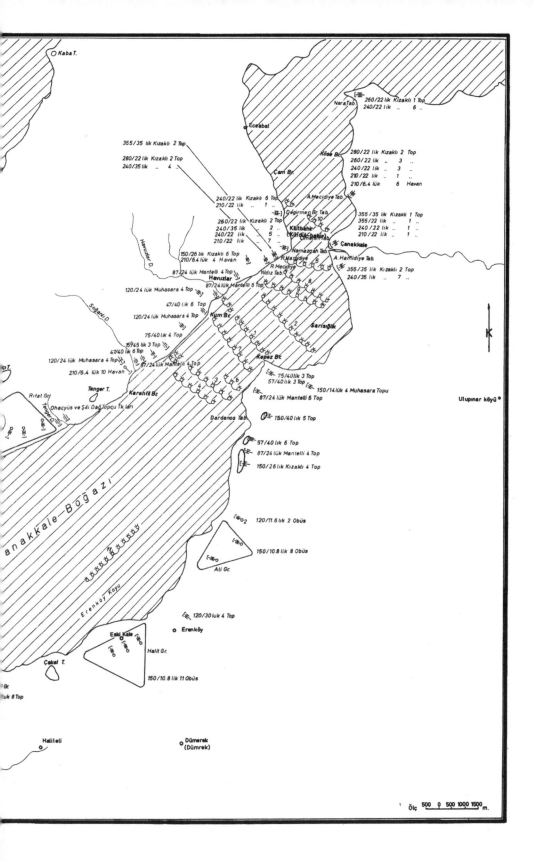

and 230 mobile guns and howitzers available for the defense of the peninsula and earlier that month Mustafa Kemal's infantry division moved forward to the peninsula to join the 9th Infantry Division. Over an eight-month period, under the direction of trained Ottoman general staff officers, a comprehensive plan was developed and implemented that put entrenched infantry units defending the likely invasion beaches and positioned large reserves in protected positions behind the beaches (the German officers remained focused on the strait defenses).[32] As in the 1913 plan, the primary objective was to slow the enemy landings and then launch coordinated counterattacks to drive the enemy back into the sea.

The plan to force the Dardanelles, steam Royal Navy battleships into the Sea of Marmara and bombard Constantinople into rubble was born in the fertile minds of the First Sea Lord Sir Jackie Fisher and the First Lord of the Admiralty Sir Winston S. Churchill. The fleet would then cut the jugular of the Ottoman Empire by severing European from Asiatic Turkey, which would force the Ottoman government into surrender. The idea had strategic clarity and logic that was almost unique among the campaigns of the First World War. Its potential for achieving decisive strategic results in an era of strategic stalemate seemed to be enormous. Later, when the naval attack failed, the plan blossomed into a land campaign, which was conceived and executed by men drenched in the classical education of public-school imperial Britain. Indeed, the 'Constantinople expedition' had the powerful emotional appeal of a new Trojan War but it too failed and at great cost.

The naval attacks

The Royal Navy began its war against the Ottoman Empire on 3 November 1914 by bombarding the forts at the entrance to the Dardanelles. Ottoman resistance to the bombardment was non existent and other similar disasters overtook the apparently hapless Ottomans at Sarikamiş in Caucasia, Basra in Mesopotamia and in the Sinai in late 1914 and early 1915. Combined with the social Darwinism of the era these events reinforced the contemporary idea that the Ottomans were weak opponents. Churchill and Fisher, ever ready to seize the moment, began to consider the idea of forcing the Dardanelles with a view towards forcing the ultimate capitulation of the Ottoman Empire. This accomplished, Russia then reeling in defeat might be re-supplied, Bulgaria might be persuaded to join the allies and three enemy fronts might be eliminated in a single stroke. It was strategy on a grand scale but it hinged on the navy breaking through the Dardanelles defenses. By late January, Churchill and Fisher had pushed the War Council into supporting such an attack. Cable traffic began to flow between the Admiralty and Admiral Sir Sackville Carden, commander of the combined fleet then operating in the eastern Mediterranean.

Carden commanded an oddly mismatched fleet that contained an assortment of some of the oldest pre-dreadnought battleships (twelve in all) in the Royal Navy, the modern battle cruiser *Inflexible* and a variety of smaller ships. He also commanded a French squadron that contained four elderly pre-dreadnoughts. The centerpiece of Carden's fleet was the ultra-modern 15in-gunned superdreadnought, *Queen Elizabeth*, which had been sent out for calibration of her guns. For minesweepers, Carden had small trawlers manned by civilian North Sea fishermen. Carden's main anchorage was Mudros Bay on the Greek island of Lemnos, which was only 50 miles from the mouth of the Dardanelles. Carden, himself, seemed to be the human reflection of his fleet and was regarded as a mediocrity by Churchill and Fisher, and as 'very second-rate' by General Sir William Birdwood (later to command at Anzac).[33] Carden's subordinates de Robeck, Wemyss and Keyes were, on the other hand, some of the most intelligent and aggressive men in the Royal Navy. Thus, in both men and in materiel, Churchill gambled on wildly asymmetric combinations to execute a mission of critical importance to the war effort.

Carden planned to force the strait in three stages. First, the fleet would destroy the outer defenses at the mouth of the Dardanelles by naval gunfire. Moving inside the strait, the fleet would reduce the intermediate defenses, which protected the successive belts of minefields that choked the narrows. Finally, after sweeping the mines his fleet would pound the inner defenses, primarily heavy coastal defense guns in fortified positions, into silence. After accomplishing these tasks the fleet would proceed into the Sea of

Marmara. It was thought unlikely that the *Yavuz*, its consort the *Midilli* or the Ottoman fleet of antique pre-dreadnoughts would choose to fight the powerful Royal Navy squadrons. Constantinople would then find itself directly under the guns of the Royal Navy. Opinion, at all levels, was mixed on the viability and the outcome of this plan. The attack was set for 19 February 1915, which by coincidence was the anniversary of the successful Royal Navy forcing of the strait under Admiral Duckworth in 1807.

The fortress command was warned of the impending attack by the Ottoman general staff, which had itself read reports taken from the Athens and Salonika newspapers on 16 February.[34] The initial assault went off as scheduled on 19 February, but the outer forts appeared little damaged. Royal Navy ship to shore gunnery against point targets was notably ineffective at this point in history.[35] Carden withdrew, then attacked unsuccessfully several times again, and finally landed Royal Marines on 4 March to blow up the 5 Heavy Arty Regt's outer forts at Kum Kale on the Asiatic side and at Sedd el Bahr on the European side of the Dardanelles. Its guns destroyed, the 5 Heavy Arty Regt was inactivated on 25 February and most of its men reassigned to the 3 Heavy Arty Regt.[36] The increased intensity of allied activity, in turn, caused the fortress command to request that the 19th Division be brought down to the peninsula from Rodosto and by the end of the first week of march most of Kemal's division had landed at Maidos. Minesweeping trawlers then began to sweep the interior of the strait in preparation for the second stage of the assault, the attack on the intermediate defenses. Every day from 2 through 8 March, squadrons of Carden's fleet shelled the intermediate defenses with small results. Carden's attacks were 'utterly lacking in vigor and determination'[37] and the minesweepers made little progress against the current flowing swiftly against them. One of seven minesweepers was sunk by Ottoman gunfire for a gain of three mines exploded. While this left the British unsatisfied, the naval activity was especially worrisome to the commander of the 9th Division, who sent a lengthy message to Cevat Pasha expressing concern over the possibility of an enemy landing at Kum Kale.[38] This so worried the Ottomans that the high command notified the 11th Infantry Division to move to the area on 9 March. The arrival of this division was intended to allow the fortress command to pull the 9th Division's regiments out of Kum Kale enabling it to concentrate on the peninsula. The French naval squadron attacked as well, unsuccessfully, on 12 March. Night minesweeping using Royal Naval volunteers to augment the civilian crews was attempted on the night 13/14 March, against a fully alerted enemy armed with searchlights and pre-ranged guns, with predictable results. Carden's staff finally and desperately began planning a full-strength and all-out attack on the Ottomans.

Carden crumbled under the stress of command and relieved himself of command on 16 March for reasons of health. He had worried himself dangerously close to a nervous breakdown, but in the end had the courage to admit that he was not the man for the job. His second in command, Rear Admiral Sir John de Robeck, assumed command of the combined fleet. In de Robeck, the fleet at last had an aggressive commander who was determined to carry the fight to the enemy. At a conference on the evening of 17 March, a confident de Robeck announced his decision to attack the following day. At the operational level, de Robeck's plan was simple and direct. The battleships would simultaneously silence the intermediate defenses and most of the inner defenses. That night the minesweepers would clear the enemy minefields. The following morning, the fleet would steam through the narrows and finish off the remaining inner defenses. At the tactical level it was quite complex and was based on thorough planning and aerial reconnaissance. The allied ships, organized into parallel divisions known as lines, advanced abreast into the narrows with detailed prearranged fire plans designed to destroy the key Ottoman forts. Observation of the fall of shot was to be assisted by seaplane support. After delivering their fires, the successive allied ranks of battleships would pull away and allow a follow-on force of minesweepers the opportunity to sweep pre planned lanes through the enemy minefields. The complex operation was put on a timetable schedule.

At 11.25 am, 18 March 1915, a squadron of the four most powerful British ships went into action by engaging the narrows forts, while older pre-dreadnoughts hammered the intermediate defenses. The howitzers of the Ottoman intermediate zone began to return fire from 120mm and 150mm pieces. The howitzer fire was heavy but comfortably inaccurate and ineffective. At 11.55 am the guns of the Dardanos and the Baykuş Mesudiye Batteries (150mm guns) began to fire and at noon the 240mm battery of the Rumeli Mecidiye Fort joined in. The allied ships pounded both the howitzer zones and the batteries. By noon many of the intermediate Ottoman forts appeared to have been silenced. Then at 1.20 pm the heavy guns of the Anadolu Hamidiye Fort (355mm and 240mm guns) opened fire. Ten minutes later an enemy aircraft appeared over the strait and the European Central Group (Rumeli Mecidiye, Hamidiye and Namazgah Forts – all with 240mm guns) began to draw very heavy fires. The allied naval gun fire cut the underground telephone cables linking the forts to the fortress command center leaving them isolated in command and control. Enemy fires began fall effectively on Anadolu Hamidiye and Rumeli Mecidiye causing casualties and temporarily silencing Anadolu Hamidiye.

French battleships closed to within 8,000m of the narrows towards 2 pm at which time the Rumeli Mecidiye Fort opened fire. The fort had been hit hard by several direct heavy shells that killed ten men and wounded twenty-four. The magazines were ablaze and out of the terror and confusion one of the most famous stories in Turkey about the naval attack of 18 March emerged. It involved a heroic corporal named Seyit, who was assigned to the coastal defence fort. The fort's main battery was equipped with four 240mm heavy guns, which fired shells weighing between 140kg to 250kg (depending on the type). Corporal Seyit commanded the third gun, which was hit by shellfire at the height of the battle damaging the auto-loading gear and rendering it technically inoperable. To the amazement of the huddled gunners, the indomitable Seyit lifted one of the rounds onto his back and carried it to the gun. Somehow he loaded the round, aimed the piece and fired the cannon. Popular histories in Turkey assert that Seyit's shell hit HMS *Ocean*, although this has never been confirmed. A famous photo was taken (that was undoubtedly posed after the battle) of Corporal Seyit carrying a shell on his back and there is a statue of Seyit on the shores of the Dardanelles commemorating this event today.

Suddenly just after 2 pm, in the middle of a recall to allow a relief squadron of British ships to move forward, the French pre-dreadnought *Bouvet* blew up and sank within minutes. This cheered the Turks, who observed the frantic efforts to rescue the handful of survivors. Howitzer fires renewed, including 210mm fire from the Tenger Havan (heavy mortar) Battery and, although a magazine fire broke out in the Namazgah Fort, the gunners there opened fire about 3.15 pm. The Anadolu Hamidiye Fort came back into action 5 minutes later by firing at *Irresistible*. Shortly thereafter both the French *Gaulois* and *Suffren* were seriously damaged by gunfire. The French squadron was essentially out of action. Undeterred, de Robeck continued to pound the Ottomans, and at 4 pm sent in his trawlers. Intense fire from the mobile 210mm and 150mm howitzers of the 8 Heavy Arty Regt in Wehrle's howitzer zone forced an immediate retreat of the minesweepers. The tide of battle continued to shift against the allies.

At 4.11 pm, the modern battle cruiser *Inflexible* struck a mine and nearly sank. Minutes later the pre-dreadnought *Irresistible* was also mined. At 5 pm, a discouraged de Robeck called off the operation and a final few rounds were fired at *Irresistible* at 5.30 pm from the Rumeli Mecidiye Fort. Although the Turkish guns were now silent, disaster continued to stalk the Royal Navy. At 6.05 pm, the pre-dreadnought *Ocean*, after attempting to tow the damaged *Irresistible* out of harm's way, also struck a mine and began to sink. Both battleships were abandoned and sank later that night. The Ottomans held the field and the strait, and their minefields were intact. Moreover De Robeck's fleet suffered serious losses. Altogether, the allies lost three old battleships sunk, and suffered two old battleships and a modern battle cruiser seriously damaged. Against this loss, the Ottomans appeared to have lost a few guns and had a handful of mines exploded. It was small return for a heavy investment.

Most of the Turkish casualties were concentrated in the Rumeli Mecidiye Fort (12 dead and 30 wounded) but overall losses were very light, totaling 97 casualties altogether.[39] There were 4 Ottoman officers killed and 1 wounded, while 22 soldiers were killed and another 52 wounded. Additionally, 3 German enlisted men were killed and 1 German officer and 14 enlisted men were wounded. On 19 March, Cevat Pasha (the fortress commander) published orders announcing the award of medals for gallantry in action.[40] The Silver Combat Medal of Distinction was awarded to Colonel Talat (commander, 2 Heavy Arty Regt), Colonel Şükrü (Engineer Corps), Lieutenant Colonel Wasillo (German advisor) and Major Nuri (Signal Corps). The Silver Combat Medal of Merit was awarded to Lieutenant Ali (fortress command headquarters), Captain Hilmi (commander, Rumeli Mecidiye Fort), Lieutenant Nazmi (Rumeli Hamidiye Fort), Captain Herschel (German commander, Anadolu Hamidiye Fort) and Platoon Commander Remzi (Dardanos Fort).

On the night of 18 March 1915, a depressed but optimistic de Robeck began to plan a continuation of the attack with a reorganized fleet. However, sometime during the next four days, de Robeck changed his mind completely. At a conference with his commanders and staff on 22 March 1915, he announced that he could not force the Dardanelles without the help of the army.[41] The failure of the naval attack now set in motion the great amphibious operation now known as the Gallipoli campaign. Participants and historians alike would question de Robeck's decision for the next eighty years and would suggest that one more push would have forced the Dardanelles.

Ottoman ammunition and the 'one more push' theory

One of the recurrent themes in the historiography of the Gallipoli campaign is the idea that the Ottoman defenses, battered by allied bombardment and short of ammunition, would have succumbed to a determined push delivered in the days following the failed naval assault on the Dardanelles of 18 March 1915. Winston Churchill, then First Lord of the Admiralty and one of the originators of the basic concept to attack the strait, definitely thought so.[42] In the abridged version of *The World Crisis*, published in 1930, Churchill pointed out 'We had only to resume a gradual naval advance and bombard to discover the wonderful truth that they had, in fact, scarcely any more ammunition. We now know what we could have so easily found out then, that for the heavy guns, which alone could injure the armoured ships, they had not twenty rounds apiece.'[43] This theme, first established by Winston Churchill in 1930, was accepted as fact and has been widely repeated by both official and popular historians through to the present day.[44] Only two contemporary historians have seriously questioned this notion.[45] Embellished by western writers over the past eighty years, this idea has created and sustained a certain 'what if' mystique in the study of the Gallipoli campaign.

Modern Turkish official histories, however, show a different situation regarding ammunition availability at the Dardanelles. While they did not have an abundant supply of shells, the Ottomans fired off only a small percentage of their available ammunition during the 18 March 1915 engagement. In fact, only four of their fourteen permanent coastal defense forts actually fired against the enemy on that day. While ammunition in these locations was temporarily depleted, substantial quantities remained nearby in the adjacent fortifications. Churchill was wrong, and his judgements on the viability of a follow-on naval attack were flawed. In actuality, the Ottoman defenses guarding the Dardanelles emerged from the day of battle in excellent condition and in a condition to renew the fight with vigor. It is very likely that further allied naval assaults to force the strait would have similarly met defeat.

The first detailed technical account of the naval attack available to the British public was Sir Julian S. Corbett's *History of the Great War Based On Official Documents, Naval Operations, vol. 2*, published in 1921.[46] Corbett noted there was the impression (particularly in Constantinople in 1915) that the Ottomans had practically exhausted their ammunition. However, he noted that the Ottoman War Office official statement contradicted that idea by establishing that 'modern ammunition for heavy guns was very short, but there was a plentiful supply of older ammunition.'[47] Following closely on the heels of Corbett's work in 1923 was the first volume of Churchill's war memoirs titled *The World Crisis*. Churchill's book was quickly serialized by *The Times* in February.[48] Churchill's second volume, which contained his account of the Dardanelles operations, was published and serialized in October 1923. According to Martin Gilbert, *The Times*, while serializing the work, 'was critical of Churchill for distorting documents and deploying "undue censure" in this account of the Dardanelles.'[49] It was in this volume that Churchill laid the groundwork for establishing in the English-speaking world the idea that the Ottomans were critically short of ammunition. He noted that the Ottomans had fired away half of their howitzer ammunition and that in one Ottoman battalion, there were thirty-six rounds remaining for the '14-inch guns and twenty-nine rounds for the 9.4-inch guns'.[50] He also asserted that the Ottomans claimed that there was enough ammunition for two further engagements of the magnitude of the 18 March. Later in the same chapter, Churchill quoted a German staff officer named Major Endres who reported that the 'Ottoman ammunition supply was so short that it would not have sufficed for a second engagement on a large scale.'[51] But, after outlining both the Ottoman deficiencies and the strengths of the Royal Navy, Churchill surmised that no positive conclusions about the success of the renewal of the naval attack could be drawn from these observations.[52]

Churchill compressed his account of the war into a single-volume abridgment titled *The World Crisis* in 1930. He asserted in his preface that 'he had not found it necessary to alter in any material way the facts and foundations of the story, nor the conclusions that I drew from them.'[53] However, it is in this book that Churchill broke the idea that the Royal Navy had only to push the attack further to discover that the Turks were about to run out of ammunition. This was a very significant change from his earlier position and came about from information published in the intervening years. Churchill amended his previous claims by quoting a German report, which stated that half of the howitzer ammunition had been expended, and that for the five 14in guns there were fifty shells apiece and a lesser number for the 11in pieces. He noted that the 'long range H.E. [high explosive], which were particularly effective against armour, were nearly entirely used up.'[54] He further noted an Ottoman report that asserted that Fort Hamidieh (*sic*) had only five to ten rounds remaining and the European batteries (Kalid Bahr) were in a similar state. Churchill took this new information directly from the memoirs of Major Dr Carl Mühlmann, a German officer on the staff of Liman von Sanders' Fifth Army during the Gallipoli campaign,[55] which were published in 1927.

Later authors compounded Churchill's erroneous assertions.

Alan Moorehead, writing in 1956, stated that the Ottomans fired off half their ammunition, 'in particular heavy guns were left with less than thirty armour-piercing shells, which alone had the power to destroy the battleships.'[56] Moorehead further asserted that the Ottomans had laid 324 mines in the strait with 36 in reserve. Robert Rhodes James, writing in 1965, mentioned an Ottoman account that claimed that most of the ammunition available for the long-range guns had been expended.[57] Philip Haythornthwaite used the same basic data in 1991 claiming that half of the ammunition was expended, including almost all for the heavier guns.[58] However, neither Churchill's claims nor the statements of the later writers are corroborated by modern Turkish historical sources.

During the combat operations that lasted from 19 February through mid-March 1915, the Ottomans fired off about 4,700 artillery shells. However, most of the firing came from the guns of 5 Heavy Arty Regt in the forts at the mouth of the Dardanelles and from 8 Heavy Arty Regt in the howitzer zone.[59] On 26 February this regiment fired 343 shells. In the action of 4 March the Ottomans fired 292 shells and a further 347 shells on the following day. On 7 March they shot off 714 shells, 51 shells on 9 March, 1,882 shells on 10 March, 28 on 11 March, 41 shells on 12 March and 974 shells on 13 March.[60] Most of the firing during this period came from the mobile howitzers and from the intermediate defenses, while firing from the powerful heavy batteries from the forts at the narrows occurred only on one day of the battle (10 March).[61] The heaviest firing from the large caliber guns came on 18 March 1915, during de Robeck's climactic attempt to force the narrows. By this date, the 5 Heavy Arty Regt at the entrance of the strait had been eliminated from the Ottoman order of battle due to bombardment and the demolitions of the Royal Marine landing parties. Most of the British accounts of the firing that day characterized the Ottoman firing as particularly heavy, and the Ottoman histories note that 2,250 shells were expended that day (see Appendix A, Table A.3). In fact, most of these were the indirect shells from the howitzers and heavy mortars. Altogether on 18 March the 3 Heavy Arty Regt fired 190 shells, the 4 Heavy Arty Regt fired 240 shells and the howitzers and heavy mortars of the 8 Heavy Arty Regt fired 1,820 shells. Although 368 more shells were expended than had been fired on 10 March (previously the most intense day of Ottoman artillery firing), comparatively few shells came from the heavy coastal guns in the forts at the narrows.

Based on his German source (Major Mühlmann), Churchill stated that 'long range H.E.' shells alone were effective against armored ships. Later Moorehead noted that 'armour-piercing' shells (AP) alone had the power to destroy battleships. The author takes these statements to mean flat-trajectory heavy ship-killing guns of the type located in the forts at the narrows. However, it is doubtful whether anybody really knew what types of shells were hitting what targets and exactly what damage which types of shells were inflicting. While it may make sense that flat-trajectory HE or AP were the most effective types against battleships, this is by no means certain, since the Ottomans fired a variety of flat-trajectory and high-angle artillery ammunition on 18 March. What is known today is that of the ammunition available to the heavy guns of 3 and 4 Heavy Arty Regts on 14 August 1914, only 201 rounds of 355/35 and 240/35 caliber were fired on 18 March 1915, and a lesser amount may have been fired on 10 March 1915. None of the remaining heavy guns (in the 210/20-355/22 caliber range) or mortars of these regiments came into action during these engagements. Assuming that the Ottomans fired perhaps 50 rounds from the 35 caliber heavy guns on 10 March, the total expended rounds (regardless of type) in these regiments would have been about 251, leaving a total available inventory of 1,030 shells of all types for these weapons. Since the shorter ranging heavy coastal guns of lower calibers had not come into action at all on either day, the Ottomans maintained an on-site inventory of at least 4,034 shells of all types for the heavy 210/20-355/22 classes of ordnance. To this must be added 1,106 210/6.4 heavy mortar shells, about 6,000 150/10.8 howitzer shells and an undetermined number of 120/30 and 120/11.6 howitzer shells. Ammunition for the lighter guns totaled up to approximately 24,000 shells. While these numbers pale in comparison to the astonishing inventories assembled on the Western Front, they are nevertheless significant. Considering that on the heaviest day of firing (18 March 1915) that a total of only 2,250 shells were expended, the Ottomans clearly had enough shells to continue the fight.[62]

Although the Ottoman official history gives an incomplete picture of the total munitions available for the defense of the Dardanelles it would appear from the data presented that the Ottomans had an adequate supply of ammunition with which to continue the battle. The powerful inner forts on the narrows that fielded the heaviest guns were the least engaged of the Ottoman forts during the period 19 February to 18 March 1915. In the immediate aftermath of the 18 March engagement, the Ottomans went to work to redistribute ammunition and to repair damaged guns and guns that had suffered mechanical failure.[63] Moreover, casualties were extremely light and the total Ottoman casualties were 4 officers killed and 1 wounded, and 22 men killed and 52 wounded.[64] Furthermore, having observed the sinking or mining of six enemy capital ships, Ottoman morale was sky-high at the end of de Robeck's aborted attack.

The dramatic differences between Churchill's 1923 and 1930 sources and the data contained in the modern Ottoman official histories may be explained by the fact that Churchill's German sources do not appear to have had access to the formal ammunition reports available to later Turkish historians. While it is evident that on 18 March 1915, the inner forts of Anadolu Hamidiye, Dardanos, Namazgah and Rumeli Mecidiye ran low on ammunition stored in on-site magazines it is also clear today that the majority of the inner forts did not fire at all on the day of battle. In some senses *The World Crisis* was written as an apologia to rehabilitate Churchill's tarnished reputation in the immediate aftermath of the First World War and it was not until the 1930s that Churchill's basic concept to force the Dardanelles began to be appreciated as sound strategic thinking. In assembling his sources Churchill only had limited access to Ottoman information and the Turkish official campaign histories about Gallipoli were available until 1936.[65] For his work, therefore, Churchill relied on incomplete German and Ottoman sources that painted a pessimistic picture of the defensive situation at the Dardanelles in the spring of 1915. This was grist for his mill and was exactly what he needed to lend credence to his arguments. Essentially Churchill prematurely seized upon partial evidence to rationalize and support his actions and ideas. Unfortunately, his work proved enormously influential and provided an unsound foundation for subsequent historical assessments.

The most lucid analysis of why the naval attack failed comes from the pen of Professor Arthur J. Marder in 'The Dardanelles: Post-Mortem'.[66] Marder explained:

> On the technical naval side, the real obstacles were the mine-fields of the narrows, against which the minesweeping was utterly inefficient, and their protecting batteries, which the naval guns never silenced. The minefields were the crux of the situation, since the old battleships could evidently be sunk by striking one mine. It could be accomplished only if the minefield batteries could be dominated while the sweeping was going on. But it was not possible for the warships to knock them out. Long-range or indirect fire proved ineffective. To be effective, the ships would have had to close in on the coastal guns and pound away, and this was not possible until the mines were cleared. Thus was the vicious circle complete.'[67]

As Marder noted, the most effective defenses of the Dardanelles were the minefields that the Ottomans began laying in August 1914. The guns simply provided covering fires to keep them from being swept up by the enemy. As previously mentioned, Alan Moorehead noted that the Ottomans laid 324 mines in the strait. Sir Julian Corbett said that the Ottomans had laid nearly 350 mines and calculated the odds that, given this number of unswept mines, only one of sixteen allied battleships could reasonably hope to reach the Sea of Marmara.[68] The Turkish histories assert that, in actuality, a total of 402 were laid in the period 4 August 1914–8 March 1915 in 11 lines numbered serially.[69]

At no time after 17 August 1914 (two and a half months prior to the outbreak of hostilities) were the Dardanelles defenses unready to receive an attack. On that date the heavy artillery regiments of the 2nd Artillery Brigade were manned and there were 133 mines laid in the strait. By 4 November 1914, the howitzers of the 8th Heavy Arty Regt were in position, as were the 40,000 troops of the Ottoman III Corps, and there were a total of

191 mines in the water. By the time of the 19 February 1915 naval attack, the Fortress Command and the III Corps had 50,000 soldiers, armed with 34,500 rifles, 16 machine-guns and 313 cannon on the peninsula (as well as 323 mines in the narrows).[70] By 25 April, the day of the allied amphibious attack, these totals would grow even more.

Without question the powerful Royal Navy had the potential, with the further marshalling of ships and men, to force the Dardanelles after March 1915.[71] However, this would obviously have entailed increased losses at a period of great danger. Clearly there was no 'open door', nor was there a period of acute vulnerability in the strait defenses, either before or after the allied naval attacks. Winston Churchill was wrong when he made the claim that the navy had the potential to force easily the Dardanelles with the forces then available to Admiral de Robeck in late March 1915. In suggesting so, he did a great disservice to both de Robeck and to the Royal Navy. Perhaps he did an even greater disservice to the historians who followed his lead in their assessments of the Ottoman defenses.

Reinforcements and reorganization

British landings at Kum Kale on 4 March alerted the Ottomans to the vulnerability of the Asiatic shore. Consequently on 9 March the experienced 11th Infantry Division, then stationed at Balıkesir on the southern coast of the Sea of Marmara, was alerted for deployment to the strait.[72] Five days later the division began to move to Ezine (southeast of Kum Kale) and, by coincidence, it closed on the town on 18 March 1915. The arrival of the new division did not alter the seaward defence at Kum Kale, which continued to be an ad hoc assortment of the 9th Division's 25th Infantry Regiment (25 Regt), the 64th Regiment (64 Regt), which was newly arrived from the 3rd Division, and several jandarma battalions. And, for the moment, the 11th Division lay in reserve.

Thus by the naval attack of 18 March, the Ottoman defence was solidified into a sort of bi-zonal configuration: III Corps under Esat commanding the middle peninsula and isthmus of Bulair with the 7th and 19th Divisions and the fortress command under Cevat, who commanded the strait defences, 9th Division – lower peninsula and Kum Kale, and 11th Division – Asiatic shore. Contrary to some western histories, which assert that the strait was split up the middle, their defenses were always unitary under the fortress commander (until the activation of the Fifth Army). The principal weakness of the defensive arrangements at this time was the failure to concentrate the 9th Division, which had two regiments in Europe and one regiment in Asia.

Ottoman training and organization

A perception exists in the western world that the Ottoman army at Gallipoli was poorly trained and poorly prepared for combat.[73] Certainly a case can be made that it was not as efficient as the German or British armies. Nevertheless, by the spring of 1915, the divisions of the Ottoman Fifth Army were very well trained. This was reflected by the records of their training programs, which showed a consistent pattern of tough and realistic battle training. Moreover, the archival record shows that Fifth Army regiments and divisions followed the tactical precepts embedded in Enver's General Orders Number 1. The regimental journals of the Fifth Army infantry divisions illustrate this.

On the tenth day of mobilization (12 August 1914) the 9th Infantry Division's 26th Infantry Regiment (26 Regt) at Gallipoli reported its 2nd and 3rd Battalions at war strength. Its 1st Battalion was on detached duty in Basra. By 15 August the regiment had 381 active soldiers, 2,092 reservists and 199 untrained conscripts assigned to its rolls and on the next day began organizing a new 1st Battalion (sometimes erroneously called the 4th Battalion).[74] Four days later, the regiment was ordered to occupy coastal observation posts and to prepare defensive positions by stationing a company at Sedd el Bahr, a platoon at Gaba Tepe, a company at Ece Limani and to bivouac the remainder at Maidos.[75] The regiment was augmented with the Bursa Field Jandarma Battalion, the divisional mountain howitzer battalion and a cavalry troop, which were attached directly to the regiment on 13 September. Its commander began combined arms training with these attachments that week. Later, on 4 October, the regiment developed fire plans from Achi Baba (Alçı Tepe) in concert with the 8th Battery, 3rd Mountain Howitzer Battalion (3 Mountain How Bn) and a 105mm howitzer battery.[76]

The division's 27th Infantry Regiment (27 Regt), also stationed in Gallipoli, was partially mobilized several days earlier on 31 July 1914, against a possible Greek amphibious threat. It was assigned an immediate mission to observe and screen the Saros Bay beaches.[77] In an accelerated mobilization, reserves flooded into the barracks and by 1 August, the regiment reported itself at war establishment (*ikmal*). On 7 August, the Gallipoli Field Jandarma Battalion, the 2nd Battalion, 9th Field Artillery Regiment (2/9 Arty Regt) and a cavalry platoon were attached to the 27 Regt.[78] On 10 September, Major Mehmet Şefik, the commander of the 3rd Battalion, took command of the regiment.[79] Under Şefik, the regiment concentrated on individual training for its soldiers throughout September and participated in division and army maneuvres in October. Beginning on 1 November 1914, the regiment participated in special training with a mountain howitzer battalion and a howitzer battery in the reserve area.[80] As the winter progressed, Şefik's frequent orders to his regiments included specific instructions that insured that the infantry-artillery team jointly coordinated their training.[81] Later, on 15 February 1915, the newly promoted regimental commander, Lieutenant Colonel Şefik was designated as the Maidos Area Commander and his regiment placed in general reserve for the III Corps. Şefik immediately began to coordinate and update the artillery fire plans from the centrally located hill mass of Kavak Tepe. The fire plans were developed for the artillery batteries of 3/9 Arty Regt and included targets in the regimental sector (which included the area later known as the Anzac beachhead).[82]

The remaining regiment of the 9th Infantry Division (25 Regt) had a similar experience, spending August and September involved in the individual training of soldiers.[83] This regiment was not assigned an immediate tactical mission and remained in training conducting maneuvres near Erenkoy until 17 November when it was moved forward to defend the beaches at Kum Kale. The divisional artillery, 9 Arty Regt, was placed in a direct support role to provide fires for the infantry regiments.[84]

Lieutenant Colonel Mustafa Kemal's subsequently famous 19th Infantry Division was activated on 1 January 1915 and was composed of the 57th, 58th and 59th Infantry Regiments (57, 58 and 59 Regts). However, the 58 and 59 Regts were sent to the

VI Corps and the division was reorganized on 9 February with the assignment of the 72nd and 77th Infantry Regiments (72 and 77 Regts). On 6 April 1915, the division itself was assigned to the new Fifth Army.[85] Probably the most lasting western impression about this division is that several of the regiments were composed of 'Arabs' and this made portions of Kemal's division unsteady.[86]

The 57 Regt was activated on 1 February 1915 in the Rodosto staging area north along the Sea of Marmara coast from Gallipoli and it received its regimental colour (*Sanjack*) on 22 February.[87] One battalion of the regiment was formed earlier on 27 January by combining the 4th Companies of the three battalions of the 19th Infantry Regiment (19 Regt), which had been training since 12 August 1914.[88] To further enhance the training of the newly formed regiment, III Corps ordered the 7th Division to send three *Mümtaz Yüzbaşıyı* (distinguished captains) to assist in training the men.[89] The regiment, although newly formed, was thus composed of very experienced ethnic Turks led by highly trained officers and was regarded by Mustafa Kemal as his most solid regiment. The regiment sailed to Maidos on 23 February and spent the next two months in 'very intensive training undergoing frequent field exercises.'[90] The 77 Regt was a VI Corps formation that was mobilized in Aleppo, Syria on 3 August 1914. By 21 August it had 47 officers and 2,347 men assigned to its rolls.[91] Ordered to Constantinople, it departed Aleppo on 28 August and arrived at the Hyderpaşa train station, in Asiatic Constantinople, on 13 September. It was assigned initially to the Second Army and began undergoing intensive individual soldier training on 27 September 1914.[92] This training consisted of demanding foot marches and field training exercises designed to harden the men. In October the regiment participated in army maneuvres. On 1 November the regiment had 64 officers and 3,179 men assigned, about a thousand of which came from the local Thracian force pools as replacements. At a ceremony attended by Enver Pasha and Cemal Pasha the regiment received its colours on 6 November at Çatalca.[93] Due to the high numbers of Arab soldiers, who did not speak Ottoman Turkish, the ceremony was translated into Arabic. The regiment spent the following months participating in field training and in maneuvres. It departed by train and steamer for Gallipoli on 23 February and came under

Mustafa Kemal's command two days later. In its first divisional orders from Kemal, 77 Regt was provided with overlays from adjacent units, situation reports concerning the 9th Division's units defending the coast and intelligence that the British would attempt to land during the hours of darkness.[94]

Other regiments in the Fifth Army had experiences similar to those of the 9th and 19th Infantry Divisions. The 19th Infantry Regiment (19 Regt) in the 7th Division mobilized at war establishment on 12 August 1914 and began intensive training shortly thereafter.[95] The division's 20th and 21st Infantry Regiments (20 and 21 Regts) were also mobilized quickly and began training throughout the fall of 1914. These regiments moved to Gallipoli in early November where they continued field exercises and maneuvres.[96] The 15th Infantry Regiment (15 Regt) in the 5th Infantry Division began its training and maneuvre cycle at full strength on 18 August 1914, with over 3,600 officers and men.[97] The 48th Infantry Regiment (48 Regt) in the 16th Infantry Division (which would deploy to the peninsula later in the campaign) had similar strength returns, began training on 16 August 1914, and on 9 September was entrained for Thrace. By 3 October 1914, the regiment was hard at work training near Keşan.[98]

The 47th Infantry Regiment (47 Regt) of the 16th Division was destroyed in the Balkan Wars but was reformed near Mersin on 15 December 1913, by combining the 1st Battalion, 125th Infantry (1/125 Regt) and the 26th Rifle Battalion.[99] On 7 August 1914, the regiment had barely 1,200 officers and men, but 11 days later had its full war establishment of 3,400 soldiers. On 23 August an artillery battalion was attached to it and with the 1st and 2nd Battalions entrained for Constantinople.[100] These troops arrived at Küçük Çekmece on 28 August and began intensive training and exercises. On 5 October VI Corps commander, Brigadier Ali Reza, inspected the regiment. Meanwhile, at the regimental depot in Tarsus, the 3rd Battalion readied itself with its authorized strength of 10 officers, 1,036 men and 105 animals. This battalion followed the regiment to Thrace. Training went so well for the 47 Regt that the Second Army commander granted the regiment a training holiday on 2 November 1914, and its commanders reported that morale was very high.[101] Thereafter, the regiment went into a four-month period of intensive training that included field exercises and maneuvres. The regiment was not present during the Gallipoli landings, but was ordered to the peninsula on 26 April 1915. Its 3,400 officers and men, 373 animals and 587 cases of ammunition were moved by train to Uzunköprü and then marched by road to the front. While on this journey the men had a hot meal every day and there were adequate rest halts. Marching 25km a day, the entire regiment arrived in Gallipoli on 29 April. Because of 'good order and discipline on the march,' the regiment was battle worthy and eager to fight.[102]

Supporting arms enjoyed similar experiences. Prior to the war, the 3rd Battery of the artillery school's 150mm Howitzer Demonstration Battalion, commanded by Captain Ali Tevfik, fired hundreds of rounds on a daily basis. It was judged by an instructor at the artillery school (Askir Arkayan) as having achieved a very high standard of training.[103] This battery arrived at Erenköy on 23 July 1914, but was later moved to the peninsula itself. Likewise, discipline and training among the coast artillery was judged good because many of the men were experienced.[104] At higher levels, the experience of the 11th Division reflected a pattern typical of Ottoman divisions. It reached its authorized war strength on 8 August 1914, and began to deploy to its war station the following week. On 8 October the division began its training regime near Bandirma.[105] This included very intensive battalion and regiment training, division and corps maneuvres, hard road marches and, unusually, the on and off loading of ships. On 14 October, the division participated in First Army field maneuvres. Training went on throughout the winter and by 3 March 1915, the division was conducting frequent night-march training. Twenty days later the division was deployed to positions near Kum Kale at Calvert's Farm where it was informed that 80,000 allies (including 50,000 Australians) were expected to invade Çanakkale.[106]

Thus by April 1915, the fighting formations of the newly formed Ottoman Fifth Army were ready to receive the allies. Most of the regiments were composed of many combat veterans of the Balkan Wars and they had been training together for periods of up to eight months. The training regimes (in the formations examined here) followed the precepts laid down in Enver's General Orders

Number 1 and included combined arms training between the infantry and its supporting arms, plenty of marches and multi-echelon field maneuvres. Consequently, confidence levels ran high and the officers and men were alert to the impending allied invasion. The evidence reflects that very comprehensive training regimes were in place prior to the arrival of Liman von Sanders.

Experience levels

The western historiography of the Gallipoli campaign tends to focus on two levels of Ottoman command – the tactical level (or division and below) and the strategic level (or army and above). Conspicuously absent from British, Australian and German works on the campaign are detailed discussions of Ottoman actions at the operational level (or army corps). A number of Ottoman army corps were deployed to the peninsula. However, the initial landings were made against the III Corps, commanded by Esat Pasha on the peninsula and against XV Corps commanded by German Colonel Erich Weber in Asia.[107] This section focuses on the III Corps as the XV Corps was so lightly engaged in the opening phase of the campaign.

The III Corps itself was organized in January 1911 at Kirkkilise (near Adrianople) under the sweeping changes of the 1910 army reorganization instruction.[108] Caught up in the Balkan Wars of 1912/13, the corps established itself by participating in every major battle of that war in the Thracian theater. In a war that destroyed large portions of the Ottoman army, it was the only army corps to survive the war organizationally intact (it began the war with the 7th, 8th and 9th Infantry Divisions and ended the war with the same divisions). During the war, the corps never moved more than 70km from its peacetime epicenter of Çorlu. Consequently, after the disastrous defeat in 1913, the III Corps did not have to conduct a major movement returning it to its garrisons nor did it have to reconstitute new formations. All other Ottoman army corps were, to a certain degree ranging from partial to total reconstitution, engaged in a significant rebuilding process. Thus the III Corps was the only Ottoman army corps (of thirteen) that was able to concentrate exclusively on operations and training in 1914.

The effects of the reorganization of the army in December 1913 further enhanced the III Corps. The reorganization eliminated the organized structure of reserve corps and divisions by establishing cadre divisions that would be filled with reservists upon mobilization. This meant that the infantry divisions of the Ottoman army were filled partially with raw conscripts but then augmented with experienced men. The mobilization of the 9th Division was typical of this generalized pattern in the army in 1914. The division was filled to about 25 percent of its authorized war establishment in August 1914 and most of the men were newly conscripted and were undergoing basic training. The mobilization called to the colours the remaining men necessary to bring the regiments to war establishment. In the summer of 1914, this pool of experienced reservists was unique (at least compared to the British and Australians) in that almost all of the men had participated in the recent Balkan Wars and had only recently been released from active duty. The III Corps' 7th and 9th Divisions, in particular, had earned strong fighting reputations in the great Balkan War battles of Kirkkilise, Pinarhisar-Lüleburgaz and First Çatalca, while under the command of the aggressive and talented Mahmut Muhtar Pasha.[109] So, in the case of these divisions, the bulk of the men were not only experienced combat veterans, but also they enjoyed a reputation as members of highly regarded fighting formations. Arguably, in 1914, the III Corps was the most experienced and well-prepared corps in the Ottoman army.

Brigadier General Esat Pasha assumed command of the III Corps on 10 December 1913.[110] He had just returned from captivity in Greece on 2 December and was already being hailed in the Empire as the Hero of Janina (or Yanya in Turkish). There are no comprehensive biographies of this man in either Turkish or English and he remains a rather obscure figure. Although a central figure in the campaign, he was overlooked by western historians and writers, who focused on the aggressively charismatic Mustafa Kemal and the capable Liman von Sanders. Nevertheless, Esat was the man on the spot commanding the III Corps on 25 April 1915 and was responsible for the initial Turkish operational posture and response on the Gallipoli Peninsula.

Born in 1862 in Yanya (modern Ioania, Greece, or Janina as it was called in 1912), Esat attended the Military Academy (*Harp Okulu*) in 1884 and then served as a regimental officer.[111] In 1887, he was selected to attend the Ottoman War Academy (*Harp Akademisi*), and graduated with the class of 1890. His performance was so exceptional (his military record reflected that he spoke German, French and Romanian) that he left for Germany on 10 November 1890 to attend the Prussian War Academy. He graduated and returned on 27 May 1894. Now a major, Esat was assigned to the Ottoman general staff, but was promoted to lieutenant colonel in 1895 and assigned to the Ottoman War Academy. By 1897, he was already a colonel and participated in the Greek War as a regimental commander. Upon his return in 1899, Esat was assigned as the chief of training at the Infantry School. He was promoted to brigadier in 1901 and spent the next several years in command of a brigade and on the Ottoman general staff. By 1908, he was the chief of staff of the Ottoman Third Army and in 1909, Esat accompanied Colmar von der Goltz on his famous inspection tour. He was assigned as the chief of infantry in 1910 and in 1911 Esat briefly commanded the 5th Infantry Division and then the 23rd Infantry Division in the Balkans.

On 26 September 1912, at the beginning of the First Balkan War, Esat was abruptly pulled from division command and assigned as the commander of the Provisional Yanya Corps. The Yanya Corps and its fortress were the linchpin in the Ottoman defenses of western Macedonia and Albania. The fortress was modern and self sufficient with a corps-sized garrison of several infantry divisions, which swelled to six infantry divisions as reinforcements arrived. Over the course of the war, Esat conducted a skillful defense as the Greek Army of Epirus besieged the city. Of note, Esat's performance in corps-level command steadily grew better as the siege progressed. His command was characterized by an ability to form quickly ad hoc groups of divisional size to hold key terrain features. These provisional groupings were assigned to senior officers and were tailored to the specific tactical mission. Esat was able to fend off numerically superior attacks and he also grew in his understanding of the modern battlefield. Although he was isolated and forced to surrender in the disastrous Ottoman defeat, Esat emerged from the war as a genuine Ottoman hero and returned from captivity to be awarded the honorific Pasha.[112] On 25 April 1915, Esat had been in command of the III Corps for over sixteen months combined with six months of recent combat experience as a corps-level commander in the Balkan Wars. It is worth noting here that neither the British or Australian armies maintained peacetime operational corps headquarters and only formed them upon mobilization in August 1914.

Photos of Esat, who appeared somewhat grandfatherly, belied his active nature and his aggressive command style. Liman von Sanders, who was no great admirer of senior Ottoman officers, used the words, 'determined and far seeing' and 'knightly and valorous' to describe Esat.[113] Ancedotal, but reflecting his personality, Esat roused himself out of bed at 2.45 am, 2 August 1914 to read personally the Ottoman army's mobilization orders.[114] In terms of objective performance indicators, as mobilization progressed, Esat's III Corps was the only corps of thirteen in the Ottoman army to meet its scheduled mobilization timetable of twenty-two days.[115] In late August the corps concentrated around Rodosto. The 9th Division moved to the Gallipoli Peninsula on 9 September 1914, the 7th Division deployed there on 29 October and Esat's headquarters followed on 4 November.[116] The 9th Division was assigned to the Fortress Command for the defense of the mouth of the Dardanelles, while the III Corps assumed control of Bulair and the Gulf of Saros. Esat wrote and issued training guidance on 8 November 1914 to his III Corps formations.[117] He specified that units conduct training that included observation techniques, combat and spot reporting procedures, alarm situations, battle-drill rehearsals, coordination with the jandarma and tactical deception measures. Throughout the winter, Esat's troops trained for war. The naval attacks of 25 February and 18 March 1915 heightened the sense that a major Allied assault on the Dardanelles was imminent.

On 7 April, Liman von Sanders returned control of the 9th Division to the III Corps and assigned Esat the mission to defend the peninsula.[118] Esat immediately prepared and issued orders to two of his three infantry divisions (the 7th and 9th) that assigned them revised coastal defence sectors and designated regiments in reserve.[119] He also directed that the division commanders coordinate artillery support and conduct artillery training with the Strait Fortress Command. Esat designated Mustafa Kemal's 19th Division as the corps general reserve and instructed Kemal to be prepared to fight either on the peninsula or on the Asian side of the strait. Importantly, he also included training guidance concerning how his units would prepare themselves for the coming fight. Esat directed that units would rehearse the manning of their fortifications during day and night. He ordered that three days a week, every unit would practice rapidly moving from their reserve areas to their battle positions (again during day and night). He specifically directed that the 9th Division's reserves (25 Regt) at Sarafim Çiftliği (Sarafim Farm) would practice route marching to Sedd el Bahr at night for operations and then return on the following night.[120] Esat was also concerned about fatigue among his troops on coastal observation duty and ordered that commanders frequently rotate them to rest areas. He was concerned about communications and directed that his divisions and independent formations practice sending messages frequently and for a selected officer to become expert in these procedures. Furthermore, he ordered them to be prepared to send messages by telephone, written reports, horse messenger, lamp and signal flags in the event of a breakdown in communications. He closed his instructions with an injunction to feed the men well during marches and the notation that his headquarters was located in the town of Gallipoli (Gelibolu).

Also in early April Esat turned his attention to the population of the peninsula. Prior to the Battle of Çatalca in the First Balkan War (1912), the Ottoman general staff ordered the army to evacuate the Christian population of Thrace.[121] This was done because the Turks felt that the numerous Greek and Bulgarian Christians living in the rear areas of the Ottoman army might rise in revolt or aid (directly or indirectly) the attacking Bulgarian army. The Gallipoli Peninsula was the historical home of thousands of Greeks, who, as in 1912, were thought to be a threat to the army. By 10 April 1915, Esat had evacuated most of them to villages across the Sea of Marmara in Asia.[122] In all, about 22,000 Greeks were evacuated from the peninsula.

Esat had a very strong and experienced command team, who had likewise served in the Balkan Wars. On the III Corps staff, Lieutenant Colonel Fahrettin (chief of staff) had served on the

Ottoman general staff in the war and Captain Remzi had served as chief of staff of the Edirne (Adrianople) fortress during the siege of 1912/13. Likewise the commanders were also Balkan War veterans. 9th Division commander Colonel Halil Sami and his chief of staff, Major Hulisi, commanded infantry regiments in the war and the division's 27 Regt commander, Lieutenant Colonel Şefik, had commanded a reserve infantry division in the fight for Salonika. Mustafa Kemal had served as the Gallipoli Army chief of operations and the 57 Regt commander, Major Avni, had served as an infantry division chief of staff in the Balkan Wars. The corps and divisions of the Fifth Army were similarly staffed and the officer commanding the Çanakkale Fortress Command (the coast defence forts and batteries) was Brigadier Cevat Pasha, who had commanded the Çatalca Artillery Command during the Balkan Wars. At lower levels the majority of the field grade and company grade officers were combat veterans as well.

There was, however, a gaping hole in the leadership fabric of the Ottoman army and it manifested itself in the absence of a long-service professional corps of non-commissioned officers (NCOs). The NCO corps, the 'backbone of the army' according to Rudyard Kipling, has long been seen as an important component of combat effectiveness. Statistics vary concerning the density of NCOs in the European armies of 1914. David Jones noted that (corporals excluded) the peacetime NCO strength of pre-war European infantry companies was Germany 12, France 6, Austria-Hungary and Italy 3, and Russia 2.[123] Another source suggested higher numbers in the German Army 18 to 20 and in the French Army 8 to 0, but these numbers surely include corporals.[124] In the Ottoman army, the pre-war authorization in an infantry company was a <u>single</u> NCO (and three officers).[125]

The men were overwhelmingly illiterate and were, for the most part, from rural or unindustrialized farming villages.[126] This was an obvious problem for which there was little remedy. Those men who could read and write, even minimally, were often quickly promoted to sergeant or corporal. Consequently, much of the training was based on direct instruction by officers or non-commissioned officers, who read to the men from books prepared specially for this situation. Examples of these included 'The Ottoman Soldier in History' (*Tarihte Osmanlı Neferi*) and 'Advice to the Brave – Gift to the Veteran' (*Yiğitlere Öğütler - Gazilere Armağan*), as well as Ottoman army training manuals.[127] The implications of this situation are far reaching, but unfortunately neither the official history, the sources examined in this study nor participant memoirs address this particular point. Of course, upon mobilization, reserve and former NCOs were recalled to the colours to fill the companies to wartime authorizations. In the case of the III Corps, the manpower pool contained recently discharged combat veterans and this probably mitigated some of the adverse effects of the acute shortage of trained NCOs.

Chapter 2
The Landings, 25 April–1 May 1915

Introduction

The second phase of the Ottoman campaign for the Gallipoli peninsula begins with the allied landing on the morning of 25 April 1915 and ends with the failure of the British and Australian offensives to achieve a decisive result. In this phase the newly activated Ottoman Fifth Army executed its defensive plans successfully and then went on to mass its forces effectively in attempts to drive the Australians into the sea. There were three sub sets of battles in this phase, two of which were decisive. On Cape Helles, the Ottoman 9th Division fought a deliberate defense from well-prepared positions falling back under pressure to hasty defensive positions before stopping the British and French. At the Anzac beachhead, Mustafa Kemal's 19th Division executed a movement to contact, followed by a meeting engagement that stopped the Australians. Kemal's force then swelled to an ad hoc provisional army corps that launched major counterattacks. These actions were decisive in that they stopped the allied advances and fatally disabled Ian Hamilton's plans. The third battle, at Kum Kale in Asia, was an allied diversion, which from the Ottoman perspective was a divisional scale fight that resulted in a French withdrawal. As the Kum Kale landing was never more than a diversion it was not a decisive battle.

At Anzac and Cape Helles, the outnumbered Turks, who were well trained and well led by Ottoman officers (rather than by German officers) fought well. However, the western view of these battles often credits Germans as the architects of victory. The memoirs of Otto Liman von Sanders published in 1928 appear to be the point of origin for many of the western myths and misperceptions concerning the Ottoman conduct of combat operations in the Gallipoli campaign. Liman von Sanders tended to weight heavily his story with the idea that he was instrumental in planning the defense of the peninsula as well as being critically engaged in the key tactical decisions that thwarted the allied landings on 25 April 1915. In particular, the memoirs lead the reader to the conclusion that Liman von Sanders himself generated the basic configuration of forces, created reserves where none had existed, galvanized the Ottomans into constructing beach defenses and obstacles, and pushed them into hard training geared to counter amphibious landings. Closely following this, the British official history of the campaign appeared in print (in 1929) and perpetuated many of the myths sown by Liman von Sanders. This chapter will attempt to separate the western historiography from the Ottoman and Turkish record of these events. Indeed, as seen in the previous chapter, Ottoman defensive preparations for the strait as well as the peninsula itself were quite mature when Liman von Sanders arrived by ship at Gallipoli on 26 March from Constantinople.

The activation of Fifth Army

An urgent message from Cevat Pasha (the fortress commander) to Enver on 20 March 1915 (two days after the naval attack) requested the release of the 11th and 19th Divisions from reserve for tactical use at Gaba Tepe and Kum Kale respectively in order to concentrate the 9th Division on the southern end of the Gallipoli Peninsula.[1] Subsequently, Enver approved the movements of the 9th and 11th Divisions but retained Kemal's 19th Division near Maidos.[2] By 31 March the entire 9th Division was concentrated on the lower peninsula together with two jandarma battalions. Furthermore, Enver warned that Hamilton had brought 40,000 French and 50,000 Australians to Mudros harbour. These messages highlight the concerns the Ottoman high command had about an allied invasion immediately after the attack of 18 March. A now thoroughly worried Enver Pasha decided to reorganize his forces on Gallipoli. On 24 March 1915, Enver requested that Liman von Sanders, who was then in command of the First Army, take control of a proposed Ottoman Fifth Army. The next day, Enver sent orders to the Ottoman general staff outlining the new command arrangements that would transfer all mobile units from the fortress command to the newly activated army.[3] The new German commander himself

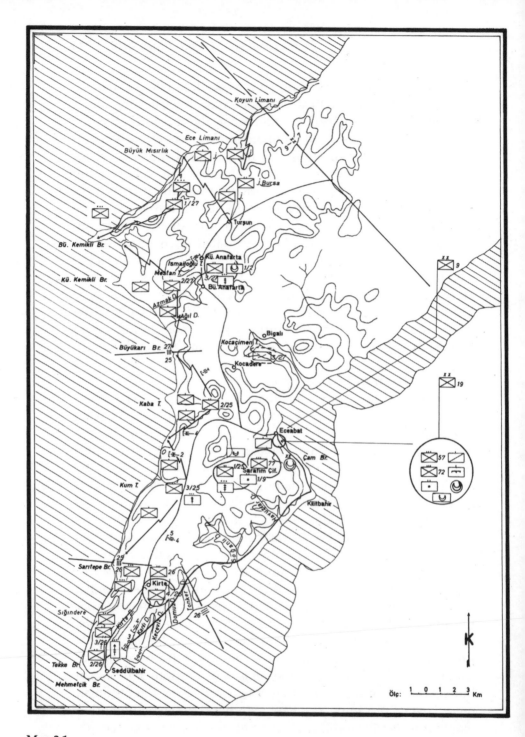

Map 2.1
9th Infantry Division, 31 March 1915. The concentration of the 9th Division on the lower peninsula is shown prior to the influence of Liman von Sanders. Not counting the 19th Division (nine battalions), there are three 9th Division battalions in tactical reserve. Because of redesignation the 1/26 Infantry is shown on this map as 4/26 Infantry. They are the same unit.

arrived on the peninsula on 26 March. The formal activation orders were published on the same day assigning the new Fifth Army the following units: Esat Pasha's III Corps (7th, 9th and 19th Infantry Divisions), Faik Pasha's II Corps (4th and 5th Infantry Divisions), a Provisional Corps to be activated under German Colonel Erich Weber (3rd and 11th Infantry Divisions), and an independent cavalry brigade.[4] But almost immediately thereafter the II Corps and the 4th Division were deleted from the Fifth Army order of battle while 5th Division was retained as an independent division. Map 2.1 shows the deployment of the 9th Division on 31 March 1915.

The new Fifth Army commander spent his first week inspecting the area of operations and concluded that allied landings were most likely at Saros Bay and/or in Asia. Meanwhile, the remainder of 3rd Division left Constantinople by ship and arrived at Erenkoy on 31 March. As a result of Liman von Sanders' analysis, the 5th Division remained at Saros Bay, while the 3rd Division proceeded to the Asian side and the area around Calvert's Farm, where Colonel Weber had set up his newly established provisional corps headquarters on 1 April 1915.[5] Colonel Weber, in turn, deployed the 3rd Division to the Kum Kale beaches and the 11th Division immediately to its south on 5 April 1915.[6] The tactical arrangements mirrored those of the 9th Division on the peninsula with company level defences on the beaches backed up by strong battalion and regimental level reserves. Over the next two weeks, minor changes were made to the tactical disposition of the combat forces and the Fifth Army staff concentrated on improving the logistical lines of communications. In particular, three rations depots and one munitions depot were moved closer to the corps headquarters and the 20m and 40m pontoons from the III Corps bridge trains were sent to the newly activated XV Corps.[7]

Over the next several days the Ottoman high command sent several machine-gun companies, four jandarma battalions and an artillery battalion to reinforce the Fifth Army. On 7 April, the Fifth Army issued Liman von Sanders' defensive operations order for the impending campaign.[8] It contained no surprises and formally assigned the subordinate corps and divisions defensive missions in their sectors of responsibility. Colonel Weber's provisional corps was formally activated as the Ottoman army's XV Corps. Liman von Sanders ordered Mustafa Kemal's 19th Division to move from Maidos to Bigalı and assigned it the mission of Fifth Army general reserve with instructions to be prepared to return to Maidos for deployment to Asia if required. There were tactical instructions dealing with artillery coordination, battle drills, day and night marches and maneuvres, and reporting procedures. However, these instructions simply restated previous Ottoman army standardized procedures that had already been implemented by the Ottoman corps and division commanders themselves.

Mustafa Kemal (later Atatürk, 1881–1938) graduated from the Ottoman War Academy in 1905. As a young general staff officer he was assigned to the Ottoman Third Army headquarters, then in Salonika (in what is now Greece). At that time, Salonika was a hot bed of revolutionary nationalist activity and Kemal became associated with the Young Turk movement. He marched on the capital with the Action Army in 1909 and served as a regimental commander in 1911 (38 Regt). After a brief tour on the general staff, Kemal was sent to Libya on 1 January 1912 to organize tribal resistance to the Italian invasion. He returned in November 1912 and was assigned to the Gallipoli Army as its chief of operations. After the Balkan War, political differences with Enver forced him to take an assignment in Bulgaria as the military attaché in Sofia and then to Belgrade as an attaché as well. Kemal returned on 20 January 1915 to take command of the 19th Division. He spoke both French and German and was known as an ardent nationalist and modernizer. His career went on to span the War of Independence and he became the first president of the modern republic of Turkey.

The Ottoman dispositions were criticized heavily by General Otto Liman von Sanders in his memoirs and the perception that defenses were poorly sited and improperly prepared has persisted to this day (he was particularly critical of the number of reserves available for counterattacks).[9] Liman von Sanders asserted that 'The positions of five existing divisions up to March 26 had to be altered completely. They were posted on different principles and distributed along the entire coast . . . there were no reserves to check a strong and energetic advance.'[10] However, the

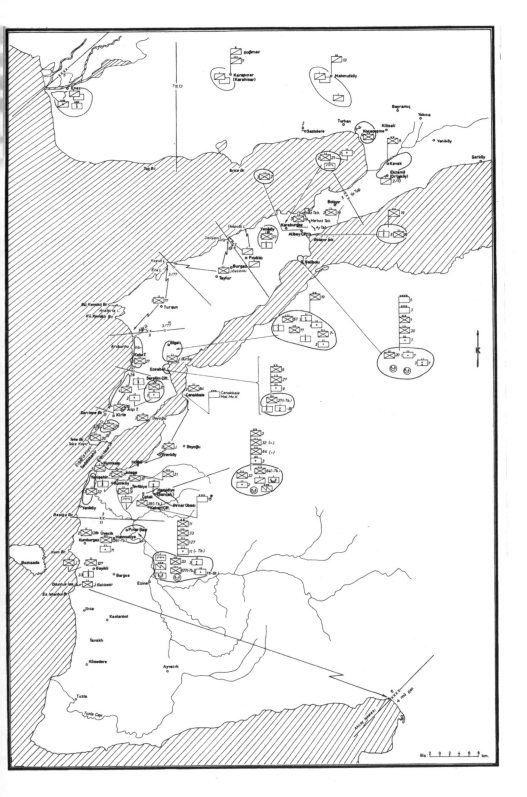

Map 2.2
Fifth Army, 25 April 1915. In its final pre-battle operational configuration the Ottoman Fifth Army mirrored the 1912 defensive plan.

Ottoman defenses were quite robust prior to the arrival of Liman von Sanders on 26 March 1915 and included substantial numbers of well-positioned reserves.[11] In fact, the Ottoman deployment on that day included twelve infantry battalions in immediate reserve. Although Liman von Sanders shifted the 19th Infantry Division north from Maidos to Bigalı, he would actually add only a single battalion to the total reserves available on 25 April.[12] Moreover, the concentration of the 3rd, 9th and 11th Divisions was already in motion before he arrived as well. Based on this evidence the impact of Liman von Sanders in the pre-battle deployment of the Ottoman Fifth Army appears minimal. Map 2.2 shows the peninsula defences as they were arranged on 25 April 1915. Readers may wish to compare them with Map 1.1 and 2.1 (see pp. 4 and 44).

The landing at Anzac, 25 April 1915

Over-reliance on English and German language sources has created an inaccurate impression of how the Turks conducted the fight at the Anzac beachhead in late April 1915. The histories of C.E.W. Bean (1923) and Nigel Steel and Peter Hart (1994) run closest to the events recorded by the Turks.[13] Robert Rhodes James (1965), Michael Hickey (1995) and Moorehead (1956) are the least accurate.[14] The most recent historian of the campaign, Tim Travers (2001), was able to gain access to the modern Turkish military archives in Ankara but could not conclude a comprehensive study of the Ottoman campaign at division or corps level.[15] With regard to the ANZAC landing all western studies have overlooked the vital role of the 27 Regt's pre-battle planning and training (the 27 Regt was, in fact, a 9th Division regiment and not a 19th Division regiment). As a group, these histories also undervalued the roles of Esat Pasha (III Corps commander) and Colonel Halil Sami (9th Division commander), and overplayed the role of Lieutenant Colonel Mustafa Kemal (19th Division commander) and Liman von Sanders. Furthermore, none of these works addressed the remarkable interplay of the message flow between the Turkish commanders, which created an enhanced situational awareness of what was happening in the field and none credited the Turks with anything other than a 'reasonably quick response.'[16] However, a detailed examination of Ottoman records illuminates how the Turks were able to focus decisive combat power at the critical point.

The 2/27 Regt, defended the coastal beaches that came to be known as Anzac. This battalion had three companies along the coast (the 6, 7 and 8 Coy) and a fourth in immediate reserve (5 Coy). They were well dug in, occupied positions that dated back to 1912 and had spent months improving both their positions and their communications. The commander was Major Halis, who had taken command of the battalion from Mehmet Şefik in September 1914. Halis was a combat veteran of the Libyan War and the Balkan Wars and, due to an eye wound, was known as 'Blind Halis'.[17] He established his command post in the fortified strong point on Gaba Tepe, which had well established communications with the supporting artillery.[18] The remaining two battalions of the 27 Regt, under the personal command of Lieutenant Colonel Mehmet Şefik, lay several kilometers behind in the 9th Division's reserve area. His attached artillery and cavalry had been under his command for almost nine months. Şefik exercised active oversight over his sector and, for example, ordered Major Halis to forward updated target overlays to his headquarters prior to the landings.[19] Just to the north, in Fifth Army reserve, lay Mustafa Kemal's new 19th Division. Kemal's units had been alerted to the acute danger of an imminent allied invasion and since late February there had been continuous coordination between the 27 Regt and Mustafa Kemal's division.[20]

The Kavak Tepe fire-planning exercise of February 1915 indicated that the Turks considered the most likely landing beach was located just to the north of Gaba Tepe (the area later known by the Australians as Brighton Beach). Major Halis' (2/27 Regt) reserve, the 5 Coy, was positioned over watching the beach for a counterattack on this landing ground. In fact, it was here at Brighton Beach that the Australians intended to storm ashore, but a misjudged landing cast them ashore instead in the narrow shelf-like cove at Ari Burnu (Anzac Cove). From the British view, this has long been seen as a serious error that upset the landings. However, had the ANZACs landed in the designated site, they would have found themselves immediately under the guns of the Gaba Tepe strong point and the 5 Coy (and in similar dire circumstances to the troops on W and V Beaches at Cape Helles).[21] By fortunate chance, the Australians came ashore in the most protected site in the 27 Regt's sector.

Despite allied attempts to remain unseen and unheard, the 8 Coy alerted the 9th Division at 2.30 am on 25 April that the British were preparing to land.[22] This news sped up the Turkish chain of command and 50 minutes later the III Corps notified the Fifth Army that landings were imminent.[23] Turkish rifle fire began at 4.20 am against the incoming boats, and 5 minutes later, effective shrapnel fire from 'batteries further south played havoc with the troops in the pulling boats.'[24] Several boats suffered direct hits with '15 pounder' shells (probably 77mm projectiles) and, by full daybreak, there were two cutters, three lifeboats and a launch aground on the beach with dead and wounded crews.[25] While not landing in the exact center of the pre-planned killing zone at Brighton Beach, there were enough Australians inside the Turkish range fans to validate the target planning that had been previously done.

The Australians began to land about 5 am and their location was immediately passed up to the III Corps headquarters. Although his soldiers were tired from night training, Lieutenant Colonel Şefik immediately ordered his infantry and artillery to begin operations to 'throw the enemy into the sea.' Based on Şefik's reports, the 9th Infantry Division commander, Colonel Halil Sami, issued orders at 5.55 am, noting that the enemy had come ashore 30 minutes before between Ari Burnu and Gaba Tepe. He also formally ordered Şefik with the 27 Regt, artillery battery and machine-guns 'to proceed to drive the enemy into the sea' and directed coordination measures with other units for fire support.[26] Halil Sami then put a 77mm battery on the road to support the 27 Regt. Duplicated copies of these orders were sent to the III Corps and also to Kemal's 19th Division for coordination purposes.[27]

By 8 am, Şefik's 1/27 Regt and 3/27 Regt, as well as his artillery, were moving along parallel routes toward Kavak Tepe. En route, he issued a short combat order that he wanted to attack and ordered his artillery to Hill 165. These were not the only Turkish forces moving into action against the Australians. Earlier, about 5.30 am, Lieutenant Colonel Mustafa Kemal alerted his 19th Division for action and ordered his cavalry troop forward to

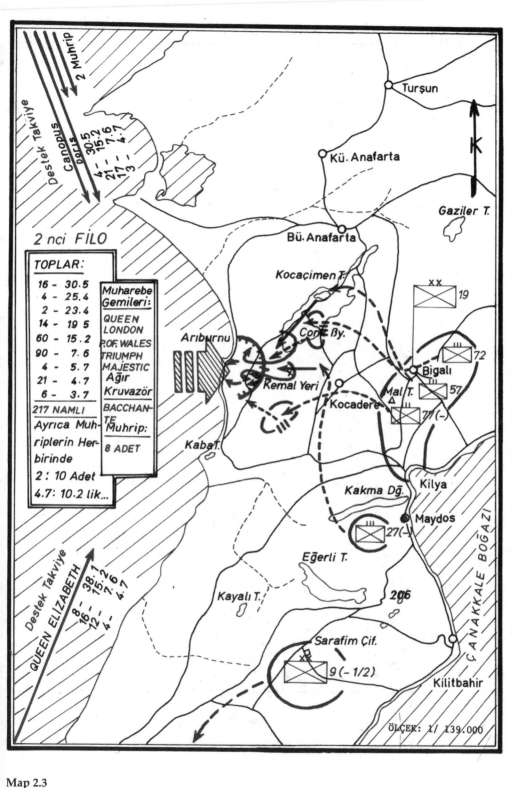

Map 2.3

Ottoman movements to Anzac, 25 April 1915. The movement of the Ottoman reserves to contain the ANZAC beachhead belies the difficulty of coordinating the actions of two divisions. What looks simple on this map was, in fact, a difficult and challenging operation.

conduct route reconnaissance of the roads to Kocaçımen Tepe (Koja Chemen Tepe about 5,000m north of Kavak Tepe, or Anderson's Knoll as it came to be called). By 7 am no orders had arrived from the III Corps and the impatient and aggressive Kemal ordered his 57 Regt, a mountain howitzer battery, and his medical detachment to Kocaçımen Tepe. He sent a situation report to III Corps outlining his intentions and his troops were marching within the hour.[28] Map 2.3 shows the routes by which Şefik's and Kemal's regiments travelled to meet the ANZACs.

There were now two separate forces moving on Anzac under different commanders. After receiving a copy of Kemal's situation report, Colonel Halil Sami, the 9th Division commander, reacted swiftly and issued new orders at 8.25 am to Lieutenant Colonel Şefik that revised and clarified the tactical chain of command.[29] These orders alerted Şefik to the fact that the 57th Regt, commanded by Major Hüseyin Avni, was soon to be operating at Kocaçımen under Mustafa Kemal. Şefik was ordered to coordinate his operations with Kemal and to receive further instructions in the Kavak Tepe area. About 9 am, Şefik's leading elements were nearing Kavak Tepe and were meeting the men of his 2/27 Regt who were conducting a fighting retreat up from the beaches. They brought with them captured enemy soldiers of the '3rd Australian' (probably from the 3rd Brigade) from the initial landings.[30] At 10.30 am, the 27 Regt was firmly in contact with the enemy; however, Şefik's planned attack was now held up by the orders to coordinate with Mustafa Kemal.

Meanwhile, Mustafa Kemal had reached Conkbayırı (Chunuk Bair) at 9.40 am with his aide where he was protected by a platoon of Şefik's 2/27 Regt. Kemal claimed in his *Report of Fighting at Ariburnu* that he met these men retreating from the Australians.[31] When he asked them why they were running away they told him that they had no ammunition left. Kemal then ordered them to fix bayonets and lie down on the ground, throwing the enemy into confusion and buying time for the 57 Regt to arrive.[32] Whatever really happened, Kemal had time to prepare a short attack order specifying that his 1/57 Regt and 2/57 Regt would attack while holding his 3/57 Regt in reserve. A cavalry officer from the 9th Division bought him a report at 11 am outlining Şefik's plan to which Kemal wrote a reply outlining his own plan and thus effectively achieving tactical coordination. Copies of these orders were sent to III Corps. The essence of Kemal's plan was that he would attack the enemy's left flank with his regiment and artillery, but would wait to begin the attack until Şefik's 27 Regt attacked the right flank. Şefik replied directly to Kemal at 11.30 am informing him that the enemy had occupied a 2,000m beachhead and that he intended to attack and advance his scouts toward Ari Burnu. He closed by saying that 'we will attack and advance together.'[33] Şefik then ordered his artillery and machine-guns to open preparatory fires. Clearly he understood both Halil Sami's guidance that he should fight under Kemal and also Kemal's tactical intent for battle management. At noon, Şefik issued his regimental attack order directing his men to 'fight like lions and drive the invaders into the sea.'[34] He oriented (centered) his regiment on a small ridge called the Kanlısırt (later known as Lone Pine). He also attached a company from his 3/27 Regt to the 1/27 Regt, thus weighting his right flank (nearest to Kemal's regiment).

Sometime between 12.30 and 1 pm, Şefik's skirmishers went forward followed by waves of infantry with bayonets fixed. Kemal's men went forward as well. They were supported by three batteries of mountain and field artillery from Hill 165, Gok Tepe and Kavak Tepe (these were Şefik's and Kemal's attached artillery and the 77mm guns that Halil Sami had sent). Kemal also took the time to order his 77 Regt forward to reinforce the left flank of Şefik's regiment and his remaining 72 Regt to reinforce his own right flank (this timely action brought the Ottoman regiments into a 180° ring compressing the Australians). This attack rocked the Australians and brought their advances to a halt. However, staunch Australian resistance brought the determined but badly outnumbered Turks to a halt (there were four Turkish battalions attacking over eight Australian battalions).

Although the Turks had delayed their counterattack by several hours from its optimum time of around 10 am, they had achieved considerable advantages by waiting until coordination was complete. Neither Şefik nor Kemal recklessly launched premature and unsupported attacks. Instead, more or less on the run they had coordinated a combined attack fully supported by artillery and machine-guns. By releasing tactical control of his

27 Regt to Mustafa Kemal, Colonel Halil Sami had effectively and informally cross-attached what might be termed a regimental combat team to the 19th Division. This insured that the senior man on the spot (Kemal) enjoyed unity of command (as well as enabling Halil Sami to concentrate on the fights then raging on the beaches of Cape Helles). A timely flow of combat reports and orders then enabled Kemal and Şefik to develop an appreciation of the unfolding events. In a 6-hour period, these men brought four infantry battalions into action (with a fifth in reserve) complete with supporting arms from reserve positions that were miles apart.

It was an unusual accomplishment and one that could not have been done without a high degree of standardization in doctrine, reporting systems and fire-support coordination. The most vivid descriptions of the result are found in Bean and Travers, who describe the severe punishment meted out to the Australians by very effective Turkish shrapnel fire and sniping. The continuous shelling and the subsequent Turkish bayonet attack initiated a disintegration of morale and effectiveness among the ANZAC, which would gather momentum as the day passed. As early as 12.50 pm, messages began to arrive at Australian headquarters declaring that they could not stand against the Turks without artillery support.[35] This is not to say that the Turks were not without problems related to artillery fire-support coordination. An urgent message at 3.05 pm from Major Avni (57 Regt) to Lieutenant Colonel Şefik (27 Regt) noted that 'our artillery is firing on our own scouts in advanced positions.'[36]

At 3.30 pm, two battalions of Major Saip's 77 Regt were moving into position on the left (the third was assigned coastal defense duties at Suvla Bay and was unavailable for operations) and Kemal launched a second powerful counterattack in concert with the five battalions of the 27 Regt and 57 Regt. This attack was supported by artillery fires from the area now known as Kemalyeri (Kemal's Place) or the Scrubby Knoll. An hour later, the three battalions of the 72 Regt, now in position on the right, attacked as well. Kemal now had ten battalions in action against the allies' eighteen.

Fortunately for Kemal, the allied battalions were poorly deployed against the Turks. This was a result of ineffective leadership at divisional and corps level. The first brigade ashore was the 3rd Australian Brigade commanded by Brigadier MacLagan. Despite landing on the wrong beach, MacLagan aggressively pushed inland toward the high ground. Then, as MacLagan was the first senior commander ashore, the commanders of the incoming 2nd Brigade and the New Zealand Brigade deployed according to his directions.[37] MacLagan, however, did not have a clear picture of the situation or the terrain and deployed the incoming battalions to reinforce his own brigade's unfolding fight (rather than deploying to expand the beachhead by seizing the key high ground). In effect, a brigade commander negated the effective deployment of his own division and the entire corps by marching toward the sound of the guns, rather than toward key terrain. As a result, the Australians were very weak at the point of Mustafa Kemal's attack.[38] Moreover, MacLagan had allowed the battalions to leave their packs and their shovels on the beach, thus forfeiting the capability to dig in quickly when counterattacked.

Meanwhile, at Esat Pasha's III Corps field headquarters on Mal Tepe it was apparent that all immediate reserves were committed to containing the allied landings and it was necessary to revise the command arrangements to reflect the on the ground realities of the battle. From a purely technical perspective, Mustafa Kemal was fighting in Halil Sami's sector. Reacting swiftly to reorganize his corps, Esat designated Kemal as the Ari Burnu Front Commander (*Ariburnu Cephesi Komutanlığı*) and attached the 27 Regt to his new command.[39] In effect, this transferred the coastline sector of the 2/27 Regt (stretching from a point south of Gaba Tepe to a point north of Fisherman's Hut) from Halil Sami's 9th Division to Kemal's 19th Division. This also formalized the cooperative working arrangement that Halil Sami and Kemal had evolved earlier in the day. Esat Pasha now had Mustafa Kemal focused on the ANZAC at Ari Burnu and Halil Sami focused on the British 29th Division at Cape Helles.

To be sure, the Turks had their share of coordination problems. Both Bean and Travers have identified correctly the loss of tactical control within the 57 Regt during the noon attack and Kemal's mishandling of the 77 Regt in mid-afternoon.[40] Nevertheless, as darkness fell on the battlefield, it was the Australians who were notably demoralized. Encouraged by his success in pushing the enemy back during the afternoon, Kemal ordered his regiments to continue with night bayonet attacks. It was during these night attacks that the Arab soldiers of the 77 Regt became disorganized and began to fire wildly into the adjacent friendly sectors. The night attacks were conducted at battalion level and, while tactically unsuccessful, served to keep pressure on the embattled Australians and New Zealanders. Remarkably, that night both ANZAC division commanders (Major General W.T. Bridges and Major General Sir Alexander Godley), although having landed 20,000 out of 24,000 troops during the day, became convinced that the Turks had the advantage and would overrun the corps at daybreak. In particular the Australians were almost paralyzed by very effective shrapnel fire from enemy field artillery and by massed enemy infantry assaults.[41] Near midnight, they shocked their corps commander (Lieutenant General Sir William Birdwood) with a joint recommendation to evacuate the beachhead.[42] Birdwood referred the decision to General Sir Ian Hamilton, who famously advised the Australians and New Zealanders to stay put and 'dig, dig, dig.'[43]

Many of the western historians of the campaign mention the issue of the reduced combat effectiveness of the 'Arab' regiments. It should be noted that the official Turkish military history of this campaign does not mention ethnicity as a factor affecting operations. However, the memoirs of the key officers of the Turkish III Corps command team do contain a variety of criticisms regarding the 'Arab' regiments. III Corps chief of staff Fahrettin noted that the 72 Regt and 77 Regt received a minimum of training (*eğitimleri de azdır*).[44] Esat noted the same and also noted that the regiments were prone to panic.[45] Mustafa Kemal mentioned that the 77 Regt made many operational mistakes (*bu alayın birçok yanlış harekatı vardır*).[46] Lieutenant Colonel Şefik's criticism of the 77 Regt was particularly strident noting that a number of the Arab soldiers hid in the bushes and had to be rounded up by Şefik's men.[47] These criticisms of readiness and training of the 77 Regt, in particular, seem to contradict the historical record established earlier in this chapter. Moreover, the ethnic composition of the regiment, strongly Yezidi and Nusayrı according to Esat and Fahrettin,[48] is contradicted by the examination of its replacement input and by modern Turkish army scholarship as well.[49] The archival record containing the daily staff journals of the 72 Regt and 77 Regt clearly proves that these units received training similar in scope and duration to other Ottoman regiments. It is true, however, that many soldiers in this regiment could not speak Ottoman Turkish and this would have had a most serious impact as the regiment launched difficult and unplanned hasty operations (the movement to contact resulting in day and night bayonet attacks on 25 April), which are reliant on verbal communications. It also appears that their performance in the movement to contact and their attacks were generally similar to the non-Arab 27 Regt and 57 Regt and it may be that this issue is overstated. Finally, Major Saip's 77 Regt performed well in subsequent operations in the defense of Gaba Tepe (famously repelling an Australian amphibious raid commanded by Captain R.L. Leane on 3/4 May).[50]

Anzac, 26 April–4 May 1915

At 1.50 am on 26 April 1915, the Fifth Army headquarters sent a ciphered telegram to Enver Pasha at the Ministry of War outlining Liman von Sanders' plans for the next few days.[51] The Fifth Army reported that the 19th Division was conducting night attacks and that the XV Corps (in Asia) was in contact with the enemy and holding the line successfully. The telegram noted that no landing had occurred at Saros Bay and that Liman von Sanders intended to send reinforcing units (two divisional equivalents) from the XV Corps and 7th Division to the 9th and 19th Division sectors. The message ended with a notation that the Fifth Army had telegraph communications with both fighting fronts, and wireless communications with the Strait Fortress Command and with the battle cruiser *Yavuz* (ex-*Goeben*). The first reinforcing units (the 33 Regt and 64 Regt) were alerted for movement concurrently with the dispatch of the telegram.

The ciphered message to Enver Pasha in the early hours of 26 April reflected Liman von Sanders' most important contribution to the decisive defeat inflicted on Hamilton's landing force. The Fifth Army commander had spent the day personally observing and evaluating the diversionary allied operations at Saros Bay and was not deceived by the maneuvre. With three divisions in contact with the enemy, Liman von Sanders committed two of his remaining divisions to the fights at Anzac and Cape Helles. In doing so, he stripped away the defenders from the Bulair isthmus and from the French front (itself a diversion) at Kum Kale in Asia. This bold decision indicates an unusually high degree of situational awareness at army level (by 1915 standards) and reflected the capability of subordinate Ottoman units to transmit accurate and timely information. This would enable Liman von Sanders to mass his forces inside the British decision cycle.

Early in the morning of 26 April (5.10 am), the 19th Division's chief of staff, Staff Major Izzettin, was already coordinating with the III Corps concerning the reorganization of forces.[52] The first of the incoming reinforcements was the mountain howitzer battalion of the 7th Division (3rd Battalion, 7th Artillery Regiment) that would go to the artillery positions at Kemalyeri. It was needed there because Mustafa Kemal's troops were exhausted from 24 hours of continuous operations, especially the men of Şefik's 27 Regt, who had been awake for 48 hours. Therefore, Kemal spent the day resting his men while pounding the enemy with his artillery and preparing to receive several more infantry regiments. He also directed that the regiments in contact take several companies out of the line to establish local reserves, and he placed his divisional cavalry squadron and a III Corps cavalry squadron a kilometer behind his center (near Kocadere) to dig a secondary line of trenches.

In the late afternoon, the dangerously tired men of the 27 Regt were barely able to repel an enemy probing attack with their rifles and machine-guns and Kemal sent in two infantry companies from the 72 Regt to reinforce them. Overall, the Turks characterized 26 April as a quiet day but that evening Kemal directed that his formations make preparations for renewing the attack and also to coordinate carefully their defences with adjacent units. At higher levels, more reinforcements were on the way by ferry to Maidos from Asia (the 64 Regt from the 3rd Division and the 33 Regt from the 11th Division, which were both XV Corps formations). In the meantime the 19th Division staff worked to prepare a battle plan to integrate the incoming regiments into the divisional sector. This began to strain the overworked division headquarters element, which consisted of about twenty officers altogether.[53] Nevertheless, Kemal and his chief of staff decided to bring the incoming 64th Regt around to the northern flank and the incoming 33rd Regt directly into the center. These rapidly marching regiments moved into position in the early hours of 27 April. Both Esat (III Corps commander) and Mustafa Kemal were concerned about the tired condition of the men but were ordered to attack by Liman von Sanders. The attack began at 7.30 am, but the newly arrived battalions were too exhausted to launch their attacks on schedule, and only the weakened 57 Regt attacked as planned. The newly arrived battalions remained in their assembly areas. In spite of this the Turks made progress with determined bayonet assaults and were able to spread panic in the allied lines. This brought a furious rain of naval gunfire on the Turks that turned them back to their start lines.[54]

Disturbed by the failure of the regiments to attack in concert, Staff Major Izzettin sent new orders to restart the offensive, and at 10 am the 64 Regt finally crossed the start lines and attacked the Australians. The remaining 19th Division regiments joined in as well, except for the newly arrived 33 Regt, which was still not ready to attack, but again allied naval gunfire blasted the Turkish attacks into oblivion. Throughout the day the Turks attacked fitfully, unable to synchronize their operations. Casualties began to mount and by 6.30 pm losses in the 27 Regt, 57 Regt and 72 Regt Regiments amounted to a staggering 30 to 40 percent. Faced with the almost certain collapse of these regiments, Mustafa Kemal decided to call off the attacks and prepare for a night assault, which would mitigate the terrible effects of the enemy naval gunfire. He was now, however, aware of the severe collapse of morale suffered by the Australians and New Zealanders on the previous night and he hoped to use this to his advantage by attacking with a force that now numbered fifteen infantry battalions (organized into two tactical groups) and nine batteries of artillery.[55] Map 2.4 shows the night attack of 27 April on the ANZAC perimeter.

The night attack began just after 9 pm as Kemal's northern group led by Major Avni, composed of the 57 Regt and 64 Regt, swept forward into the enemy's trenches 'like a wave.' There was intense fighting at close quarters but heavy ANZAC rifle and

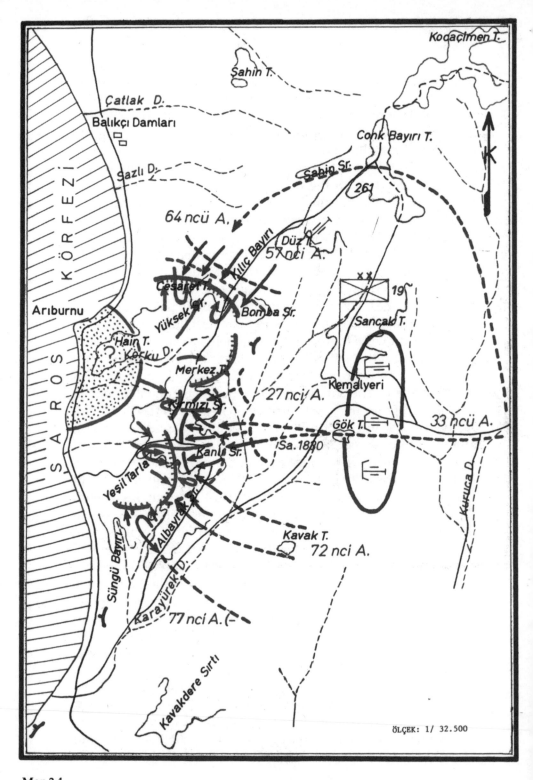

Map 2.4
19th Division attack, 27 April 1915. Vigorous sequential Ottoman counterattacks battered the ANZAC beachhead from multiple directions compressing and containing it on 25 April. The counterattacks were well supported by the centralized artillery positions.

machine-gun fire drove the Turks back. Shortly thereafter, his southern group of the remaining four regiments, led by Lieutenant Colonel Şefik, launched their attack. Kemal committed every available man to the attack (leaving no reserves at all). Again the Turks broke into the enemy trenches but the attacking regiments, exhausted and depleted from two days of combat, could not break through. Moreover, Turkish soldiers from various regiments became badly mixed in the confusing fighting in the dark. Kemal sent an urgent request to Esat Pasha for reinforcements, but received a negative response that all available III Corps units were committed to action. The night attack then frittered away to series of small actions and eventually collapsed.

The tempo of battle slowed on the following day as each side sought to consolidate gains and stabilize its lines. The ANZAC had grown to twenty-one infantry battalions and now outnumbered the 19th Division in the battle area. The operational finesse exhibited by the Turks on 25 April began to deteriorate noticeably in the following days. The likely culprit for this degradation of command was the vastly increased number of regiments that the 19th Division now had under its command, although this is not specifically mentioned as a problem in the extant record. Yet the Anzac beachhead continued to attract incoming reinforcements like a magnet and the 125 Regt arrived on 28 April. This regiment was given a brief rest period in the center of the Turkish positions near the artillery. Good news from Enver Pasha also arrived promising that Ottoman forces held in general reserve near Constantinople would soon be on the way to the front.[56] Encouraged by this development, Liman von Sanders ordered the renewal of the attack and ordered the remainder of the 5th Division south from Saros Bay to join the fight. The III Corps ordered the 19th Division to absorb the incoming 5th Division regiments and to plan yet another major attack to drive the Australians into the sea.

Mustafa Kemal now had about 24 hours at his disposal to put together a plan for a decisive attack. He decided to launch a three-pronged assault, supported by an artillery preparation, with his main effort in the center. To accomodate this he reorganized his reinforced division into a Right Wing Column under Major Avni (of 7 battalions from 4 regiments), a Centre Column under Lieutenant Colonel Ali (of the 6 battalions of the 14th Infantry Regiment (14 Regt) and 15 Regt), and a Left Wing Column under Lieutenant Colonel Ali Şefik (of 6 battalions from 4 regiments).[57] Although the main effort seems under strength, it was composed of the fresh and organizationally intact regiments of the 5th Division, serving under the command of its divisional commander, Lieutenant Colonel Ali. Backing up Ali's 5th Division regiments was a battalion of the 125 Regt in reserve. Kemal ordered 22 machine-guns (from 6 detachments), 3 field artillery batteries and 7 mountain artillery batteries to support the main effort. The artillery spent most of the day of 30 April repositioning their guns to support the attack. Essentially, Mustafa Kemal was launching a divisional scale main effort of fresh men, supported by two simultaneous brigade-scale supplementary attacks of tired men, and he planned to throw over 18,000 infantrymen into the fight. The divisional orders reached the company officers in the front-line trenches in the early evening hours.[58] Kemal reckoned that success was achievable based on his knowledge that morale among the Australians was almost shot and he felt that once his men broke into the enemy trenches that his opponents would collapse.[59] He was also confident that his artillery would continue to have an especially demoralizing effect on the enemy. There were some lingering and worrisome questions about the reliability of the of the Arab soldiers of the 77 Regt, but Kemal kept these troops on the far right flank where a failure would not endanger the decisive main attack. That night the troops rested in anticipation of the coming attack.

At 5 am on 1 May 1915, the Turkish artillery began to deliver preparation fires on the enemy trenches. Because of ammunition shortages, the preparation was scheduled to last just 15 minutes, at which time the infantry would attack. The center and left columns went over the top on time but the right column was delayed somewhat. The distance between the trenches (no-man's-land) was about 200m in the critical center sector, and, unfortunately for the Turks, it was open ground. A 'wall of heavy machine gun and rifle fire' immediately greeted the Turks, although enemy artillery fire was weak and ineffective.[60] The

Turks suffered huge casualties, but small groups managed to reach the Australian lines where hand to hand fighting using bayonets and knives broke out. The Turkish attacks faltered and ground to a halt in the face of fierce resistance. Learning that all three attacks were failing, Mustafa Kemal committed his reserves at 10.30 am in support of his center column. However, by noon, all of his column commanders reported that the massive attack had failed, although some ground had been gained on the left flank. The Turkish artillery firing had died away to nothing because of ammunition shortages. Kemal was discouraged and was tempted to call off his offensive. But, in the early afternoon, an Ottoman radio detachment intercepted an Australian transmission that indicated that their tactical situation was critical. Enthused by this news, Kemal shared it with Lieutenant Colonel Şefik, the Left Wing Commander, and started to reorganize his command for a night assault.[61]

A division attack order was issued at 4.30 pm that placed two battalions of the just arrived 13th Infantry Regiment (13 Regt) immediately behind the line as reserves. The day's fighting had resulted in some gains and there were locations along the front where there was a mere 10m between the two armies. Kemal's attack was timed to begin at midnight on the left and then at 2 am in the center and on the right. By sequencing his attacks in this manner, he hoped to draw enemy reserves away from his main effort. This action became famous as the night attack of 1 May 1915. Unfortunately for the Turks, the Australians were alert and were observing their fronts. Again, the Turks ran into a withering barrage of machine-gun and rifle fire and, although the attack went off as scheduled, they were unable to punch through the enemy lines. By 3 am, Mustafa Kemal acknowledged failure and called off the attacks. Ottoman losses were terrible and the allies estimated that at many as 10,000 Turks were killed (the official Turkish military history admits to 6,000).[62] The attacking regiments were shattered. For example, the war diary of the 15 Regt noted that over 960 officers and men were killed and wounded that night.[63]

One final event happened at the end of this period that is noteworthy because it involved the tarnished 77 Regt which was holding an extreme left-flank position in the Gaba Tepe strong point (this was the 'Arab regiment' that had disappointed Mustafa Kemal on 25 April 1915). About 4.30 am, 4 May, the Australians launched a daring *coup de main* raid on Gaba Tepe led by Captain R.L. Leane of the 11th Battalion, AIF.[64] The Australians attempted to land on a narrow beach and assault the seaward flank of Major Saip's strong point. Leane's men were supported by the direct fire of two battleships. Saip's men were surprised and he reported that the artillerymen supporting him fled their guns under heavy fire leaving his regiment unsupported. Nevertheless, they held the high ground and Leane's assault failed mainly because he was unable to cut through the heavy defensive wiring. He decided to withdraw from the beach under fire. Interestingly, the men of the 77 Regt withheld their fire as Leane loaded his walking and stretcher-borne wounded on lighters and then resumed firing. About 7 am, the raiding force was entirely withdrawn from the narrow beach. Mustafa Kemal was extremely pleased with the performance of Major Saip's 77 Regt and mentioned the regiment's success in his orders of the day.[65] This small victory rehabilitated the regiment's reputation and restored Kemal's faith in its ability to hold ground.

From the Turkish perspective, the Ari Burnu (Anzac) landings and battles were a division-level fight that expanded to a corps-level fight in a matter of days. The Ottoman command structure anticipated a major enemy attack in the area and planned accordingly. As the battle unfolded, Mustafa Kemal (with a tiny headquarters) exercised effective command and control and maintained continuous coordination between units. There was a much higher degree of situational awareness and confidence on the Ottoman side, which enabled them to maintain the operational and tactical initiative although they were consistantly outnumbered. After the first half day ashore, the ANZAC simply waited, worried and dug. The Turks failed by a narrow margin to throw them back into the sea. This speaks more to the overall tactical dynamic in 1915 rather than to poor performance levels on the part of the Ottoman army.

The primary failure on the part of the Turks was that they allowed an unopposed landing on the narrow shelf-like cove at what became known as 'Anzac Beach'. This was a result of their careful pre-battle analysis that indicated the Ari Burnu Beach (known as 'Brighton Beach' to the allies) was the logical landing spot. In effect, the Turks disregarded the cove since it was, militarily speaking, an unsuitable landing point for a large-scale operation. This failure enabled the Australians to land there (albiet unintentionally) and to put ashore most of an entire corps of infantry in a 24-hour timespan. This brought the Fifth Army to the edge of disaster. Nevertheless, effective pre-battle coordination and rehearsals enabled the Turks to recover from this miscalculation and they, in turn, then brought the ANZAC to the edge of disaster. It was, in Wellington's words, 'a near run thing.'

The landings at Cape Helles, 25 April 1915
The story of the Ottoman side of the battles that raged on the southern tip of the Gallipoli Pensinsula on 25 April 1915 is more accurately told in the allied official histories and by later historians than the story of the Ottoman side of the ANZAC landings.[66] The Cape Helles battles were dramatically different from those fought by the Australians that day because they were fought mostly on the landing beaches themselves. The day's fighting revolved around the desperate struggle to get off the landing beaches and onto the high ground beyond. The difficulty encountered by the British as they attempted to land on contested beaches would later be repeated in the Second World War in Sicily and Normandy. Like those later campaigns the British attacked deliberate defensive positions that were strong pointed and which were held by well-led, well-trained and confident troops.

The Ottoman defense of Cape Helles (or Sedd el Bahr to the Turks) was unitary at the tactical level and was the responsibility of the 26 Regt. This regiment had occupied the area on 19 August 1914, and had been working on improving the defenses for over eight months. Moreover, it was reinforced by direct support artillery, cavalry, jandarma and engineers, which were task organized under its commander. During this period, the regiment usually put two battalions into the beach defenses and maintained one battalion in reserve.[67] The baptism of fire for many of the younger soldiers of the regiment came from naval gunfire during the allied naval attacks of 25 February, 3 March (during which it lost four men killed and fourteen men wounded) and 18 March 1915. Although bloodied, morale within the battalions of this veteran regiment remained very high.[68]

As Ottoman army reinforcements poured into the area in March and April 1915, it was possible to bring the entire 25 Regt from Asia to the peninsula (thus consolidating the entire 9th Division). Colonel Halil Sami placed this regiment into the reserve positions occupied by the 26 Regt and on 21 April he was able to shift the entire 26th Regt into the Cape Helles beach defenses.[69] Thus on the eve on the allied invasion, Halil Sami now had a fully trained and fully manned infantry regiment defending the southern beaches of the Gallipoli Peninsula. Notably, the young regimental commander Major Hafız Kadri had orchestrated the Achi Baba (Alçı Tepe) artillery fire-planning exercise of 4 October 1914 (previously discussed) and was fully familiar with the terrain and the associated defensive plans. Major Kadri and his staff went to work on the morning of 22 April to reestablish and finalize the coordination of the defense and rapidly issued orders that would take effect on 24 April. Kadri's regimental order was sixteen paragraphs in length and described in detail the revisions to the occupation of the defensive works by his men.[70] Kadri paid close attention to his artillery support and tied 150mm and 105mm howitzers, field gun batteries and 37mm quick-firing guns directly in support of his infantry battalions. He ordered that map overlays showing these plans be made and distributed to his commanders, as well as to the adjacent fortress command. He also personally supervised the relief in place of his reserve battalion by the incoming 25 Regt.

As finally configured on the morning of 25 April, Major Kadri deployed his 3rd Battalion (3/26 Regt) in the Sedd el Bahr defenses and his 1st Battalion (1/26 Regt, which is sometimes referred to in western histories as the 4th Battalion from its origin as a reconstituted replacement on 16 August 1914 for the original 1st Battalion in Yemen) in the Kum Tepe defenses. In the center, he maintained three companies of his 2nd Battalion in regimental reserve (2/26 regt), while positioning the 6th Company (6 Coy) of this battalion on the western coast (thus linking the Sedd el Bahr and Kum Tepe positions). Kadri positioned his regimental command post and his regimental reserve in the village of Krithia (Kirte). Most of his artillery was positioned on the eastern slopes of the peninsula where it was somewhat protected from allied naval gunfire but the observers remained on the Achi Baba (Alçı Tepe) high ground that was the dominant terrain feature of the lower peninsula.[71] Behind Kadri's regiment, Lieutenant Colonel Irfan's 25 Regt waited in general divisional reserve. Although well-balanced, these dispositions were based on the primary tactical assumption (dating back to 1912) that the enemy would choose to land at the tip of the peninsula and fight northward.

The 9th Division artillery regiment commander, Lieutenant Colonel Mehmet Ali, was likewise making final preparations for the coming battle. After attaching three artillery batteries to Şefik's 27 Regt, he had forty-four artillery pieces of various types remaining and available in the southern half of the divisional sector.[72] Most of these were attached in direct support of the infantry and were registered on the landing beaches.[73] Coordination between the guns and the newly positioned infantry was increased. Mehmet Ali also had on call priority of fires for two 105mm and one 150mm howitzer batteries from the nearby Strait Fortress Command. To these batteries he gave orders that their first priority was against allied ships forcing the Dardanelles but, absent that situation, to be prepared to fire on Sedd el Bahr (to their rear) against allied landing operations. He further reminded all of his artillery batteries that the infantry-artillery team required organization and discipline in order to be effective.[74] Map 2.5 shows the reinforcing strait artillery as well as the command arrangements.

Whereas the fighting at Anzac on 25 April proved to be essentially a movement to contact resulting in a meeting engagement followed by hasty Ottoman attacks, the fighting at Cape Helles was characterized by direct British assaults on an enemy strong-point system. It was more like the fighting then raging in France and, consequently, was far more violent, resulted in far more British casualties and also culminated in a large number of Victoria Crosses being awarded for acts of gallantry. The British threw almost the entire strength of the regular 29th Division at the very tip of the Gallipoli Peninsula with the objective of driving northward to seize the high ground of Achi Baba (Alçı

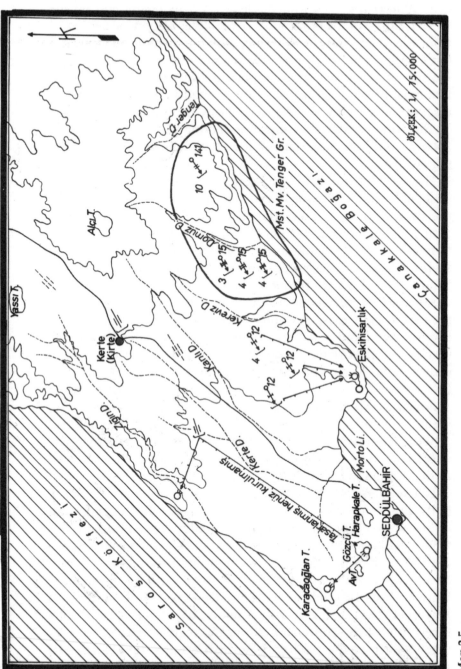

Map 2.5
Supporting artillery units at Cape Helles. The positions of the fortress's Tenger Artillery Group, which were available to supplement the Fifth Army's organic artillery, are shown on this map.

Tepe). Defending against this large array of forces, which was backed up by significant naval gunfire assets, was the single 3/26 Regt commanded by Major Mahmut Sabri and composed of about a thousand soldiers .

This battalion had two companies (10 and 12 Companies) employed in beach defense. These companies each deployed two platoons in strong points (fortified with wire and trenches) on the low hills overlooking the landing beaches of Ikiz Koyu (X Beach), Teke Koyu (W Beach) and Ertugrul Koyu (V Beach). The third platoon in each company was in reserve and positioned in defilade behind the hills. Major Mahmut Sabri maintained his battalion command post, two infantry companies (9 and 11 Companies) and his attached engineer company in general reserve about a kilometer inland from the landing beaches. It was a classic defensive arrangement characterized by the positioning of ready reserves for reinforcement and counterattacks. Additionally, the battalion had an artillery battery positioned southwest of Krithia for direct fire support. Alerted to expect an imminent allied landing, Mahmut Sabri wrote new orders for his battalion on 23 April 1915, to ready them for the coming fight.[75] He directed his platoon strong points to engage the enemy ships and landing craft at ranges of 200–300m with violent fires. He told his platoons that they would be reinforced by his reserves once he knew the direction of the main enemy attack. He told them to be brave and patiently to make their preparations. This was not an order to die in place at all costs as Mahmut Sabri identified the location of his battalion first-aid station at Harapkale and, further-more, identified the 'middle road' as being the best route to take there because it was covered from enemy fires. The men of his battalion received this order on the morning of 24 April. It was the last one that they would receive before the British began landing.

The night of 24/25 April was quiet and moonlit. In spite of the light breeze and waves, the Turkish sentries could hear enemy ships and, occasionally, an enemy aircraft. As early as 3.20 am the 7th Coy (2/26 Regt) adjacent to Sabri's 3/26 Regt alerted the III Corps of enemy activity off Teke Burnu.[76] At 4.30 am, the British naval bombardment began from three directions, fully alerting the Turkish defenders on the tip of the peninsula. Although he had suspicions about where the British would actually land, Major Mahmut Sabri decided to await reports from his company commanders, which arrived about 6 am. These added nothing to his situational awareness but he sent a situation report to the regimental command post anyway outlining the strength of the naval forces bombarding his positions. He completed his report with the words, 'the battalion is ready and will perform to the final degree.'[77] About the same time, the 12 Coy's platoons observed over forty boats in lines heading for Teke Koyu (W Beach). At the 400m range line, Turkish heavy machine-guns began to engage the lead boats, but the riflemen witheld their fire until the British were within 40m of the shore. The British landing was centered on the beach and, therefore, directly into the center of a prearranged Turkish 'beaten zone.'[78] The forward Turkish platoon reported at 7.05 am that an actual landing (as opposed to a demonstration or feint) was underway.[79] At nearby Sedd el Bahr (V Beach) at 6 am, the men of the 10 Coy observed, with great puzzlement, in the middle of masses of boats, a steamship (the converted collier *River Clyde*) heading inshore. At the 400m mark, the Turks began to engage the enemy with machine-guns and light artillery. At 6.30 am, five of twenty enemy boats became separated from the main body and the Turks engaged them with very heavy rifle fire. The steamship continued on until it grounded out in the surf and it was apparent to the Turks that it contained hundreds of enemy soldiers as well as numerous machine-guns. The ship immediately became a magnet for heavy Turkish fire as the company commander directed rifles and machine-guns against it. The Turkish official history refers to the *River Clyde* as a Trojan Horse.

Reports reached Major Mahmut Sabri at his battalion command post at 9.07 am from the 10 Coy commander that indicated that the *River Clyde* was a 'bankrupt operation.'[80] Nevertheless, Mahmut Sabi felt that the presence of this ship confirmed that Sedd el Bahr was the enemy's main effort and he ordered his 11 Coy forward (then in battalion reserve). This would give him about 300 rifleman on his critical left flank.[81] Meanwhile and simultaneously, the enemy also landed at Ikiz Koyu (X Beach), Zengindere (Y Beach) and Morto Koyu (S Beach). In doing so, the British hoped to confuse the Turks and cause them to disperse and expose their reserves. Of these landings, only Y Beach fell outside of the 3/26 Regt's sector. Responding to this dangerous situation with his remaining 9 Coy, Mahmut Sabri decided to reinforce the hills north of Teke Koyu (known to the Turks as Karacaoglan Tepe). From the high ground there, his 9 Coy could dominate X Beach. He ordered the company to make haste and deploy to Karacaoglan Tepe in order to restore the situation.[82] Mahmut Sabri now had his entire battalion committed to the fight and it was barely 10 am in the morning. However, he had taken the time to request reinforcements earlier and the 26 Regt ordered the 7th Company (from the 2/26 Regt) forward from Krithia at 6.50 am that morning.[83] Mahmut Sabri initially planned to place this company in battalion reserve and sent a message to the company commander enroute ordering him to make haste. However, in an unusual display of initiative, with heavy enemy fires falling along his intended route of march, the 7 Coy commander decided to bring his company into action immediately and attack the enemy landings at X Beach. The Turks regarded this as a fortunate decision since it placed an infantry company in contact on the north flank of the British landings there and so prevented a breakout.[84] As has been described in the extant literature of the Gallipoli campaign, the battles for the V, W and X Beaches were bloody in the extreme. This was because these actions brought the British main effort directly into the teeth of the Major Mahmut Sabri's well-prepared defenses. The Turks in their strong points on the high ground held the British on the beaches for most of the day of 25 April and it was not until the early evening that the British managed to seize the positions of the 10 Coy and the 12 Coy.

Throughout the day a constant stream of reports and orders connected the Turkish defenders with their higher headquarters. At 9.30 am, the commander of the 26 Regt, Major Kadri, urgently requested reinforcements from the 9th Division by telephone.[85] This was followed by a stream of situation reports forwarded from Major Mahmut Sabri that described the deterioriating situation in his sector. The Turkish official history characterized the division commander, Colonel Halil Sami, as slow to react to the situation at Cape Helles.[86] According to the official history, at 2.15 pm, the 9th Division headquarters 'finally' issued orders to the 25 Regt (the division reserve) to advance its 3/25 Regt for a counterattack.[87] It appears that Halil Sami was focused on Şefik's 27 Regt movement to the Ari Burnu (ANZAC) landings and was hesitant to commit his only reserves.[88] Nevertheless, 30 minutes later, the soldiers of the 3/25 Regt were on the road from Sarafım Çifğili. Travelling through Krithia, the battalion came under heavy enemy naval gunfire, turned west towards Sari Tepe (over-looking Y Beach) and moved into attack positions.

The artillery coordination and preparations of Lieutenant Colonel Mehmet Ali paid off around 2 pm when the guns of the fortress began to fire in support of the two divisional artillery batteries then in action. A five-piece 105mm howitzer battery and a five-piece 150mm howitzer battery pounded S and Y Beaches.[89] Additionally, several 120mm howitzers captured from the Bulgarians in 1913 fired 250 rounds as well. Nevertheless, the situation on the tip of peninsula grew steadily worse for the Turks. At 3 pm, Mahmut Sabri reported that he had committed his entire command and that the situation on Ay Tepe was in doubt. At that moment, 9th Division commander Colonel Halil Sami still retained two reserve battalions of the 25 Regt as well as their supporting field artillery battery, but was reluctant to commit them since they were his only remaining reserves. Once committed, Halil Sami would lose any ability to influence the battle. However, he decided to execute a counterattack from Zengindere (later called Gully Ravine by the British) with these last-remaining reserves and he informed his commander at III Corps of his decision.[90]

Casualties were mounting rapidly. The 7 Coy experienced many soldiers killed, including the company commander, who led a bayonet charge against the British.[91] Halil Sami hesitated again and, for reasons that are not clear, did not issue attack orders immediately (as he had indicated to III Corps) to the waiting battalions of the 25 Regt. This was a serious mistake that cost the Turks dearly. Halil Sami's early morning stellar perfor-mance seemed to deteriorate as the day progressed.[92] The delay likely caused the loss of the Ay Tepe strong point at 5.40 pm and increased the pressure on the adjacent strong point on Gözcübaba, which then came under direct attack.[93] Written and telephonic reports to this effect from both regiments reached Halil Sami, who was north of Krithia in the artillery area, confirming this tactical disaster and pointing out that the piece-meal commitment of reserves was at fault. At 6.30 pm, Colonel Halil Sami belatedly issued orders deploying the remaining two battalions and the machine-gun detachment of the 25 Regt to Teke Koyu and Sedd el Bahr. He also ordered them to move rapidly and close on the enemy landing areas that night.[94]

One of the most well-known vignettes in Turkey about the battle is the heroic story of Sergeant Yahya (Yahya Çavuş) of 12 Coy, 3/26 Regt, who defended Gözcübaba after the fall of Ay Tepe.[95] As evening fell, a column of Irish troops, heavily supported by direct flanking machine-gun fire from four guns brought ashore that evening by the Munsters, began to move off Ay Tepe toward Gözcübaba. With his officer down Sergeant Yahya found himself in charge of five squads of infantry (sixty-three men altogether) and he took command of the position and the situation. Under heavy attack, the Turks beat off several attempts to take the strong point. When the Irish broke in and seized part of the trenches, Sergeant Yahya led a bayonet coun-terattack that ejected the enemy from the position. Later that night British fires enfiladed Gözcübaba and the Irish were able to push the survivors off the hill. Sergeant Yahya lived to tell the tale and was decorated for his actions.

In a very complex division order, Halil Sami directed two companies of the 1/25 Regt and a machine-gun platoon to reinforce the 3/25 Regt (then marching down Gully Spur toward Y Beach) for a night attack on the British. He ordered the 1/25 Regt headquarters and its two remaining companies and machine-gun platoon to Sedd el Bahr to reinforce Mahmut Sabri's badly battered 3/26 Regt with orders to 'clean up the beaches.'[96] The 2/25 Regt and two companies were sent to reinforce the 8th Company (8 Coy) at Eskihisarlik (S Beach), and its remaining two companies were kept in reserve at Yassi Tepe (where Halil Sami himself intended to spend the night). This deployment of half-battalions in the evening contrasts with the morning deploy-ment of entire battalions. Halil Sami's apparent lack of situational awareness contrasts significantly with Mustafa Kemal's height-ened situational awareness that the Australians had conducted a single massive landing at Ari Burnu. Moreover, Halil Sami's detachment of the 27 Regt to Mustafa Kemal (or about one-third

Map 2.6
3/26 Regt situation,
25 April 1915. This map
shows the movement of
reinforcements through
Kirte (Krithia) to support
the 3/36 Infantry. For the
Ottomans, Tb refers to
battalion and Bl refers to
numbered Ottoman
companies (i.e. 7th
Company). For the British
Bl refers to the total
number of companies
committed to the beach.

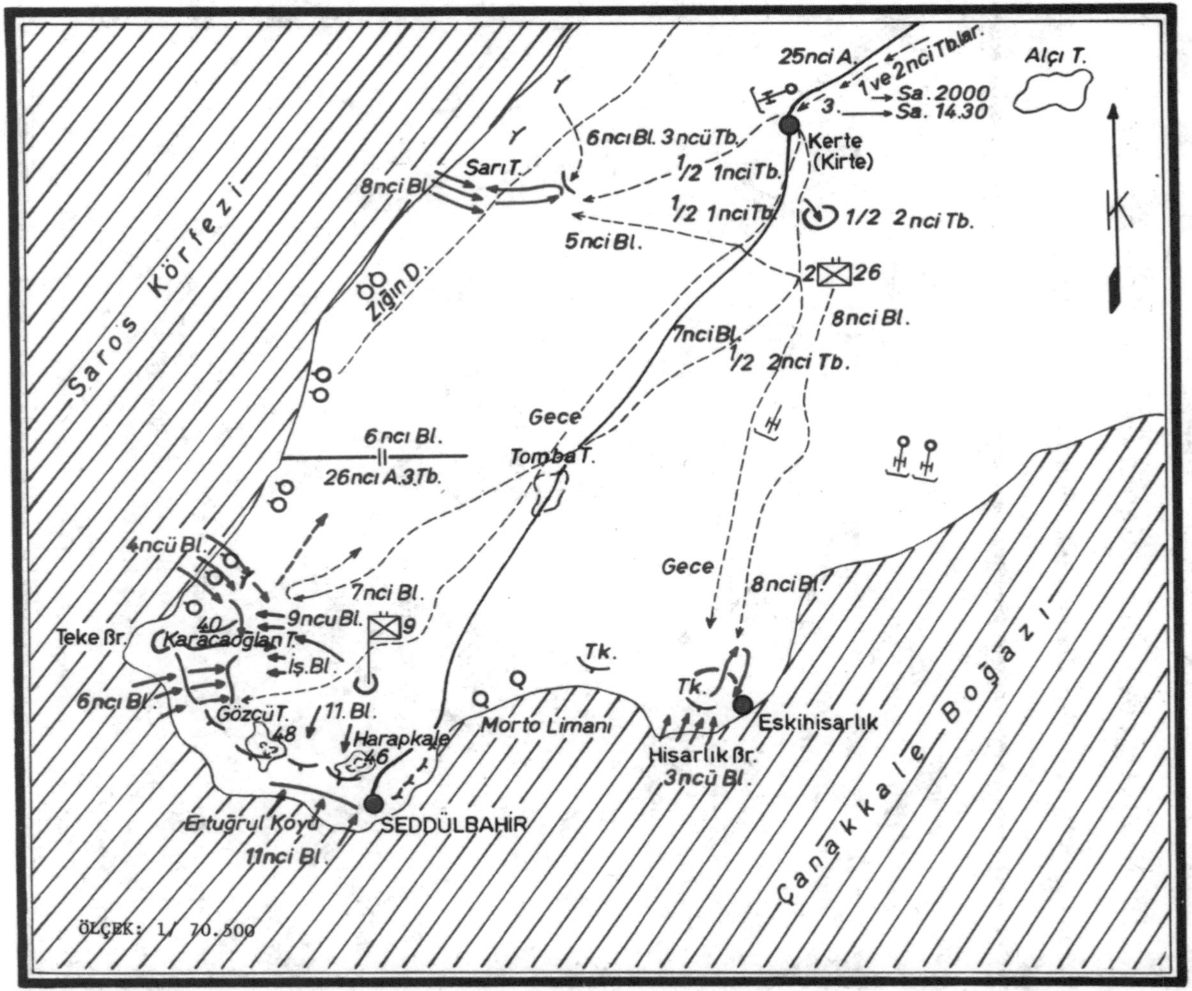

of his combat power) left the 9th Division with only two infantry regiments to oppose the Cape Helles landings. Clearly, Colonel Halil Sami was unsure exactly where the allied main effort at Cape Helles was and, consequently, felt compelled to disperse his increasingly scarce reserves to cover all of the landing beaches. The British plan to stage multiple landings on Cape Helles to confuse the Turkish defenders was, therefore, very successful at the tactical level. Map 2.6 shows the routes of 3/26 Regt on 25 April 1915.

At 1 am on 26 April 1915, advance runners (messengers) from the 1/25 Regt arrived at the command post of Major Mahmut Sabri to coordinate its arrival. Sabri quickly crafted a plan to retake the lost high ground of Ay Tepe and sent it back by runner to the incoming battalion commander. Mahmut Sabri's plan envisioned that the fresh troops of the 1/25 Regt would march directly to attack positions by 2.30 am and begin preparations for a night bayonet assault on Ay Tepe.[97] To insure maximum control, Mahmut Sabri linked the incoming battalion's 3 Coy with his own 9 Coy and the incoming 4 Coy with the survivors of his own 12 Coy. This insured that the incoming troops were aware of where both the enemy and the tactical objectives were located. He ordered his own 11 Coy to retake Gözcübaba, which had fallen earlier that night, at the same time. The incoming machine-gun platoon (two guns) was ordered to support the advance on Ay Tepe. Finally, the incoming battalion commander was directed to remain in reserve at Harapkale with one platoon of infantry. Mahmut Sabri's attack was scheduled to begin at 3.30 am. As complex as this operation was, the night bayonet attack began on schedule, but a wall of British rifle fire, machine-gun fire and grenades hit the advancing Turkish infantry.[98] This was soon followed by effective naval gunfire support. Mahmut Sabri immediately committed his reserve platoon under the 1/25 Regt commander in a last ditch attempt to retake the position. The battle see-sawed back and forth, and Mahmut Sabri received conflicting reports of success on his left flank. Although some parts of the Ottoman trenches occupied by the British were taken, Mahmut Sabri's attack collapsed after an hour's fighting. The difficult first 24 hours of the battle then ended with Sabri's battalion of about a thousand men having lost over 500 soldiers killed. Significantly, the battalion did not collapse and maintained its cohesion.

Although Mahmut Sabri's counterattack failed, it was a remarkably ambitious undertaking. It must be noted that his combat orders insured that the incoming fresh troops were taken in hand by his experienced men who knew the terrain. Taken overall, Sabri's plan was sound and maximized the troops that he had available. The plan showcases the flexibility with which the Turks were able to cross-attach companies and battalions from one regiment with another. Mahmut Sabri was able to orchestrate on short notice the integration of a battalion from the 25 Regt with his own battalion of the 26 Regt. Moreover, he was able to maintain his 'grip' on the situation throughout the difficult first 24 hours of the battle. Considering that Mahmut Sabri's single battalion fought almost twelve British infantry battalions to a standstill, his achievement was singularly impressive.

Cape Helles, 26 April–1 May 1915

On the morning of 26 April, the British 29th Division had all of its infantry ashore and was preparing to bring in its artillery. Some of the infantry battalions had suffered terrible casualties in the landings but, nevertheless, the division intended to push inland toward its main objective of Achi Baba (Alçı Tepe). It was quiet in the early hours and the Turks spent the time preparing supplementary trench lines in their rear. But then at 9 am British machine-guns opened up on the Turks and infantry began to push off the high ground. The Ottoman positions were still under the control of Major Mahmut Sabri. With his limited and tired forces, he fought a delaying battle throughout the day that slowed the British advance to a crawl. Mahmut Sabri had the remnants of about three infantry battalions under his tactical command and was opposed by fourteen weakened British infantry battalions. There were no other Ottoman troops immediately available in the lower peninsula to reinforce him. Throughout the day, he conducted a deliberate withdrawal to a new defensive line centered on the high ground of Yalçi Tepe. Here the front stabilized on the supplementary trenches that Sabri had prepared. Sabri reported at the end of the day that he had lost 6 officers and 630 men from his pre-battle strength of 1,128 officers and men.[99] However, he estimated that he had inflicted between 2,600 to 3,000 casualties on the enemy. Colonel Halil Sami reported that night to Esat Pasha that the 9th Division had lost 10 officers and 1,887 men from the 25 Regt and 26 Regt.[100] However, reinforcements were about to arrive.

Travers claimed that the Allies could have advanced much farther on 27 April because 'Liman von Sanders and the Turks were a little slow to react to the landings.'[101] This is doubtful because reinforcements were already on the way and the first fresh battalion arrived about noon on 27 April. This was the Bursa Jandarma Battalion, which was sent to the 26 Regt. As will be seen at different points in the campaign, the Ottoman *seyyar jandarma* (field jandarma or gendarmerie), although something of a para-mililitary rural police force in peacetime, were well trained and were a tactical asset for the Fifth Army. Later that afternoon, Major Halit's 20 Regt (from the 7th Division) arrived after a hard march from the neck of the peninsula (Bulair). This regiment was very experienced and very well trained.[102] Colonel Halil Sami decided to employ the fresh 20 Regt on his right flank and to consolidate the remainder of his forces under the command of the 26 Regt on his left flank.[103] Later in the day, Mahmut Sabri's exhausted troops (a mix of men from the 25 Regt and 26 Regt) were pulled off the line as the 20 Regt conducted a relief in place and were repositioned in the 26 Regt's sector. In sum, the 9th Division, now brought back up to a 3-regiment configuration, had a fresh regiment (over 3,000 men) on the west side of the Gallipoli Peninsula, a composite regiment of equal strength on the east side and a spent mixed regiment in reserve.

Because of the relative calm on 27 April, Halil Sami decided to conduct a local attack with his fresh troops before the Allies could consolidate their gains.[104] In turn the 9th Division headquarters ordered a night attack by the 20 Regt and 26 Regt with the bayonet to seize the enemy trenches. The commander's intent was to push the Allies out of their trenches and Halil Sami scheduled the attack for 1 am on 28 April. In his divisional orders Halil Sami directed that the attacking regiments bring up the divisional engineer company and that defensive trenches were to be prepared by the time dawn broke. The divisional order was passed down the chain of command but it 'choked on the details.'[105] There was considerable confusion concerning previous orders and tactical dispositions that conflicted with the attack order. In particular, the commander of the incoming 20 Regt was concerned that one of his three battalions had been previously placed by Halil Sami in division reserve. The division resolved this by allocating command of the 3/25 Regt to reinforce the 20 Regt. The 26 Regt retained its 2/26 Regt and 3/26 Regt and was additionally given the 1/25 Regt and the Bursa Jandarma Battalion. These changes were made in the evening and resulted in the finalized attack order being considerably delayed. The result was that pre-combat preparations and rehearsals were incomplete and some units were notified of the attack only an hour before its start.[106] The attack began on time but was poorly organized because of the haste with which the division had co-ordinated the operation. The preparations necessary for a difficult night attack (route reconniassance, rehearsals and troop rest) were incomplete. The predictable result was a failed attack that made only a slight impression on the Allies.[107] In fact, the Turkish attack failed to delay a major allied attack that began at 8 am on 28 April.

The allies, under Major General Hunter-Weston, had spent the day of 27 April preparing for a corps-level attack designed to seize the village of Krithia. Hunter-Weston had fourteen British infantry battalions and five French infantry battalions, and although he had little field artillery ashore, he had the guns of the combined allied fleet at his disposal. Halil Sami had ten badly battered infantry battalions, but reinforcements were now fast arriving. The fresh 2/15 Regt (from the 5th Division) and two battalions of the 19 Regt (from the 7th Division) were arriving that morning from the north. These reinforcements gave the Turks good odds against their enemy and, apparently undeterred by the failure of his night attack, Halil Sami issued new combat orders to his men. His orders confirmed that 'the assault forces scattered by the night attack should withdraw to the defensive lines.'[108] At this point in the battle, Halil Sami reorganized his division into what amounted to two battle groups, which he designated as 'wings'. This was a doctrinal Ottoman army response to the accumulation of mixed reinforcements from various units that placed them under a single commander. Simultaneously at Anzac Mustafa Kemal was applying the same organizational technique. Halil Sami placed Major Halit of 20 Regt in command of the Western Wing and Major Kadri of 26 Regt in command of the Eastern Wing (thus dividing his front into two halves). Then he ordered the incoming battalions and machine-gun detachment of the 19 Regt to take over the defensive line on the east flank of the 20 Regt. Moreover, the Bursa Jandarma were attached to the 19 Regt as well and the 2/15 Regt positioned in reserve near the village of Krithia. Halil Sami directed that the reorganization for combat must occur rapidly and he ordered that the trenches be manned and held to the 'final degree.'[109] Finally, Halil Sami ordered his regimental commanders to update the trench map overlays of their positions and send copies to him at his command post on Yassi Tepe.

There was much confusion as incoming troops received contradictory information concerning their routes. This was because the roads south of Achi Baba (Alçı Tepe) were dangerous because of Allied naval bombardment. This caused the march tables to appear 'eccentric' and the confused reinforcements turned around several times before revised orders correctly identified the routes.[110] This delayed them by about 3 hours. Nevertheless, the head of the column of the incoming 19 Regt passed Yassi Tepe about 4 am and arrived at the front at 7 am, 28 April 1915. With difficulty, the reinforcements began to filter into the forward trenches. Other forces were moving forward as well and Halil Sami attached two heavy machine-gun detachments to the forward regiments. In turn the divisional artillery commander, Lieutenant Colonel Mehmet Ali, modified the fire control center on Achi Baba (Alçı Tepe) by centralizing the 9th Division's artillery into two groups supporting the Eastern and Western Wings of the front. The Turkish official history of the campaign notes that this was an 'elastic arrangement' that placed all of the guns supporting the Western Wing (20th Infantry Regimental sector) under a single battalion command.[111] The new western artillery group headquarters was then operationally disconnected from the Alçı Tepe observation and command posts and reestablished on Yassi Tepe. In the Eastern Wing (26 Regt sector), the Alçı Tepe posts remained in operation and were then further augmented by a heavy artillery group from the Strait Fortress Command.[112] This badly needed reinforcement added about 24 artillery tubes to the divisional artillery. The reorganization and centralization of artillery took the firing batteries away from their mission of direct support linking them to individual Ottoman infantry regiments and placed them in what is called general support. While somewhat less responsive to the needs of lower echelon infantry commanders, this system enabled the Turks to mass artillery more effectively under trench-warfare conditions.

Not all of Halil Sami's defensive arrangements were complete when the Allies attacked at 8 am on 28 April. Making matters a bit worse, Esat Pasha identified Mustafa Kemal's attempt to drive the Australians into the sea as the III Corps main effort.[113] This relegated Halil Sami's fight to a secondary effort (although Esat Pasha intended to eliminate the Cape Helles beachhead after dispensing with the ANZAC) and, consequently, he received fewer reinforcements and support than Kemal. Halil Sami reported to III Corps headquarters that morale was very high but that his forces had not yet completed their preparations. Moreover, he was worried about the reinforcement flow drying up.[114] Nevertheless, the 9th Division was in good shape to receive an attack as a result of Halil Sami's hard overnight work. Hunter-Weston's attack was hastily coordinated and employed British regulars, Indians, Royal Naval infantry and the French.[115] These troops were not trained for cross-attachment and had never worked together. Unfortunately, the attack lacked adequate field artillery support (only twenty-eight field guns were ashore) and was not rehearsed. The British 29th Division was ordered to push north to seize Krithia and Yassı Tepe, while the French attacked to shield their right flank. Once these objectives were in hand, Hunter-Weston intended to wheel east and seize Achi Baba. By 1915 standards, the plan was tactically complex and, moreover, required multi-national coordination.[116]

Over ten battalions of British infantry stormed the 20 Regt's forward trenches. In many locations, they broke thorough but were confronted immediately by locally positioned platoon-sized Ottoman reserves. However, the local reserves were quickly decimated by Royal Navy gunfire and the Ottoman regimental commander requested the release of the 9th Division's reserves. Halil Sami ordered the reserves forward (2/15 Regt) at 10 am.[117] On the Ottoman eastern flank, the allied attack enjoyed more success. This sector of the Ottoman line was held by the tired soldiers of the 25 Regt and 26 Regt, both of which had been severely handled on 25 April. Shortly after 11 am Major Kadri reported that the enemy was collapsing his front and that his men had been forced to retreat from the forward trenches. He had committed almost all of his reserves and he urgently requested assistance.[118] Halil Sami responded by ordering the just-arrived 19 Regt forward from its position 5km behind the lines. While moving forward the regiment was taken under heavy naval gunfire around 11.30 am which slowed its advance and caused casualties. Thus by about noon, the Ottoman 9th Division was in serious trouble and a distressed Halil Sami decided to authorize a withdrawal to the Alçı Tepe–Yassı Tepe line. Orders to this effect were sent out to the regimental commanders.[119] Fortunately for the Turks, however, the regimental commanders were not yet ready to concede their positions and, in fact, Major Halit of the 20 Regt kept the retreat authorization secret from his battalion and company commanders. In the eastern sector, the intrepid Major Mahmut Sabri put together a hastily scraped organized reserve force of survivors from his own battalion and launched a company sized counterattack at 3 pm. Simultaneously, the delayed 19 Regt, after a brief consolidation on Uç Tepe at 1 pm to reconstitute itself after the naval gunfire attack enroute, arrived and launched a timely bayonet attack to the right of Mahmut Sabri's men. These attacks were well supported by the centralized Ottoman artillery and 'great results were achieved with fires and target plans.'[120] This counterattack was the death knell of Hunter-Weston's offensive and the 'tired and disorganized' allies began to retreat and dig in.[121] This ended the first phase of the Gallipoli campaign at Cape Helles.

The landing at Kum Kale, 25 April 1915

From the allied perspective the French landing at Kum Kale was an operational diversion to distract Liman von Sanders. At the tactical level, the landing was limited to a small strip of land between Kum Kale and the tiny village of Yenişehir and was designed to keep Ottoman direct fire from the ongoing landing at Cape Helles. The task was allotted to the French division under General d'Amade, who was instructed to pull out in 24 hours and redeploy his forces to reinforce the 29th Division at Cape Helles. He committed a colonial regiment with some artillery and engineers and planned to land around 6 am. Shelling by the navy began early but unexpectedly strong currents kept the French from landing until 10 am. Nevertheless by 11.15 am, Kum Kale was in French hands. Ottoman resistance was feeble and was limited to some machine-gun firing. The French spent the remainder of the day disembarking the regiment and at 5.30 pm began to push toward Yenişehir. However, in the meantime, strong Ottoman reinforcements came up and held the village against four French attacks over the following 3 hours.

The weaker Ottoman reponse in Asia was notably different from the strong responses at Anzac and Cape Helles. The enemy came ashore easily and there were no Ottoman counterattacks throughout the day. The reason for this was a lack of continuity of command and control. Colonel Erich Weber's newly established XV Corps took over the sector from the Menderes Detachment, itself a provisional formation of the fortress command. Weber then shifted new troops into the area as reinforcements arrived. Previously in February the Kum Kale beaches were weakly screened by a battalion of a depot regiment (esentially a training outfit composed of raw recruits undergoing basic infantry training) but by 18 March, the 64 Regt had arrived to hold the beaches in strength. Then as the 3rd Division arrived, the 64 Regt was pulled back near Calvert's Farm, while the 2nd Battalion, 31st Infantry Regiment (2/31 Regt) took its place.[122] By 25 April, the platoons of this battalion's 6th Company (6 Coy) were entrenched in Kum Kale, Yenişehir and in between on the Orhaniye mound. Thus in a month's time, responsibility for the Kum Kale sector, at the operational level, passed from the fortress to the Fifth Army, while, at the tactical level, control of the beaches passed between the battalions of three different regiments. Because of these changes, detailed planning and rehearsals such as those enjoyed by the 9th Division on the peninsula were notably absent. Nevertheless, the 3rd Division staff conducted tactical planning and issued instructions for night bayonet attacks on allied lodgements.

The first reports of heavy enemy naval activity and expected landings went up the chain of command about 3.30 am from the 6 Coy reaching the 3rd Division headquarters 30 minutes later.[123] The division commander, German Colonel August Nicolai, alarmed his entire force and put the remainder of 31 Regt and the 2nd Battalion, 39th Infantry Regiment (2/39 Regt) on 'stand by' to deploy. Subsequent reports from 6 Coy at 7 am indicated that the enemy was landing at Cape Helles but that nobody was landing at Kum Kale.[124] At 9 am reports changed to indicate that landings now appeared imminent and Nicolai ordered Lieutenant Colonel Hüseyin Nurettin, the 39 Regt commander, and the battalions that were standing by forward toward Kum Kale. He was told to plan for a daylight attack and a mountain gun battery was attached to his command (this countermanded the previous tactical plan involving night bayonet attacks). Finally at 9.53 am the troops in Kum Kale reported that the enemy was landing. In the fighting that followed one platoon leader was killed and another wounded as the 6 Coy was pushed out of the village. It is unclear why the French landing succeeded so quickly but it is important to note that these positions were not as strongly developed as those on Cape Helles. Nevertheless, a report from the 6 Coy commander at 11.30 am indicated that although he had lost Kum Kale morale remained high.[125] This was likely due to the arrival of the 3/31 Regt in the nearby village of Yenişehir, whose commander immediately sent two platoons forward to assist the 6 Coy in order to form a perimeter around the French lodgement. Lieutenant Colonel Nurettin arrived in Yenişehir at 2.20 pm followed 10 minutes later by the 1/39 Regt. This regiment's second battalion arrived soon after and Nurettin began to deploy his men forward while ordering his attached mountain battery into firing positions in Yenişehir itself. Not counting his 6 Coy, then in contact with the enemy, Nurettin now commanded an ad hoc 'regimental battle group'[126] of three battalions, one of which was from a different regiment. He began to plan for an attack on an enemy force that he estimated as one battalion reinforced with an artillery battery. In the meantime, his soldiers repulsed several French attacks advancing on Yenişehir.

Unlike Mustafa Kemal and Lieutenant Colonel Şefik, Nurettin had little opportunity prior to 25 April to rehearse and plan for a coordinated multi-regiment assault. Afternoon faded into evening and Nurettin was unable to organize his battalion commanders quickly enough to launch a daylight attack. Understandably upset by these delays, Colonel Nicolai went to Yenişehir at 6 pm, but after seeing the situation for himself he then rapidly reconsidered the situation and authorized a night attack. Nurettin planned to use his own 3/39 Regt to fix the enemy with heavy fires, while the other two battalions of the 39 Regt attacked Kum Kale abreast on the right flank. The attack began at 7 pm supported by machine-gun and artillery fire. The men of the 39 Regt pressed home their assault, which actually broke through the French field works into the southern end of Kum Kale village. Unfortunately, Nurettin was opposed by the entire 6th Regiment Mixte Coloniale, which had a battery ashore of the famous French 75s in direct support as well as naval gun fire from the French fleet. After hand to hand fighting the first Ottoman attack was beaten off by 9 pm with heavy losses.

In the meantime, Nicolai ordered the uncommitted 1/31 Regt forward to reinforce Nurettin, which duly arrived on the scene about 1 am, 26 April. Knowing that reinforcements were on the way, Nicolai and Nurettin planned to conduct a second night assault using these fresh troops. By 2 am, the 1/31 Regt had moved through the tried survivors of the 39 Regt's battalions to attack positions in the lines of the 6 Coy. The men were hastily organized and led forward at 3 am across 300m of open ground, once again driving inside Kum Kale village. Again there was bitter hand to hand fighting in the dark. There was much confusion on both sides but a determined French counterattack crushed the Ottoman assault and the fighting was over by 4 am. The fighting was so fierce that it appeared to the French that the Turks had launched seven attacks throughout the night. Concerned that the French might follow up their victory with a follow-on attack of their own on the Orhaniye mound, the Turks began to dig in. However, a large number of Ottoman survivors, from both regiments' previous attacks, remained in Kum Kale village unable to return to their own lines across the 300m of open ground. This situation led to an unforunate incident about 7 am,

26 April in which a French officer (Captain Rockel) under a white flag was apparently murdered in violation of the laws of war. The modern Turkish official history noted that this likely happened because the tired and isolated survivors were confused and dispirited and, while awaiting the arrival of higher ranking French officers, renewed fighting broke out during which Rockel was killed.[127] In any event, a large number of survivors surrendered to the French, who then shot an Ottoman officer and eight soldiers in retaliation for the death of Rockel.[128]

Stunned by losses in the heavy night fighting the 39 Regt reported to the 3rd Divsion that it had lost significant numbers of company grade officers and that the situation was dangerous.[129] A series of reports were exchanged between the regiment and the division over the course of the day. The reports noted that the battalions had bled heavily because exposure to French fire was like 'being blown apart from an atomizer' and that a French attack was expected. More bad news followed when the regiment reported that Lieutenant Colonel Nurettin had apparently been killed as well as a large number of soldiers.[130] At that moment both Colonel Weber and Colonel Nicolai were conferring in Ciplak, near the ruins of Troy, and they immediately ordered the commander of the 31 Regt, Lieutenant Colonel Ismail Hakkı, forward to take command at the front. However, he did not arrive at the command post north of Yenişehir until 4.40 pm. The Turks began to plan for a renewal of the offensive that night after dark. Reinforcements were also arriving, the 2nd and 3rd Battalions, 32nd Regiment (2/32 Regt and 3/32 Regt), which arrived at 6.30 pm. Unknown to the Turks, however, the allies had already decided to pull out the French that morning and the French re-embarked, abandoning the Kum Kale lodgement soon after dark. A survivor of the night attack, Corporal Ibrahim, who lay hidden in the ruins of a Kum Kale house, then returned to his own lines with this news.[131] The next morning, Weber formed the survivors of the 39 Regt into a provisional detachment under the command of Geman Major Schierhaltz.

Ottoman losses were exceptionally heavy, 45 officers and 1,690 men altogether (17 officers and 450 men killed, 23 officers and 740 men wounded, and 5 officers and 500 men captured or missing). The Fench lost a total of 20 officers and 766 men.[132]

Considering that the Ottoman losses came from just three and a half battalions in an 18-hour period, the intensity of the action is self evident. The tactical response of the 3rd Division was much less coherent that the actions of the 9th Division and the 19th Division. There are several explanations for this. First, the original 3rd Division was deconstructed in December 1914 to provide individual regiments as reinforcements for distant theaters. Its original organic regiments (7th, 8th and 9th Infantry Regiments) were all detached and the division was reconstituted by combining replacement regiments from different divisions (the 31st and 32nd Regiments came from the 11th Division, while Nurettin's 39th Regiment came from the 13th Division) and, moreover, half of the divisonal artillery came from the 8th Division. The division itself arrived in the sector in penny packets in late March and early April 1915, coming under the command of a newly activated corps headquarters. The institutional continuity enjoyed by III Corps and, particularly, by the 9th Division was sadly lacking at Kum Kale. In spite of this, Weber, Nicolai and Nurettin mounted a regimental-sized counterattack on the French that nearly succeeded in retaking the village on the night of 25/26 April 1915. Given these conditions and understanding the difficulty of night attacks in 1915, their performance might be considered exemplary.

Ottoman corps-level operations

On 25 April 1915, a constant stream of combat reports began to flow into III Corps headquarters beginning about 3 am. As has been previously described, Esat's staff passed on all reports to the Fifth Army headquarters. Within several hours, as the scope of the ANZAC landings clarified, Esat became concerned that the landings at Ari Burnu endangered the original plan that gave defensive priority to the southern end of the peninsula.[133] About 8 am, Esat rode out by automobile from his headquarters in the town of Gallipoli to Bulair to brief Liman von Sanders, who was observing the activity in Saros Bay. Esat came with maps and overlays to make a case for shifting reinforcements south. He met the Fifth Army commander in the central redoubt of the Lines of Bulair where Liman von Sanders was observing the allied ships cruising in Saros Bay. Esat requested the immediate release of his

7th Division, which was refused by Liman von Sanders; however, the Fifth Army commander agreed to give priority of effort to the Ari Burnu landings.[134] This meant that the reinforcement flow would be directed to Kemal rather than Halil Sami at Cape Helles. Liman von Sanders then directed Esat to board a ship to Maidos and take personal command of the battles raging on the southern part of the peninsula, while he remained at Bulair to judge for himself whether the British were conducting a feint there.[135]

Before departing Esat wrote a hasty order to his 7th Division ordering them to remain in place, but informing them that his headquarters was moving to Maidos. He also warned them to be prepared to move south quickly if ordered.[136] He returned to Gallipoli and boarded Steamboat No. 62 at 11 am bound for Maidos. He arrived and proceded to Mal Tepe, a hill nearer the Ari Burnu front, where he established his headquarters at 2 pm.[137] There at Mal Tepe in the late afternoon, Esat made his most important contribution to opposing the landings by changing the divisional boundaries and sectors to accommodate the improvised mixing of the 9th Division and the 19th Divisions at Ari Burnu (previously discussed). By appointing Kemal as the 'Ari Burnu Front Commander' and attaching the 27 Regt to the 19th Division, Esat effectively transferred the coastline sector of the 2/27 Regt to Kemal. This formalized the ad hoc command structure and unified the Ari Burnu front under a single commander, Mustafa Kemal.

Esat's actions at this stage of the battle reflected an understanding of modern command and control that was unusual for its time. Within a span of 12 hours, Esat had identified what he believed was the enemy's main effort, approved the execution of very successful decentralized counterattacks, briefed the Fifth Army commander and requested reinforcements, restructured his divisional sectors in the heat of battle and moved to the critical point where he could personally control the III Corps' main effort. In an era of detached high command, Esat's performance was uniquely active and reflected his understanding of the modern tactical dynamic.

Colonel Weber in XV Corps began to receive a similar stream of reports at about the same time as III Corps. Weber had three potential coastal landing areas of tactical concern (from north to south): the village of Yenikoy, Little Besika Bay and Big Besika Bay. The 3rd Division held the coast to a point south of Yenikoy from which the 11th Division held the coast to a line parallel with the inland town of Ezine. Kum Kale itself was, apparently, not thought to be as likely a location for a major landing as the larger bays to the south. After learning that Nicolai alerted his own 3rd Divison in the early hours of 25 April 1915, Colonel Weber put the adjacent 11th Division on alert at 6 am with orders to put two-thirds of the soldiers into their defensive trenches. Soon after that concentrations of allied ships in Besika Bay made it seem that landings were imminent there. However, as the French landings were delayed it remained unclear to XV Corps where the allies might actually land. After the French finally landed at Kum Kale, Weber waited for a larger landing which he expected on one of the three principal beaches to the south. Finally at 3.35 pm he sent the 126th and 127th Infantry Regiments (126 Regt and 127 Regt) forward to positions overlooking both Little and Big Besika Bays. These regiments would remain there, held in place by the French naval demonstrations. Meanwhile, Lieutenant Colonel Nicolai's regiments went into action at Kum Kale and stabilized the situation there by mid-afternoon.

In addition to the French landing, Colonel Weber also had to contend with Liman von Sanders, who began to order XV Corps to send aid to the hard-pressed III Corps. At noon on 25 April Weber was ordered to send an infantry regiment to Maidos to reinforce Esat.[138] Weber responded that the French had landed at Kum Kale entirely occupying his 3rd Divison. He continued by insisting that landings were expected in 11th Division's sector as well and he maintained he was unable to send troops. The Fifth Army staff then sent an urgent message ordering Weber to send a regiment from 3rd Division immediately and ordering Weber to reinforce 3rd Division by shifting 11th Division units north-ward. These messages were transmitted through the telephone exchange of the fortress command and, unfortunately, Weber's reply was misrouted and arrived late (at 5 pm).[139] Thus as evening fell no reinforcements had been sent to III Corps. An infuriated Liman von Sanders sent a third message demanding that Weber's nearest regiment be dispatched immediately and that Weber must send a second regiment as well. In order to accomplish this rapidly, three Ottoman general staff officers went to work via telephone. They were Staff Captain Nihat, XV Corps chief of operations, Fortress chief of staff Lieutenant Colonel Selahattin Adil and III Corps chief of staff Colonel Fahrettin. Nihat put the 64th Regiment on the road at 8.15 pm to the town of Çanakkale where Selahattin Adil had ships waiting at the piers. The regiment arrived at Kilye pier in Maidos at noon on 26 April where Fahrettin had guides waiting to bring the regiment to its staging area behind the Anzac beachhead. Shortly thereafter Nihat dispatched the 33rd Infantry Regiment in train, which duly arrived on the peninsula shortly after noon as well. It was commendable staff work performed by trained Ottoman general staff officers and the excellent staff coordination between three headquarters allowed Mustafa Kemal to launch powerful counterattacks on 27 April using well-trained and fresh troops. Over the next several days, when it was clear that the French were gone for good, XV Corps would lose all but two of its regiments to the gathering battles on the peninsula and in early May the corps headquarters itself would be sent over to assume control of the southern zone.

The reports of the III Corps and XV Corps commanders and staffs were consolidated by the Fifth Army under the direction of the chief of staff, Colonel Kazım. The speed of transmission of information to Enver in Constantinople was quite rapid with the Ottoman general staff often having possession of information within 2 hours of an event. Messages were ciphered and assigned a log number and a priority. High-priority messages were carefully managed to insure positive control. The time it was sent and the time the general staff acknowledged receipt were logged in as well as the time that the acknowledgement was passed to the commander or duty officer.[140] The bulk of the message traffic between the Fifth Army and Constantinople were sent by telegram over the civilian wires of the Administration des Telegraphes de L'Empire Ottoman (*Devlet-i aliye-i Osmaniye Telgraf Idaresi*). Additionally, the Çanakkale fortress maintained wireless communications with the ships of the navy anchored at Istiniye and in the Golden Horn and it was possible to pass information rapidly via this means as well.[141]

After action considerations

The first week of combat on the Gallipoli Peninsula ended badly for Ian Hamilton, who had expected to be in positions overlooking the strait after pounding through the Turks. The British badly underestimated the Ottoman army and were surprised by its tactical capability and levels of proficiency, especially its rifle marksmanship and its delivery of effective artillery fires. For their part the Turks thought they might push the enemy back into the sea and were surprised by the enemy resistance, especially at Anzac.

If there is a singular observation about why the Turks were able to stop Hamilton so completely it is that they were able to operate inside the British decision cycle. As a military doctrine the concept of 'getting inside the enemy's decision cycle' was articulated by the United States Army in its AirLand Battle doctrines of the late 1970s. It is based on the idea of leveraging fresh intelligence and information about the enemy in a way that enables a force to react faster than the enemy. It depends on a number of factors such as empowering commanders with the authority to act and training them to use their own initiative to acomplish the mission. On the ground in real combat the essence of operating inside the enemy's decision cycle is succinctly captured by the American Confederate cavalry General Nathan Bedford Forrest's famous maxim 'Get there firstest with the mostest.' On the Gallipoli Peninsula in 1915, the locally outnumbered Turks showed up most of the time with more troops, more favorably positioned, in the hands of more active commanders. How they managed this deserves consideration.

The Ottoman army's reporting system was, in comparison to the allied system, much more effective because of its standardized formats and bottom-up driven requirements. The Fifth Army commanders, at every level, were consistantly in possession of accurate and timely information that enabled them to make rapid and effective decisions. This also created a superior condition of situational awareness for army, corps and division commanders, which enabled them to calculate and take risks. Cumulatively, these factors led to the capability to mass the available forces effectively and efficiently. This was enhanced by the army's ability to task organize regiments and battalions at will between divisions and corps. This seemingly effortless ability to cross-attach units was a result of the triangular division architecture as well as a result of the hard-won experiences of the Balkan Wars. The generation of combat power by the Ottoman army, then, was really an expression of its doctrines and methods rather than the simple accumulation of men and weapons. Four operations illustrate this point: Şefik and Mustafa Kemal's co-ordinated attack on 25 April, Kemal's subsequent massed night attacks, Mahmut Sabri's defence of Cape Helles and Nicolai's massing at Kum Kale. In each case the Turks brought their forces to the right place in time to thwart the allied offensives.

Finally, in the author's opinion, the most significant mistake made by the Turks in the Gallipoli campaign occured in this phase. Enver Pasha eventually sent thirteen additional Ottoman army infantry divisions to the Gallipoli front to reinforce the Fifth Army's original six divisions. Had he sent six to eight divisions immediately from the massive force pool then held in Thrace in the late spring of 1915, these could have had a dramatic affect on the Ottoman attacks in phase three of the campaign – possibly leading to the destruction of the Anzac and Cape Helles bridge heads. This was a significant strategic error that immobilized critical military assets when they were most needed. There were two reasons for this: Enver thought that the Russians were about to launch a corresponding amphibious invasion on the Bosporus strait and, moreover, he worried about a Greco–Bulgarian alliance attacking western Thrace. That he thought these things were possible highlights the generalized weaknesses in strategic thinking and planning which affected the Ottoman high command throughout the war. As the British managed to throw away their victory so too did the Turks manage to discard the possibility of a campaign of annihilation.

Chapter 3

Stalemate, 2 May–6 August 1915

Introduction

The third phase of the Ottoman campaign for control of the Gallipoli Peninsula is characterized by Ottoman attempts to seize the initiative through offensive action. It is also clearly differentiated by the formation of corps-level operational groups to control the fighting on two separate fronts (Anzac and Cape Helles). Additionally the fighting itself shifted from single-division battles to multi-division battles coordinated by corps-level headquarters. In terms of Ottoman campaign strategy, this phase was marked by heavy reinforcements sent to the Fifth Army for the explicit purpose of conducting large-scale offensive operations designed to drive the allies off the peninsula. This phase also began a period wherein German commanders played a more direct role in tactical and operational leadership positions during offensive operations on the peninsula.

This phase ended in stalemate for both the Turks and the allies. Ottoman casualties during these months were particularly heavy largely because the Turks were engaged in both deliberate and hasty offensive operations. Similar problems emerged that affected both combatants as they struggled to understand and overcome the dynamics of trench warfare. These problems included: inadequate preparation time for planning sophisticated operations, inadequate artillery support and a lack of specialized munitions (such as high-explosive shells), the inability to cross no-man's-land in coherent formations and the inability to reinforce properly successful penetrations of the enemy's lines. Cumulatively, these problems led to both the allies and the Turks being able to penetrate the other's lines to a depth of 500–1,000m but then, unable to reinforce these penetrations for further advances, being subsequently driven back by vigorous counterattacks. In these assaults, both sides were unable to control the attacks in a manner that maintained unit integrity and these battles ended with the attacking formations hopelessly intermixed and leaderless.

Ottoman operational reorganization, May 1915

At the end of April 1915, the Ottoman III Corps found itself fighting on two separate fronts (Anzac and Cape Helles) and commanding regiments that cumulatively totalled over seven infantry divisions. At Anzac, Mustafa Kemal, a lieutenant colonel, was commanding a corps equivalent of troops with his tiny divisional headquarters. A similar situation existed at Cape Helles and, moreover, Esat was forced to divide his attentions between two separate fronts. On 28 April, the 15th Division was inbound as a reinforcement and the time had arrived for the Fifth Army to reorganize its forces to fit the ongoing campaign. On the night of 28/29 April, Liman von Sanders sent orders activating a Southern Group (*Guney Grubu*) to control the forces at Cape Helles, however, the group remained under III Corps command.[1] In the absence of an available headquarters, he ordered the commander of the 5th Division, German Colonel Eduard von Sodernstern, to assume command of both the 7th Division (commanded by Colonel Remzi) and 9th Division (commanded by Colonel Halil Sami) effective at 9 am the next morning. Accordingly von Sodernstern established his new headquarters and, while learning about the situation from Halil Sami, was joined by Captain Carl Mühlmann and Colonel Hans Kannengiesser, who had been sent to assist by Liman von Sanders. None of the Germans spoke Turkish so an Ottoman reserve officer (who was an Arab) was assigned as a translator. This was the entire staff of the Southern Group – three Germans and an Ottoman reservist.[2] Nevertheless, von Sodernstern was quick to act issuing his first orders at 3 pm, which divided the Southern Zone into Right and Left Sectors, under Colonels Halil Sami and Remzi respectively.

The 7th Division's 21 Regt began to arrive by steamboat from Bulair at 8 am with Colonel Remzi, the division staff and a field artillery battalion arriving by 2 pm. Most of the division was in sector by midday 29 April 1915. Also on this day, the inbound 15th Division was afloat in the Sea of Marmara and the Ottoman general staff ordered the 16th Division to the peninsula from its reserve areas around Kirklareli as well. All of these reinforcements were destined for the Southern Group and Liman von Sanders ordered von Sodernstern to prepare an offensive operation. The next day was spent quietly moving the incoming regiments of the 7th (32 Regt and 39 Regt) and 15th Division (126 Regt and 127 Regt) into the area. Altogether, by day's end, von Sodernstern was able to mass 13 battalions from 9 regiments totalling 10,460 officers and men.[3] Meanwhile, Enver was pressuring Fifth Army to attack the invaders and Liman von Sanders, in turn, pressed Esat and von Sodernstern for action. On the afternoon of 30 April, von Sodernstern received orders from Fifth Army ordering him to conduct a night attack on 1/2 May 1915 using units from all three divisions then in sector.

Units at the front spent the day conducting reconaissances of no-man's-land, which was generally about 600m wide and the reports were consolidated at sector headquarters. The divisional orders were prepared and distributed about 3.30 pm. The 9th Division's attack order reveals the simplicity of the operation, 'tonight at 10 pm the entire division will attack the enemy. From 8 until 10 pm, units will conduct reconnaissance and fire to harass the enemy.'[4] Altogether the Turks placed 18½ battalions supported by 3 machine-gun companies and 10 artillery batteries against a combined Anglo-French force of 30 battalions, supported by 30 machine-gun companies and 23 artillery batteries (not counting the powerful guns of the allied fleet).[5]

The night attacks of 1/2 May and 3/4 May

The Right Sector attacked promptly at 10 pm with a first wave composed of the 20 Regt under Major Halit attacking down Gully Ravine. To his left the 25 Regt, now commanded by the veteran Major Kadri, advanced as well in the clear night air. Losses were heavy in the confusion of the night attack as the Turks reached the British trenches. Recognizing he was outnumbered, Halit urgently requested reinforcements and at 1 am the 9th Division ordered its three reserve battalions forward (from the 126 Regt). However, it took over an hour to bring them down from staging areas near Krithia and they did not reach the British trenches until past 3 am, by which time the Ottoman assault had ground itself

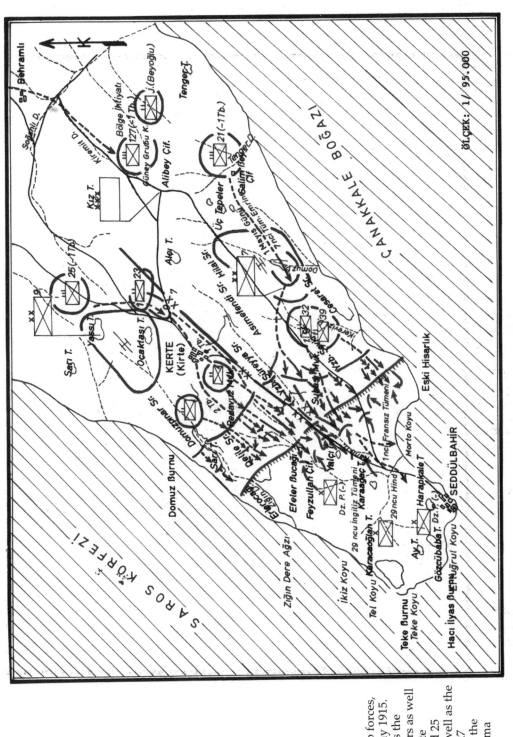

Map 3.1
Southern Group forces,
attack of 1/2 May 1915.
This map shows the
divisional sectors as well
as the immediate
reserves (21 and 25
Infantry (-), as well as the
area reserves 127
Infantry (-) and the
Beyoğlu Jandarma
Battalion).

to a halt. Nevertheless, the fresh troops threw themselves forward but were stopped by British counterattacks. The Turks began to retreat while allied artillery and naval gunfire punished them all the way back to their own trenches. In the darkness companies and platoons became hopelessly intermixed and lieutenants often found themselves in command of company sized groups.[6] The enemy followed this up with counterattacks at 7.30 am, 2 May. Map 3.1 shows the night attacks of 1/2 May at Cape Helles.

Colonel Remzi's Left Sector attacked the French lines at 10 pm also with battalions from the 21 Regt, 19 Regt and 26 Regt from right to left. Remzi's trenches were closer to the enemy (200m in some places) and as a result the 7th Infantry Division's aggressive attack was more successful, breaking through the French lines at one point and advancing nearly to Morto Bay. Prompt reinforcement of the French by battalions of the Royal Naval Division salvaged the situation and assisted them in driving the Turks back. Remzi's reserves (a battalion each from the 32 Regt and 39 Regt) went in at 2.10 am, too late to reenergize the failed attack, which collapsed soon after under French counterattacks.

By 3 am von Sodernstern received reports from both divisions that his offensive had failed with heavy casualties, which were especially severe among the junior officers. The modern Turkish official history suggests two reasons for the failure of the 1/2 May night attack.[7] First, the Southern Group staff consisted of only three people, who were simply unable to process the reports in time so as to be able to reinforce the success of Remzi's Left Sector. Von Sodernstern had parts of the 15th Division standing by for just such a contingency. Secondly, the central tactical telephone exchange that was located in Krithia, closer to von Sodernstern and Halil Sami than to Halit, repeatedly broke down under fire. In turn, this caused greater disruption in the flow of information to and from the Left Sector.[8] Encouraged by their defensive success, the British and French launched a major counterattack across the entire front at 10 am, 2 May, which failed completely within an hour. However, it did serve to delay Ottoman attempts to untangle the intermixed units and reestablish effective command and control. Shelling by the allied fleet was especially damaging on 2 May and losses over the preceding 24 hours were heavy with the 9th Divison losing 59 officers and 3,964 men, while the 7th Division lost another 2,000 soldiers.[9] On the plus side, the 16th Division arrived on the peninsula, as did a twelve-gun machine-gun detachment from the German ships anchored off Constantinople. But after a brutal 24 hours of combat the Southern Group spent the night of 2 May quietly recovering its strength.

The remainder of the 15th Division closed on reserve staging areas in the Left Sector after a 25km road march, which left the soldiers exhausted. Nevertheless, von Sodernstern regarded these reinforcements as fresh troops and, although the 7th Division had suffered severe casualties, he began to plan for another night attack. As a result of the previous success against the French, and also because the 9th Divison had been in continuous action since 25 April, von Sodernstern decided to launch the main effort in the Left Sector.[10] The relative proximity of the French trenches compared to the deeper no-man's-land on the British front was an additional factor but the 9th Division was ordered to conduct a support attack anyway. Unfortunately, his orders surprised the division commanders, who were trying to reconstitute their battalions. Throughout the day of 3 May, the Southern Group staff (three officers) feverishly put together a plan. Staff Captain Nihat worked the telephones with East's chief of staff to shift additional artillery shells south to support the attack.[11] Meanwhile, the 15th Division commander and chief of staff spent most of the day at the Southern Group headquarters trying to get a grip on the situation. Von Sodernstern's final attack order was not released until 7 pm because it had to be translated from German into Ottoman Turkish.[12] He organized an eight-battalion assault supported by five artillery batteries to attack at 11 pm that night and he ordered the troops to carry only their rifles, leaving their packs behind. His plan involved the 7th Division passing the 15th Division's 38th Infantry Regiment (38 Regt) and 45th Infantry Regiment (45 Regt) through its lines, whereupon these regiments would attack in columns. Von Sodernstern clearly expected success because he held two battalions of the 56th Infantry Regiment (56 Regt) in reserve and warned its commander to be ready to conduct 'pursuit operations.'[13] He sent the third battalion of the regiment to weight the 9th Divison's supporting attack. Finally, he notified his divisional commanders that he intended to shift his headquarters forward from the vicinity of Alçı Tepe to the 7th Divison command post at 7 am, 4 May to better control the battle. The Turkish official history noted that there were a number of 'very bad' errors in the translated orders due to translator error. In the 7th Divison the final orders did not reach the regimental and battalion commanders until well past 8.30 pm.

The French held their lines with twelve battalions supported by thirty-three artillery pieces and a dozen heavy machine-gun companies. The attack began quietly at 11 pm but immediate French fires turned the Ottoman assault into a giant engine of screaming men shouting 'Allah! Allah!', which broke into the French trenches. By 12.30 am the Turks had penetrated almost to the Morto Bay beaches and the 38 Regt commander requested the release of the reserves for pursuit operations. Unfortunately, the telephone lines to von Sodernstern were again destroyed by enemy fires and 2 hours passed without action.[14] On the right flank the 9th Divison's supporting attack made a minor penetration of the British lines but was rapidly crushed. As dawn approached von Sodernstern, apparently unaware of the success gained by the 15th Division, gave the order to retreat. The battered survivors returned leaving 3,900 dead and wounded behind – a loss rate of 40 percent in 10 hours.[15] Captain Nihat prepared reports to Fifth Army outlining the failure. The Southern Group had lost over 10,000 men in a 4-day period. III Corps commander, Esat Pasha, was especially critical of these losses and complained to Liman von Sanders about von Sodernstern's performance. In fact, the attacks failed because the planning was rushed and procedures to circumvent the breakdown of communications were impossible to put in place in the time available. Of note, the Ottoman army recognized the bravery and achievements of its soldiers and formations. The 19 Regt, which had been involved in the night attacks of 1 May, was badly worn down and was committed again in the second night attack on 3 May. The regimental commander, Lieuetnant Colonel Alman Sabri, who survived and rallied his men was awarded the Silver Battle Medal of Distinction (*Muharebe Gumus Imtiyaz Madeliyi*) for 'high achievement' on 9 May 1915.[16] Other commanders and regiments received similar honors.

On 5 May 1915, Liman von Sanders issued orders revising the tactical groups commanding the various zones of the battle area. He designated the Asian shore as the Anatolian Group (*Anadolu Grubu*), the Cape Helles area continued as the Southern Group (*Guney Grubu*), the Anzac area was designated as the Northern Group (*Kuzey Grubu*), and the vulnerable northern Aegean beaches were designated as the Saros Group (*Saros Grubu*). Group commanders assumed full tactical authority over all forces in their sectors regardless of unit affiliation or organization. The III Corps staff became the nucleus of the new Northern Group and Esat Pasha took over the direct control of the fighting at Anzac from Mustafa Kemal. The III Corps formations fighting at Cape Helles were detached from his command at the same time. Mustafa Kemal returned to his role as a division commander, but would later emerge as a group commander.

Although Liman von Sanders memoirs assert that von Sodernstern was lightly wounded about this time, the Turkish official histories assert that he was taken sick, removed from duty and sent to Constantinople on 4 May 1915. To replace von Sodernstern, Liman von Sanders appointed Colonel Weber and Weber's XV Corps staff formed the nucleus of the Southern Group's new headquarters staff. Coming from the relatively quiet Asian shore, the XV Corps staff were shocked by the con-fusion and bloodletting that had characterized the Cape Helles battles of early May.[17] Indeed, it took two more days to sort out the survivors and to reorganize them back into their organic units. Whether Liman von Sanders lost confidence in von Sodernstern is unclear from either German or Turkish sources, but it is unlikely because Colonel Weber was the more senior officer and was already in command of a corps headquarters (whereas von Sodernstern was a divisional commander). In the same way that Esat took over from Mustafa Kemal, Weber took over from von Sodernstern and, importantly, Weber brought with him a corps-level staff of 15 officers and 164 soldiers (as well as 91 animals) with which to plan operations more effectively.[18]

In the middle of the reorganization, Liman von Sanders received a 'surprise telegram' from Enver Pasha proclaiming the battles on the peninsula of supreme military and political importance to the empire and, moreover, promising reinforcements to continue the attacks.[19] Liman von Sanders would continue to receive such 'suprises' because the Ottomans had bypassed him (and the Germans) by establishing direct communications between Enver and his classmate, Colonel Kazım, the Fifth Army chief of staff, who independently sent reports to the general staff.[20] Colonel Kazım believed that the attacks should continue without pause so that the British and French would be unable to dig deep and comprehensive trench lines. The allies, for their part, were under similar pressure from London to break through what they believed were weakened Ottoman divisions holding hasty field works. Fortunately for the Turks, it was Ian Hamilton who decided to attack first.

The Second Battle of Krithia (6–8 May)

The second allied assault intended to seize the Achi Baba heights (Alçı Tepe) was a combined Anglo-French general attack using about 25,000 troops, of which only 4 battalions were fresh (125th Brigade). Hunter-Weston, in overall command, used a scant two-day period to plan the attack and repeated many of the Turkish problems, including inadequate reconaissance, the temporary combining of brigades into ad hoc divisions, incomplete orders that reached the troops too late and, most importantly, employing spent soldiers who were in a state of total exhaustion. The 3-day offensive was a daily series of dismally unoriginal direct frontal attacks, which consumed 6,500 allied casualties but gained almost no ground.

From the Ottoman perspective, the allied attacks preempted premature Ottoman attacks and actually allowed the Southern Group to continue its reconstitution. Although the British thought there were about 20,000 Turks on hand, modern Turkish histories assert that there were about half that (10,000) available supported by 24 machine-guns and 40 artillery pieces. As the attacks began about 10 am on 6 May, reports reached Weber and he reacted immediately by alerting his general reserve (38 Regt and 45 Regt). The British attacks failed completely while the French actually reached the Ottoman lines forcing Colonel Remzi to commit his divisional reserves (19 Regt and 21 Regt), which threw back the enemy. Casualties were comparatively light. The next day the allied attacks were delivered more strongly forcing Weber to commit the 45 Regt to halt the penetration in the 7th Division's sector. Urgent reports from the Southern Group to Fifth Army seemed to present an alarming situation by stressing the overwhelming numbers of enemy soldiers (twenty-eight battalions).[21] On 8 May Hunter-Weston mounted his final attacks and, once again, Ottoman resistance and the timely commitment of reserves prevented penetrations. Although the French enjoyed more success than the British, at no time was the Ottoman position seriously threatened. In fact the 45 Regt and most of the 9th Division's 26 Regt were never committed from their reserve positions. Overall Ottoman losses totalled less than 2,000 killed and wounded.

Based on a contemporary letter about the battle from Captain Mühlmann, Professor Tim Travers asserted that a crisis of command existed in the Southern Group during the time of Second Krithia.[22] Travers presents Weber's German chief of staff, Major von Thauvenay, as convincing Weber (as well as notifying Admiral von Usedom) to order the Southern Group to retreat to the Soğanlıdere Line behind Alçı Tepe. This would have been a monumental mistake because it voluntarily conceded the high ground to Hunter-Weston while, at the same time, doubled the length of the front lines. A concerned Mühlmann then went directly to Liman von Sanders, who immediately ordered the Southern Group to stand fast. This incident is not mentioned in the Turkish official history and perhaps the dispute stayed entirely within German channels. It is hard to fathom Weber contemplating a deliberate retreat to Soğanlıdere, especially considering the allied failure to penetrate the Ottoman defences and, moreover, in view of the fact that Weber retained several regiments of uncommitted infantry in reserve throughout the battles. Professor Travers also related that von Thauvenay was thereafter relieved of his duties, however, he remained in his position as chief of staff until the week of 8–12 June when he was replaced by Lieutenant Colonel Salahattin Adil.[23]

The night attack of 18/19 May 1915
On 13 May, Enver notified Fifth Army that powerful reinforcements were on the way, which included the 2nd and 12th Infantry

Divisions.[24] The 2nd Division was one of the army's premier divisions from the I Corps in the capital. It was well trained and consisted of its original organic infantry regiments. It was commanded by Lieutenant Colonel Hasan Askeri, brother to the famous guerilla commander Süleyman Askeri.[25] The 12th Division was similarly well trained and, moreover, Enver promised to send artillery and also to accelerate the flow of replacement soldiers to the Fifth Army corps to fill the depleted ranks to authorized strength (*ikmal*). With this information Esat presented Liman von Sanders with an offensive concept, which was based on the idea that the allies main effort at Cape Helles created an opportunity to attack a weakened Anzac perimeter.[26] He also noted that he had two fresh regiments from the 16th Divison on hand as well as additional 210mm and 120mm artillery and he requested one of the incoming divisions. The 2nd Division began arriving from Constantinople on 11 May and received telephonic orders to move into its staging area at Sarafim Farm two days later. Because of the threat of allied aerial observation the divison marched at night. On 14 May, it received orders committing it to the Northern Group. A second telephonic order at 11.15 am on 17 May sent the division and regimental commanders to Esat's headquarters on Mal Tepe where the III Corps staff had been intensively planning an attack on Anzac.[27]

The mood and morale in the Northern Group was very optimistic as evidenced by a report from Colonel Mustafa Kemal, which highlighted the positive effect that shelling three torpedo boats and six transports forcing them to withdraw had on those watching from the Ottoman positions.[28] Kemal was also well pleased with the available artillery, the presence of the 2nd Division and with troop morale. In reply, German Major Raymond carried secret and special orders to Kemal alerting him to the fact that the Northern Group would attack within the next 24 hours. The formal offensive authorization from Fifth Army arrived at the group headquarters at 1.50 pm, 17 May and specified the attack time as 3.30 am, 19 May 1915.[29] The orders stipulated that the entire 2nd Divison would march from Sarafim Farm at 7.30 pm on 18 May, leaving packs and baggage behind. Esat was tasked to provide the incoming 2nd Division soldiers

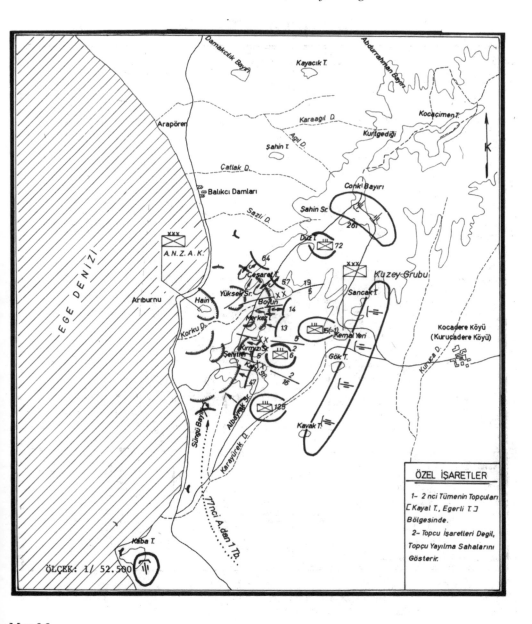

Map 3.2
Attack on Anzac of 19 May 1915. This map shows the general regimental positions within the divisional sectors and the growth of the Ottoman artillery positions. The headquarters of Esat Pasha's Northern Group is located on Kemalyeri (Scrubby Knoll).

with a hot meal as they arrived in their tactical assembly areas. The 2nd Division infantry and artillery regimental commanders were directed to meet at 5 pm that day to recon the routes and assembly areas and to rehearse the movement with their battalion commanders on the morning of 18 May. The attack was to be carried out by two wings and all attacking units were to be in their final positions by 2 am on 19 May. In turn Esat moved his group headquarters to Kemalyeri (Scubby Knoll) that day and sent his subordinates their warning orders on the afternoon of 18 May. Map 3.2 shows the night attacks of 19 May at Anzac.

The actual operations order for the night attack of 18/19 May 1915 was released at 8 pm finalizing what the subordinate commanders already knew: Kemal's 19th Division would attack the north, the 5th Division the center, the 2nd Division the Kanlısırt area (Lone Pine) and the 16th Division the south.[30] In addition the Gaba Tepe detachment was to throw a battalion in to support the left flank of the 16th Division. The commanders were ordered to minimize noise, especially the mass fixing of bayonets, as well as to leave all packs and heavy gear behind. When the assault waves entered the Anzac trenches the Ottoman artillery was to begin shelling the beaches and reserve areas to prevent Australian reserves from reinforcing the front lines. All

Table 3.1

Attack Strength, Northern Group (Excluding Artillery and Corps Support)

Unit	Battalions	Infantrymen
19th Division	13	10,966
5th Division	8	6,000
2nd Division	9	10,946
16th Division	12	13,400
1/77 Regt	1	800
Total	43	42,112

Source: T.C. Genelkurmay Başkanlığı. *Birinci Dünya Harbinde Türk Harbi Vnci Cilt, Çanakkale Cephesi Harekati (Amfibi Harekat)* (Ankara: Genelkurmay Basımevi, 1979), p. 195.

preparations were kept secret and Esat retained the 33 Regt as his corps reserve. The intent was clear in that a massive simultaneous human wave was to be launched at 3.30 am on a scale hitherto unseen on the peninsula. The actual number of infantrymen committed by the Northern Group is worth recording because it exceeded the estimated 30–40,000 Turks suggested by the British official history.

Altogether Esat had over 50,000 men committed to the attack, which would launch 4 divisions abreast on a front 3½km wide. Esat reckoned that he would pay a heavy price in blood, 30 percent of the men committed, but that in 6½ hours, the Anzac beachhead would be eliminated.

In turn the subordinate division commanders issued their own orders organizing their attacks. Mustafa Kemal deployed the 64 Regt and the veteran 57 Regt on the right and left respectively and he specified that each regiment provide thirty handpicked men to maintain contact between the regiments and the adjacent 5th Division. He retained the 72 Regt as his reserve and ordered its guides forward at 2 am so that as the assault proceeded they would know the routes through no-man's-land. Kemal intended to be able to commit his reserves at the decisive moment.[31] In Lieutenant Colonel Hasan Basri's 5th Division, the 14 Regt and 13 Regt were positioned on the right and left respectively, while he maintained the 15 Regt (of two battalions) in reserve. Hasan Basri was especially concerned about the flat terrain and lack of cover to his front and wanted Kemal's adjacent 57 Regt to conduct a vigorous and highly visible demonstration to distract the defenders so that his men might gain more ground without excessive casualties. He also warned his commanders not to let the massive wave disintegrate into pieces as men became casualties.[32] Hasan Askeri's newly arrived 2nd Divison seems to have conducted a relief in place taking over the trenches of the 33 Regt, which was then drawn back into reserve. He placed his 4th Infantry Regiment (4 Regt) on the right and his 5th Infantry Regiment (5 Regt) on the left leaving his 6th Infantry Regiment (6 Regt) in reserve. Hasan Askeri was concerned about tactical control of units moving forward in darkness as this was his division's first taste of combat. Accordingly he reminded his field and company grade officers to lead their men from the front and he stressed the importance of conducting an extremely violent bayonet attack giving the Australians no chance to recover. Hasan Askeri also moved guides from the 6 Regt forward at 2 am but he was worried because he had been informed that the Australians in this sector conducted a daily stand to well before dawn broke. Of the four division commanders attacking that day, Hasan Askeri was clearly the most anxious because he moved his divisional band into the forward trenches and ordered it to sound trumpets and drums at 3.40 am to be immediately followed by a complete playing of the *Motherland March (Vatan Marşını)*.[33] Colonel Rüştü's now veteran 16th Division placed the 47 Regt and 48 Regt on the right and left respectively with the 125 Regt in reserve and gave them similar instructions as the other divisions. The final unit on Esat's left flank was Major Saip's 1st Battalion, 77th Infantry Regiment (1/77 Regt), which came up independently to screen Rüştü's left.[34]

Unfortunately for the Ottomans, British RNAS aerial reconnaissance had picked up on the large masses of Turks unloading at Akbaş pier moving toward Anzac and the Australians had, likewise, noticed a lull in the ordinarily heavy daily fires on 18 May. Accordingly, both ANZAC divisions were warned at 5 pm to expect an assault. As darkness fell the 12,500 Australians holding the perimeter were shelled heavily and at 3 am, 19 May, they stood to arms in their trenches and readied themselves for an assault. They had not long to wait and 30 minutes later the Turks came rushing out of their trenches. Dawn was just breaking over Anzac.

Kemal's 57 Regt was able to seize parts of the Australian's first line of trenches largely due to the favorable dead ground that masked their attack. Hasan Basri's 14 Regt was also able to take some trenches but its sister 13 Regt 'ran out of luck that night' and dawn found it stopped cold still some 40m from the enemy trenches.[35] The soldiers of Hasan Askeri's 2nd Division, shouting 'Allah, Allah' and singing the *Motherland March*, fared the worst and were mown down like wheat in the open ground by Australian machine-gun and rifle fire. His commanders, trapped in no-man's-land, tried to lead small groups of the hardy Turkish askers forward but to no avail. Hasan Askeri committed his reserve in another attempt to break through with fresh men at 4.30 am. But at 5.10 am he sent a message to Esat reporting that 'the attack is halted, the entire reserve is expended, the assault has failed with very heavy losses of officers and men, and many survivors are fleeing back to friendly lines in disarray.'[36] Colonel Rüştü's 16th Division apparently achieved some small degree of surprise because of the quietness of its preparations but the adjacent inexperienced 2nd Division's noisy attack ended that quickly. By 5 am all but a single company of the 48 Regt of Rüştü's division, which had taken part of the Australian's forward trenches, were stopped as well. Such success as the Northern Group achieved lay in only a handful of company sized elements sitting in the Australian trenches.

As the reports of failure poured into the group's new Kemalyeri headquarters, which was located just a kilometer behind the 2nd Division's trenches, Esat decided to continue with daylight attacks.[37] Kemal launched his uncommitted 72 Regt on his right flank and renewed the fight with his battalions in contact. A bloody see-saw battle then raged in Kemal's sector with his attack stalling at 7 am, followed by an Australian counterattack at 7.30 am that pushed the 64 Regt back to its lines at 9.30 am. The 57 Regt held on to its gains past noon but Kemal pulled them back at 3.30 pm. The 5th Division renewed its bloody attacks until 10 am before quitting. The shattered 2nd Division was hopelessly mired with its battalions intermixed around the few surviving cadres of leaders and was unable to renew the offensive. The 16th Division attempted to renew the attack but Colonel Rüştü was very concerned about his open right flank as the 2nd Division had returned earlier to its own lines leaving his forward regiments exposed. Moreover, Royal Navy gunfire support was hammering his reserve regiment so severely that it could not deploy forward and Rüştü called off the attacks at 10 am as well. A discouraged Esat telephoned Fifth Army at 11.20 am to report the failure of the offensive after 7 hours of combat.[38] He praised the heroism of his soldiers and blamed the singularly heavy Australian machine-gun and rifle fire for the defeat. He noted that casualties were high, amounting to 50 percent in some units, but that he had yet to receive the strength returns from his divisions. Liman von Sanders then ordered the 2nd Division pulled out of the line for duty as the Fifth Army reserve. Losses were extremely heavy among the 2nd and 5th Divisions.

Table 3.2
Division Casualty Returns, 19 May 1915

Division	Officers		Soldiers		Totals
	KIA	WIA	KIA	WIA	
19th Div	6	7	333	748	1,094
5th Div	8	14	1,017	1,432	2,471
2nd Div	24	54	1,455	2,734	4,267
16th Div	13	22	547	926	1,508
1/77 Regt		17		127	144
Totals	51	97	3,369	5,967	9,484

Source: Fifth Army Report Divisional Losses, 19 May 1915, ATASE Archive 3474, Record H-14, File 5-38, reproduced in T.C. Genelkurmay Başkanlığı, *Birinci Dünya Harbinde Türk Harbi Vnci Cilt, Çanakkale Cephesi Harekati (Amfibi Harekat)* (Ankara: Genelkurmay Basımevi, 1979), p. 211.

In addition to the above losses, the 16th Division reported 486 men missing, making a grand total of losses in excess of 10,000 men. Officer losses in the fresh 2nd Division, which included the division chief of staff and two regimental commanders, were especially high reflecting the ardour and zeal with which previously unblooded men went into battle. The Northern Group's offensive failed primarily because it depended on the element of complete surprise rather than a preliminary bombardment closely tied in time to the assault waves. Instead, the Australians were ready and waiting. Even so, the sheer scale of the attack, some 30,000 men in the initial wave, itself should have led to some larger degree of success and it is a tribute to the resolute bravery and fire discipline of the Australian infantry and machine-gunners that it failed so utterly. Famously, a temporary cease fire was arranged so that the surviving wounded trapped in no-man's-land might be recovered and the dead might be buried (who within days began to rot causing acute hygiene problems in the Australian trenches). Negotiations arranging the 'Anzac armistice' dragged on but finally on 24 May from 7.30 am to 4.30 pm a mutually satisfactory cease fire was conducted during which some 3,000 odd dead Ottoman soldiers were buried on the spot.[39] Subsequent modern Turkish analysis points to inadequate supplies of artillery ammunition which forced Esat to forego a conventional artillery preparation, the massing of the 2nd Division which exposed the operation to aerial observation, and the attempts to relieve units on the front after dark as contributing factors to the failure. With the complete failure of the 19 May attack, Liman von Sanders ordered the aggressive Esat to suspend offensive operations as it was now clear that the Australians were more than capable of holding their own against almost any number of Turks who could reasonably be ranged against them. Operations at Anzac now entered a period of relative quiet.

The Third Battle of Krithia (4–6 June 1915)
The 12th Division began unloading at Akbaş Pier at 9 am on 16 May and began moving to positions in the Southern Group. On 20 May, Colonel Nicolai warned Liman von Sanders that the army's posture at Kum Kale was dangerously weakened by the loss of the 11th Division. Alert to the possibility of a renewed allied landing in Asia, the Ottoman general staff put the I Corps (commanded by Mehmet Ali Pasha) and the 1st Division on movement orders south. Liman von Sanders assigned these units to the Kum Kale area and attached the 3rd Division to I Corps on 28 May 1915. Tidying up the operational area, Enver assigned Staff Colonel Feyzi's XVI Corps to the Saros Bay area. In the meantime, Hamilton was planning another attack to break through to the high plateau overlooking Kalid Bahr (Kalıtbahr). Colonel Weber's Southern Group was in fair shape as June began with the 9th Division (7,000 men) holding the right and the 12th Division (8,600 men) holding the left. In close reserve he had 4 battalions of the 7th Division and 11 battalions under Colonel Şükrü's 15th Division north of Soğanlıdere (some 18,500 men), as well as about 25 batteries of artillery. Each division on the front lines had an engineer company attached to assist in fortification construction. The Turks had the opportunity to dig in and Halil Sami's experienced 9th Division was especially well prepared with overhead cover and electricity. Importantly, the Turks developed and rehearsed counterattack plans.[40] Against them

Hamilton massed about 22,000 French and 24,000 British infantry with another 7,000 British infantry in reserve. Hamilton also planned to conduct a diversionary attack from Anzac to draw Ottoman attentions.

Mustafa Kemal's soldiers reported Australian attacks at Anzac at 5.15 am, 5 June which resulted in successful counterattacks about an hour later. The main effort began against the Southern Group at 8 am as the French hit Colonel Salahaddin's 12th Division penetrating the 34th Infantry Regiment's (34 Regt) lines to about 175m. However, by noon the regimental commander had restored the situation with a counterattack of his own immediate reserve (3rd Battalion, 34 Regt). However, on the division's right flank the Royal Naval Division's bayonet assault penetrated more deeply forcing Salahaddin to commit his divisional reserve, the 22nd Infantry Regiment (22 Regt), which restored the lines by 1 pm. The British attacks against the 9th Division were more successful with the British 129th Brigade (42 Div) penetrating about 500m and the 88th Brigade (29 Div) almost as deeply. Halil Sami's companies fell back to their second line of trenches in these sectors but held on to the front against an Indian brigade on the division right flank. Halil Sami fed his immediate reserves into the fight (2/25 Regt) to contain the enemy and moved more reserves forward (the remainder of the 25 Regt). By late afternoon, the British attack was stalled and the Turks were pushing them back and reclaiming their forward trenches, Meanwhile, Weber also pushed reserves forward to backstop any breakthrough. By the end of the day the discouraged allies called off the attack. The British official history asserts that the battle was lost because Hunter-Weston used his reserves to attack the Ottoman lines still held by the Turks, in effect, reinforcing failure while the successful brigades were left unsupported and vulnerable to Ottoman counterattacks. Moreover, the author, Aspinall-Oglander, speculated that a victory was possible because the Turks appeared disorganized and 'all would have been lost' with a continuing British attack.[41] However, as none of the Southern Group reserves were actually committed and were in good positions as night fell on 5 June, it is hard to imagine a different outcome. In fact at 7.30 pm that evening Liman von Sanders sent a message to Enver reporting a successful defence

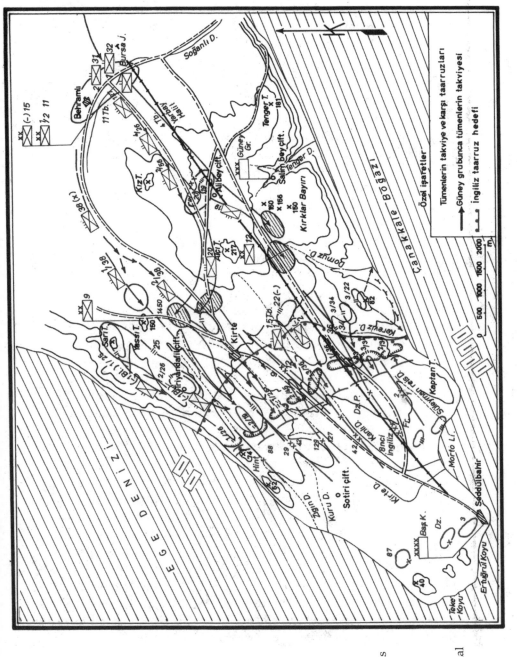

Map 3.3
Third Krithia, first day attacks and Ottoman counterattack, 4 June 1915. This map illustrates the importance of the positioning of Ottoman reserves in depth. The allied attacks are halted by divisional tactical reserves as the group reserves move forward as a contingency measure.

and indicating that Weber intended to counterattack. Map 3.3 shows the allied attacks of 4 June 1915.

Colonel Weber's staff worked through the night sending reports to Fifth Army at dusk, and then at 4.45 am and 8.30 am.[42] The final report indicating that the 9th Division had regained control of its forward trenches and subsequent reports from the divisions to Weber indicated that the enemy was tired and weakened. Consequently, Weber ordered the 9th Division to counterattack that night at 3.30 am (6 June) with bayonets fixed on unloaded rifles using a large formation of two columns. Weber sent reinforcing battalions from the 2nd and 12th Divisions with orders to be in the tactical assembly areas not later than 1 am. Altogether Colonel Halil Sami had eleven infantry battalions (five in the right and six in the left column) for the assault. His division staff prepared supplementary orders which went out to the adjacent divisions at 12.15 pm, 5 June outlining his plans. The 4 Regt commander, Lieutenant Colonel Nazif, was ordered to control the right column, while 127 Regt commander, Lieutenant Colonel Hasan Lüftü, was ordered to command the left and they were warned that large numbers of enemy dead and wounded lay in their path which might cause difficulty. Supporting Halil Sami, the adjacent 12th Division organized a reserve group on its right flank to put pressure on the enemy trenches.[43] Follow-up instructions ordered the division artilleries to support the assault as well after the attack had been discovered by the enemy.

The attacking troops began moving forward about 1 am packing into the trenches of the 5 Regt. They went over the top as scheduled at 3.30 am, 6 June and disappeared into the British trenches. Reports filtered back at 6 and 6.45 am indicating that the right column had seized the first line of enemy trenches and the left column was similarly successful and had taken five enemy machine-guns. There had been heavy fighting inside the British lines for over 1½ hours. Throughout the fight the Ottoman artillery attempted to suppress the allied guns but with no success. The Ottoman attacks ground to a halt as the British counterattacked to stabilize the line. Colonel Weber noted in his after action report that fighting continued for the remainder of the day but these resulted in no changes to the general situation. Third Krithia ended with heavy losses on both sides. The British

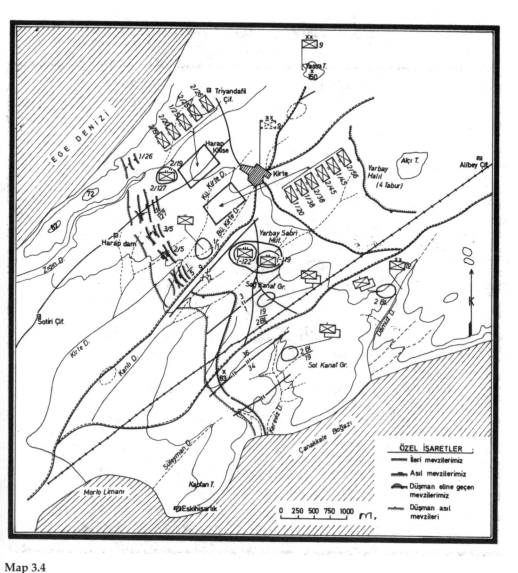

Map 3.4
Arrangements for 9th Division attack and general situation, 1 am, 6 June 1915. The use of gigantic assault columns composed of five or six battalions from different regiments is shown on this map. The 9th Division commander intends to displace his headquarters on Yassa Tepe forward to Kirte.

and French lost about 4,500 men and 2,000 men respectively. Ottoman losses reported in combat returns were curiously lopsided with 52 officers and men killed and 4,965 officers and men wounded.[44] However this does not square with the 9,000 casualties reported to Liman von Sanders on 9 June or the 6,000 reported by Colonel Weber, of whom 'at least one third died.'[45] In any case, because of the losses on both sides heavy fighting at Cape Helles subsided until late in the month. Map 3.4 shows the night attacks by columns of 6 June at Cape Helles.

Reorganization (mid-June 1915)

Alert to the stalemated situation on the peninsula, the Ottoman general staff ordered the II Corps headquarters (commanded by Brigadier Faik Pasha), the 6th Infantry Division, and three jandarma battalions south. The 6th Division joined XVI Corps on coastal defence duty on the narrow peninsula neck at Saros Bay, while the II Corps headquarters and the 6th Division's 18th Infantry Regiment (18 Regt) continued onward to Cape Helles and Anzac. By this time in the campaign the Ottoman divisional orders of battle were hopelessly confused with many regiments cross-attached from their original organic parent formations. Nonetheless, the Ottoman divisions continued to maintain their combat effectiveness by easily adapting to the situation.[46] On 7 June 1915 Liman von Sanders began to feel nervous about the Kum Kale shore and informed the Asia Group commander (also I Corps commander) Mehmet Ali to review the defensive arrangements of his formations. On that day he also issued orders, which relieved and replaced several division commanders, including the 9th Division's Halil Sami, who was sent to Constantinople after forty-four continuous and intense days of combat.[47] Colonel Kannengiesser replaced him in command of the division. Von Sodernstern was also formally replaced in 5th Division by Lieutenant Colonel Hasan Basri. Of note, a small but prescient change was made in the Northern Group by assigning a Bavarian major named Wilhelm Willmer to command an ad hoc detachment, the Anafarta Müfrezesi, to watch Suvla Bay.

On 8 June the Fifth Army staff conducted a conference for the group chiefs of staff at which the Southern Group chief of operations, Staff Captain Mehmet Nihat, presented a forty-eight page paper about the recent battles at Cape Helles. It was apparently at this conference that a fatigued Lieutenant Colonel von Thauvenay presented the tactical situation in the Southern Group as 'hopeless' and pleaded for fresh reinforcements,[48] an act that led to his relief as group chief of staff that very day. The concerns surfaced at the conference generated dialogue about taking advantage of the current operational lull in combat to conduct relief in place operations moving the Southern Group divisions in contact to the rear and replacing them with fresh units. The Fifth Army staff concurred and ordered the group to go ahead with this concept. The Southern Group acted swiftly by issuing orders the following evening (perhaps leading to the conclusion that Mehmet Nihat anticipated this and had already devised such a plan).[49] Colonel Weber ordered the 9th and 12th Divisions to pull back on the night of 11/12 June, while at the same time the 11th, 7th and 2nd Divisions would relieve them in the lines from right to left respectfully. While putting fresh men in the trenches this also put three divisional headquarters forward to relieve the strain on senior commanders as well. Conducted under conditions of great secrecy for fear that the allies would discover and take advantage of the dangerous maneuvre, the relief in place went off successfully.

Liman von Sanders remained concerned about the depleted condition of his divisions and began to press the Ottoman general staff for reinforcements and replacements. Enver rebuffed his requests but within days wired Liman von Sanders that the political situation allowed him to send assistance to Fifth Army. Between 13 and 16 June the Fifth Army and the general staff traded messages about exactly what was required on the peninsula, but Enver did not commit any actual forces. Finally, on 17 June, Liman von Sanders sent off a message to Enver requesting authority to move II Corps, 4th and 6th Divisions, south to Cape Helles,[50] prompting Enver to reply immediately that he did not want these units committed to combat piecemeal (*parça parça kullanmak*).[51] However, Enver also promised to dispatch the Second Army headquarters from the capital area and the 8th Infantry Division, then entrained near Smyrna (modern Izmir) enroute from Palestine, to reinforce Fifth Army. Once these formations were in situ at Saros Bay, Liman von Sanders would be free to move his divisions south. On 19 June, the general staff put 5,000 replacements into the pipeline to Fifth Army to bring its depleted formations up to strength. Of course this number was insufficient to replace casualties of the magnitude suffered by Fifth Army and Liman von Sanders asked for more. He also requested that Enver direct Major General Cevat Pasha, the strait fortress commander, to release artillery and ammunition to the Fifth Army. Liman von Sanders based this on the principle that the strait was unlikely to be attacked, Enver concurred, and on 21 June Cevat released three batteries of 150mm howitzers and one battery of 105mm guns to the Fifth Army.

Kereves Dere (21–22 June)

After the front-wide attacks of early June at Cape Helles failed, Hamilton authorized Hunter-Weson to conduct smaller divisional-scale attacks to seize locally favorable objectives. By this time, the Southern Group had forty-two infantry battalions on hand, but these were considerably weakened from weeks of combat. Strength returns from the Southern Group chief of staff (Lieutenant Colonel Hüseyin Selahattin) on 20 May showed 26,022 men present for duty out of an authorized strength of over 42,000, with losses reported as 16,178.[52] He also noted that the 'old divisions' were notably reduced compared to the newly arrived divisions, in particular the 7th Division was at 50 percent strength and the 9th Division (six battalions) was at 33 percent strength, while the 11th, 12th and 15th Divisions varied between 80 and 90 percent strength. Oddly, the report did not list the strength of the 2nd Divison but other reports list its 1st Infantry Regiment (1 Regt) and 6 Regt with 1,800 men each and the 5 Regt with 1,500 men, putting this division at 50 percent of its authorized strength.

The French launched the first of these smaller attacks on 21 June at Kereves Dere, which the Turks call the Battle of 83 rakımlıtepe (Hill 83). The attack was planned with two regiments assaulting at 6 am after a 45-minute artillery preparation. The French objectives included the hill and two Ottoman redoubts known as the Haricot and the Quadrilateral. Ammunition was plentiful and the French left no details undone. The objectives

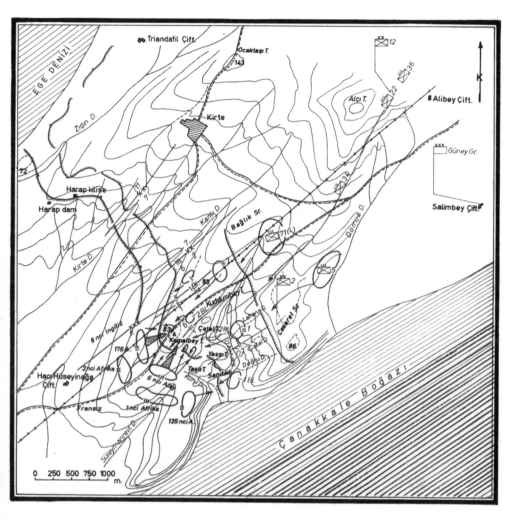

Map 3.5
Battle of Kereves Dere, attack and counterattack, 21–22 June 1915. The Battle Kereves Dere is known to the Turks as the Battle of Hill 83, which is shown on this map. The limited nature of the attack is apparent.

were held by 600 men of the 2nd Division's 1/6 Regt, who had been in position since 13 June.[53] Although their trenches were only about 200m from the French, they knew that their sister battalion, the 2/6 Regt, lay behind them in immediate reserve.[54] Map 3.5 shows the attacks of 21–22 June 1915.

The French assault broke into the right-flank Ottoman trenches but failed on the left. The fighting was bitter and the 2/6 Regt was committed around 7 am. A half hour later, Lieutenant Colonel Hasan Askeri had the 5 Regt and 71st Infantry Regiment (71 Regt) moving forward from reserve positions. Moreover, at 10.25 am Colonel Weber put the 34 Regt from the 12th Division lying in reserve near Alçı Tepe on the road south as well. However, none of these reserves were needed as the 6 Regt was able to hold the French by themselves and most of the French were pushed back by mid-afternoon. The 2nd Division chief of staff, Captain Kemal, who had come forward to assess the situation was severely wounded and evacuated to a field hospital, where he died four days later. Nevertheless, by evening Hasan Askeri was able to report that the French attack was finished and that the 1/6 Regt had reclaimed 150m of trench taken by the enemy. He also noted that he had substantial reserves in place to prevent further attacks.[55] He followed this up at 1 am with a report noting that Hill 83 was firmly in his hands and that he intended to counter-attack at 2 am with two infantry battalions of the 34 Regt. But, by 4.45 am the attack had collapsed and Hasan Askeri ordered his artillery commander to provide the retreating men with artillery fire. He spent the early morning of 22 June moving reserve companies into position as well as pulling 4,000 sand bags out of reserve for use. At 5 am, Lieutenant Colonel Cemil, commander of the 36th Infantry Regiment (36 Regt), was startled to see an Ottoman steamer named the *Haliç* steam into view to recover some casualties on shore.[56] In spite of allied shelling and the presence of two enemy destroyers, the *Haliç* performed its mission and withdrew safetly. The Turks were greatly cheered by this event. The French renewed their assault at 2.15 pm against the right flank of the 1 Regt, which took very heavy casualties in its 1st Battalion then holding the shoulder of the hill. A comprehensive situation report from the commander of the 34 Regt, Major Yümnü, noted that the French attack was particularly fierce and well supported by hand grenades and artillery fire.[57] The major also reported the loss of 699 men out of the 1,894 soldiers that he had on hand at dawn in a period of just 3 hours.

The battle frittered away into the night of 22/23 June and a half-hearted French attack on the Quadrilateral failed the next day. Minor fighting continued until 25 June before the French quit. The battle ended with the French in possession of some of the forward Turkish trenches on Hill 83. Fifth Army reports to Constantinople on 25 June reported at least 79 officers and 5,800 soldiers as casualties over 4 days of combat.[58] The French reported about 2,500 casualties but the Turks claim that this is only the number of dead and that many more were wounded. The 2nd Division was so weakened by the battle that Weber decided to pull it to the rear replacing it in line with the fresh 12th Division.

Gully Ravine (28 June–5 July 1915)

Hunter-Weston launched his second divisional attack on his left flank along an axis of attack defined by Gully Ravine or Zığındere. The Ottoman 11th Division opposed British attack, which lay entirely within this division's defensive sector. Colonel Refet commanded the division composed of the 33 Regt, 126 Regt and 127 Regt and the key village of Krithia lay just 1,500m behind his forward positions. Refet had about 8,000 men on hand and he maintained his headquarters on Ocaktaşi Tepe (Stone Oven Hill). Two battalions of Lieutenant Colonel Sabri's 33 Regt held the right, on what that British called Gully Spur, while two battalions of Lieutenant Colonel Mustafa Şevki's 126 Regt held what the British called Fir Tree Spur. Each regiment held one battalion in immediate reserve. Refet held the 127 Regt in divisional reserve. According to the Turkish histories Refet was not expecting an attack and was focused on anti-aircraft defenses and coordination with the adjacent 7th Division. As the 4th Division had mostly arrived and the 6th Division was enroute the Fifth Army believed the tactical and morale situation to be well in hand. Map 3.6 shows the attack on Gully Ravine of 28 June 1915.

Opposing Refet was the British 29th Division under the command of Major General de Lisle, which was reinforced with

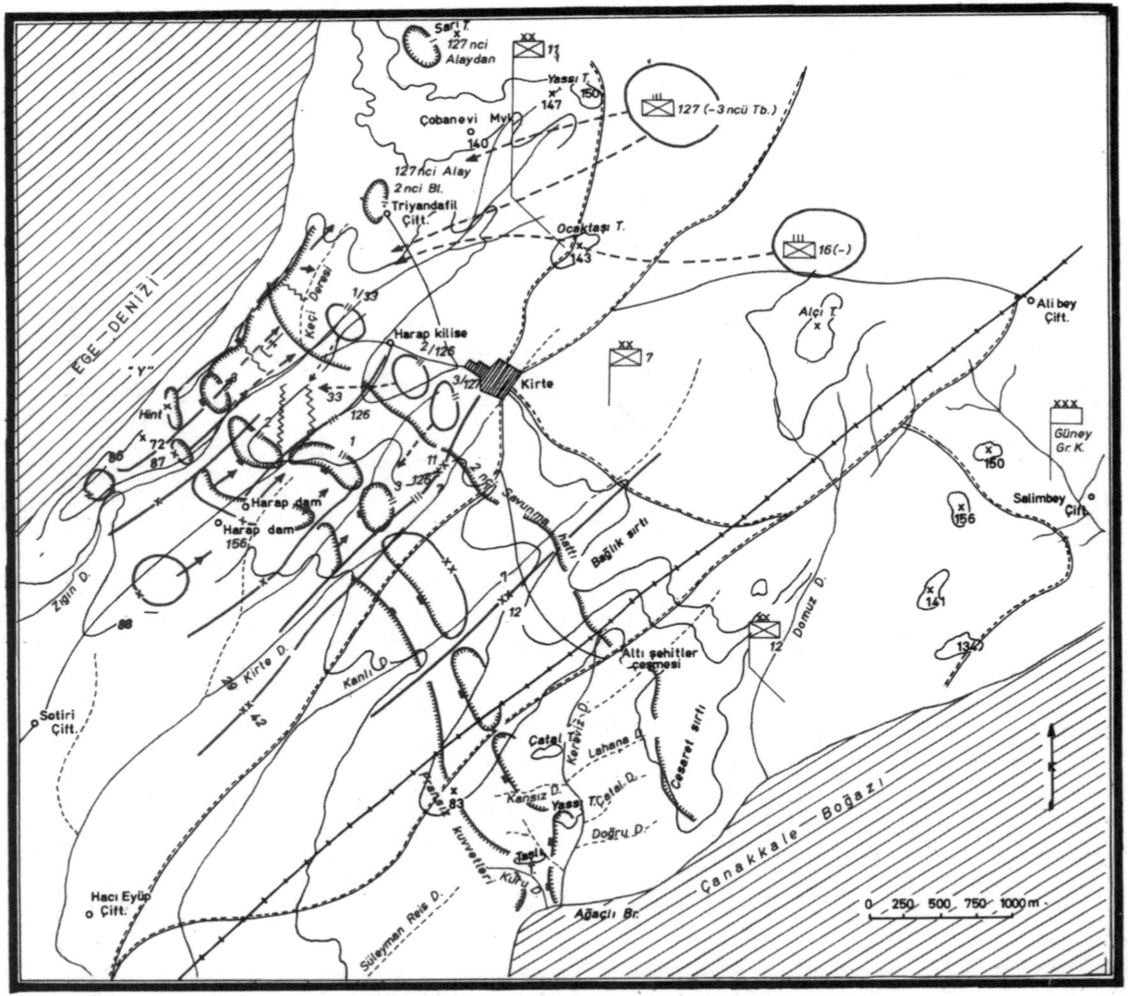

Map 3.6
Gully Ravine, Southern Group defensive situation and British attack, 28 June 1915. The Battle of Gully Ravine is known to the Turks as the Battle of Zığındere. The open nature of the Ottoman right flank is apparent from this map.

an Indian and a territorial brigade. The British were extremely well prepared and had very up-to-date maps based on recent aerial observation. They only had seventy-seven British and French artillery pieces but had a cruiser and two destroyers available for naval gunfire support as well. Harrassing fires began about 2 am, 28 June 1915 and the main bombardment commenced at 9 am. Lieutenant Colonel Sabri sent situation reports to the division headquarters at 9.20, 9.55 and 11 am, the last reporting a major ground attack on his lines that started at 10.45 am.[59] As the Ottoman positions were incompletely wired in the British seized the forward trenches within minutes, which was also reported to division. Lieutenant Colonel Mustafa Şevki followed suit reporting the attack but also that his lines were holding. His telephone lines were cut by fire at 11.30 am. As noon approached, Indian troops had advanced over a thousand meters on the extreme right flank nearing what they called the Nullah. Accurate situation reports enabled Colonel Refet to understand the danger and he ordered Lieutenant Colonel Hasan Lüftü's 127 Regt forward to blocking positions behind the 33 Regt, while simltaneously reporting to the Southern Group his situation and the fact that he had committed his divisional reserves.[60] At the same time (noon), Colonel Weber released the Southern Group's immediate reserve, two battalions of the just-arrived 16th Infantry Regiment (16 Regt) from the 6th Infantry Division, which was located only 1km east of the 11th Division head-quarters, to Colonel Refet's control.[61] Refet immediately used these forces as well as Lüftü's regiment to conduct a violent counterattack on the Indian brigade which raged for about 3 hours. By 4.30 pm, Lüftü was able to report that he had pushed the enemy back and partially restored the situation.[62] However, an Anglo-Indian salient shaped like a thumb still extended north along the coast threatening the Ottoman flank. As darkness fell, Colonel Refet coordinated with the 6th Division to receive a machine-gun company as well as sending out orders solidifying his lines. He was especially concerned about the salient on his right flank and directed two companies of the 16 Regt to extend their lines over the cliffs and down to the beaches. Returns from the day's fighting indicated that 10 officers and 2,012 soldiers were casualties (398 killed, 781 wounded and 843 missing).

Message traffic on the night of 28/29 July between Liman von Sanders and Enver resulted in orders to Colonel Weber to counterattack using the incoming II Corps formations. Weber began to plan accordingly and early on 29 July he appointed the II Corps commander, Brigadier General Faik, as Right Wing Commander. At 7.30 am, Faik, who was fluent in German, had a telephone conversation with Liman von Sanders to discuss the overall situation. An hour later, Colonel Weber placed the 7th and 11th Divisions directly under Faik's command.[63] He also ordered the 12th Division to prepare to launch small raiding parties to support Faik's assault. For his part, Liman von Sanders ordered East's Northern Group to return five battalions of the 9th Divison, which was reconstituting itself behind Kum Tepe, to Weber's control. The new 9th Division commander, Colonel Kannen-giesser, had several battalions on the way by midday. Brigadier General Faik spent the morning receiving reports from his new divisions and putting together his plans. He also sent word to his incoming 1st Division for the 124th Infantry Regiment (124 Regt) to accelerate its movement into the combat zone. A report from Colonel Refet arrived at II Corps headquarters at 1 pm, which recommended a night attack. Refet's report noted that his units were still intermixed from the previous day's fighting and that he could not reorganize them entirely until nightfall. He also noted the excessive casualties suffered by the 33 Regt, which had been reduced to 11 officers and 928 men.

Faik spent the afternoon positioning his artillery near the Triyandafıldçiftliği (Triyandafil Farm), moving his incoming units into position and finalizing his orders. As the remaining regiments of the 6th Division were slow to arrive, Faik also organized a provisional regiment from battalions of the 17th Infantry Regiment (17 Regt) and 18 Regt.[64] Nevertheless, through sheer determination Faik issued his corps attack order at 6 pm.[65] At 7.30 pm the artillery preparation would begin and 30 minutes later, from right to left, the 124 Regt, 16 Regt, 33 Regt and 126 Regt, the infantry would assault. In addition to the divisional artillery batteries, two 150mm howitzer batteries lent their fire and the incoming 1st Division was ordered to man the third defensive line by 8.30 pm. The previously prepared raids by the 7th and 12th Divisons were ordered forward to confuse the enemy as well.

The provisional regiment remained as Faik's reserve. Faik's attack went off as scheduled but quickly bogged down in the face of heavy machine-gun and artillery fire. By midnight, battalions of 16 Regt had seized the enemy's first line of trenches but the 124 Regt had made little progress. Reports from the regimental commanders requesting time to reorganize arrived at corps head-quarters at 2 am, 30 June. Reluctant to give up, Faik sent warning orders to 1st Division commander, Lieutenant Colonel Cafer Tayyar, to ready the 71 Regt for a follow-up assault. This attack was hastily organized in the dark and launched prematurely. Unsurprisingly it was 'scattered rather than concentrated' and failed under intensive machine-gun fire.[66] A disappointed Colonel Weber forwarded Faik's situation report outlining the failure to Fifth Army by telegraph at 5.50 am, 30 June 1915.

Faik was undeterred by these reverses and began to plan for further attacks using the relatively fresh 1st Division. However, because of the disorganized state of the II Corps, only a minor attack was attempted on the night of 1 July with no results. That night messages from Liman von Sanders poured into Faik's head-quarters encouraging him to wipe out the British salient on the Turk's right flank. At 9.45 am, Faik sent a warning order to Lieutenant Colonel Cafer Tayyar to ready his men for further assaults. This was followed several hours later by an attack order specifying a 3 pm assault time with a follow-on attack at 6 pm. Apparently, Cafer Tayyar could not put things in order quickly enough and his division attack order specified a revised attack time of 6 pm, which was to be carried out with bayonets and hand grenades.[67] This was believed feasible because the British trenches in front of the 71 Regt and 124 Regt were only about 50m away. The assault force was composed of the 3rd Battalions of three regiments (the 70th Infantry Regiment (70 Regt), 71 Regt and 124 Regt) under the tactical command of Major Reşat (commander of the 3/70 Regt), who was directed to load the men up heavily with hand grenades. The 2nd and 1st Battalions, 70 Regt were assigned missions of assault-force reserve and division reserve respectively. The attack order encouraged the men to pray before the assault and ended with the exhortation that those who died would be kissed by God. Cafer Tayyar reck-oned that his men had enough time to prepare for this operation.

The attack began badly with little of the artillery support that had been planned and the advance stalled causing Major Reşat to commit his reserve. Reşat himself was seriously wounded at 6.30 pm and he later wrote in an after action report that his battalion Imam, Hüseyin Efendi, then led the attack with many soldiers following him from the 9 Coy and 10 Coy. The officers manuevered the assault into the trenches, but pushing the enemy back was 'like pushing mud.'[68] The attack continued by platoons advancing at the cost of many dead, but the enemy trenches were taken. In fact these were the former Turkish trenches known to the British as J12 and J13. Major Şerif, commander of the 3/124 Regt who had assumed command, was able to report a successful operation to Cafer Tayyar by 11.30 pm that night. Telephone conversations between Cafer Tayyar and Faik at 4.45 am, 3 July resulted in Faik ordering the attack to continue at 5.20 am. However, by 10.30 am it was clearly apparent that the 1st Division was incapable of further attacks.

Fortunately for the Turks, the Fifth Army commander had secretly set units in motion to reinforce the Southern Group. Previously on 1 July Liman von Sanders ordered the Asia Group commander, Brigadier General Mehmet Ali, to deploy to the peninsula with his I Corps staff and the fresh 3rd Division. By 12.30 am, 3 July the corps headquarters and the advance parties of the 3rd Division were arriving on the peninsula. Accompanying Mehmet Ali was his corps chief of staff, German Major Eggert, and Staff Captain Tevfik. In addition to these forces the Fifth Army had accelerated the flow of the 5th Division inbound from the north as well. Early in the afternoon of 3 July Liman von Sanders arrived at the Southern Group's headquarters at Salimbeyçiftliği to confer with Colonel Weber. Mehmet Ali and his staff had arrived there earlier in the day and, after a brief nap, were working with Weber's staff. The outcome of this meeting was a massive change in the operational posture of the group and a revised offensive plan to attack the next day. Orders began to go out immediately at 2.40 pm to the 4th Division (then in reserve) to relieve the 12th Division (then in the line) beginning at 9 pm that night. In addition, the 4th Division was ordered to shift six 47mm naval guns and 1,800 shells west to support the offensive. By late afternoon, Mehmet Ali began to issue orders directly to the commanders of the 3rd and 5th Divisions to plan for an attack the next day at 3.45 am. However, further discussions by the combined staffs slowed the tempo as Liman von Sanders realized that delaying the offensive by one day (to 5 July 1915) offered a higher prospect of success because the incoming units were arriving more slowly than expected and needed both preparation and rest.[69]

The extra day of planning enabled Mehmet Ali to construct a plan launching six battalions of the 3rd Division to the west of Gully Ravine and four battalions of the 5th Division to the east. He held two battalions of the 5th Division in immediate reserve just south of Triyandafıldçiftliği. While in comparison to earlier Ottoman attacks, the infantry force seemed lighter than past practice, the artillery plan was significantly more complex. The Ottoman artillery was organized into a Right Wing Group under Lieutenant Colonel Asım and a Left Wing Group under Lieutenant Colonel Adil.[70] This centralization of artillery assets mirrored the successful artillery command arrangements used in the Battles of Çatalca in the Balkan Wars.[71] Lieutenant Colonel Asım and his staff spent the time intensively studying and mapping the British positions, which could be observed directly from Alçı Tepe. He organized his group into 2 components, a light group composed of 14 field-artillery batteries, 2 mountain-gun batteries and 1 mortar battery and a separate heavy group of 105mm, 150mm and 210mm howitzers. The light group was assigned detailed fire plans designed to suppress the fires of the British trenches. The heavy group, which was under the command of Major Rıfat, was assigned a counter battery mission to suppress the British artillery. Lieutenant Colonel Adil's plan for the Left Wing was equally detailed. This was the most well-coordinated artillery plan employed by the Turks on the peninsula since 25 April. It reflected an understanding of the weaknesses of earlier failures. Altogether, Mehmet Ali planned to throw 6,930 men from the 3rd Division and 6,765 men of the 5th Division into the attack and all were fresh and well rested. Confidence levels were running so high that Liman von Sanders personally invited the Austro-Hungarian military attaché, General Pomiankowski, accompanied by Fifth Army chief of staff, Lieutenant Colonel Kazım, to view the attack from Weber's headquarters on 5 July

1915. Liman von Sanders hoped to persuade Pomiankowski to press his government to attack Romania and restore direct communications with Constantinople.[72]

Over the night of 4/5 July, the assaulting battalions moved into attack positions in the forward trenches of the 1st Division, which was then holding the line. The attack began with 30 minutes of demonstration fires in the 7th Division's sector and then at 3.30 am Lieutenant Colonel Asım's light artillery group opened fire on the British trenches. Ammunition shortages limited the preparation fires to 15 minutes, at which time firing stopped while the Ottoman infantry went forward. The artillery, now reinforced with Major Rıfat's heavies, shifted to the south to pound the British artillery positions. The men went forward with fixed bayonets at 3.45 am commanded on the right by the 39 Regt commander, Lieutenant Colonel Nurettin, and on the left by the 31 Regt commander, Lieutenant Colonel Ismail Hakkı. To the left, the adjacent 11th Division launched a supporting attack using the 13 Regt and 15 Regt. Unfortunately, according to the British official history, the Ottoman artillery bombardments caused little damage to either the British trenches or to the British artillery. The Turks broke into the first line of British trenches but at terrible cost. Platoons were 'cut in half' and then 'cut into quarters'.[73] On the right, Nurettin sent a terse report back at 5.30 am saying 'The enemy trenches are completely in our power. Losses are excessive. It is dangeous for the regiment to advance. I am digging in.'[74] On the left, Lieutenant Colonel Ismail Hakkı sent back a similar situation report to the 3rd Division noting that he had seized the forward trenches suffering many dead and wounded but that heavy fires kept his men pinned (sheltered) in the enemy's trenches.[75] These reports were quickly passed up the chain of command to Mehmet Ali, who was working out of the Southern Group headquarters. In order to continue the attack, he passed orders to his reserve to move forward.

British machine-gun and artillery fire was fierce and at 6.50 am they began to counterattack with ready reserves. They began to take back their trenches from the Turks, information that was quickly passed back from the 3rd Division by its German commander, Colonel Nicolai. Now worried that the attack might fail, Mehmet Ali directed his reserves to reinforce the 3rd Divison and sent two engineer companies to Nicolai as well. About this time, the men of the 1st Division were shaken by streams of demoralized Ottoman soldiers retreating back to safety under intense British machine-gun fire. At 8.20 am, Colonel Nicolai was able to report that the two reinforcing battalions had entered the fight. However, by 9 am, he sent word back that the battle was a great struggle and was not going well. Meanwhile, on the left, the Turks had penetrated 500m into the enemy lines but were also being counterattacked. His immediate reserves expended, Mehmet Ali rounded up an engineer company and three uncommitted infantry platoons from the 13 Regt and 15 Regt and sent them forward. However, none of his efforts were sufficient to salvage the operation and the 1st Division commander reported at 11.45 am that the 31 Regt (3rd Divison) and the 15 Regt (5th Division) were retreating through his lines.[76] He followed this up with a second report noting that the 39 Regt (3rd Division) was coming back through as well. By this time, Colonel Nicolai was also on the telephone with I Corps chief of staff, Major Eggert, updating the corps headquarters with the bad news. Undeterred by failure, Mehmet Ali had Eggert notify Fifth Army that he

Table 3.3
Southern Group Losses (Killed, Wounded and Missing), 28 June–5 July 1915

1st Division	2,853
4th Division	963
6th Division	2,932
7th Division	265
11th Division	3,311
12th Division	534
Total	10,858

Source: Southern Group Report Divisional Losses, 5 July 1915, ATASE Archive 1/217, Record H-23, File 202 reproduced in T.C. Genelkurmay Başkanlığı, *Türk Silahi Kuvvetleri Tarihi Osmanli Devri Birinci Dünya Harbinde Türk Harbi Vnci Cilt 3ncu Kitap, Çanakkale Cephesi Harekati (Haziran 1915–Ocak 1916)* (Ankara: Genelkurmay Basımevi, 1980), p. 207.

wished to continue the attack but was having difficulty organizing the preparations because there was not enough time available. Therefore, Eggert passed on the news that I Corps was suspending offensive operations but would resume them in 24 hours. As darkness fell, Liman von Sanders left the Southern Group headquarters and returned to his own headquarters at Yalova.

Casualties from Mehmet Ali's attack were heavy. Of 6,930 officers and men in the 3rd Division, 1,401 were killed, 1,555 were wounded and 226 were missing as dawn broke on 6 July (3,182 altogether).[77] The 5th Division suffered less heavily with 758 killed, 726 wounded and 359 (1,843) out of a beginning total of 79 officers and 6,383 men.[78] When these losses are combined with the casualties from the other divisions for the entire period, Ottoman losses for Gully Ravine approached 16,000 men.

The Ottoman army's training and personnel system attempted to replace these casualties but the scale of losses exceeded its immediate capacity. For example, the 6th Division received 1,000 replacements on 6 July and distributed 500 men each to the 16 Regt and 17 Regt.[79] This left an overall shortfall in authorized combat strength of almost 2,000 men. Over time, however, the Ottoman divisions on the peninsula were periodically reconstituted to full strength.

Ottoman operational reorganization, July 1915

On Tuesday evening, 6 July 1915, Fifth Army sent orders to the Southern Group informing Colonel Weber that the Ottoman general staff had ordered the I Corps headquarters and the 3rd Division to return to the Asian side of the strait. This movement was the precursor of a major reorganization of the Southern Goup designed to inject fresh commanders and forces into the battle area. In truth both Enver and Liman von Sanders were very unhappy with the tactical situation in the Southern Group. According to a later report written by the group operations officer, Staff Captain Nihat, regarding the attacks of 29/30 June, Faik's II Corps operations were characterized by an exceptionally slow tempo.[80] Nihat also asserted that Colonel Weber was preparing plans to withdraw to the Soğanlıdere line and that preparations for pulling back thirty-five artillery batteries were also in place. He continued that he understood from a telephone conversation with Fifth Army chief of staff, Lieutenant Colonel Kazım, that Liman von Sanders wanted to set matters right in the Southern Group (Kazım, it must be remembered, was in constant contact with his academy classmate, Enver Pasha). After Mehmet Ali's failure, Nihat continued, there was a consensus that Weber, although a good soldier but having been engaged in combat continuously since 6 May, was tired and dispirited. There was clearly a crisis of confidence at the end of the first week of July 1915 in the ability of Colonel Weber to continue in command.

Both Fifth Army and the Ottoman general staff were aware of the increasing strength of the allies at Cape Helles, which indicated that the fight for Achi Baba (Alçı Tepe) and the plateau overlooking the strait was the allied main effort. Ottoman intelligence reports confirmed an accurate appraisal of the increases in allied strength at Cape Helles that included the landing of the Royal Naval Division, the Indian brigade and the 52nd Lowland Division (Territorial), and dismounted Australian cavalry.[81] Intelligence regarding the composition of the second French division was also very accurate and compehensive.[82] As a result, Ottoman reinforcements went to Colonel Weber to oppose Hunter-Weston at Cape Helles rather than to Esat Pasha to oppose Birdwood at Anzac. At the same time, the staffs were aware of the heavy losses suffered by the Southern Group.[83] These factors coalesced around the gathering opinion that a change was needed at the tip of the peninsula. On 6 July 1915, Enver sent Liman von Sanders a telegram informing him that Vehip Pasha, the commander of the Ottoman Second Army, would take command of the Southern Group.[84] Accompanying Vehip were some of the Second Army staff officers, who would combine with the Southern Group staff to form a new group headquarters. Moreover, the Ottoman XIV Corps (8th and 10th Infantry Divisions) and V Corps (13th and 14th Divisions) were put on orders to deploy to the Southern Group as well. This was to become effective on 9 July after which Colonel Weber would return to Gemany.

Mehmet Vehip (later Kaçı, 1877–1940) was Esat Pasha's younger brother and he had graduated from the War Academy. In the early 1900s he served as chief of staff of the Diyarbakır

Infantry Division and as commander of the Ezincan Military School. By 1909 he was a member of the Ottoman general staff corps and moving up rapidly. In the Balkan Wars he served with Esat in the Yanya Corps as chief of staff during the siege. In 1914, Vehip was in command of the 22nd Infantry Division in the Hijaz, which at that time was engaged in counterinsurgency operations. He returned in the spring of 1915 to command the Ottoman Second Army. After service on the Gallipoli peninsula, he returned to reform the Second Army in the fall of 1915. Later in the war, he commanded the Ottoman Third Army and the Caucasian Army Group. Vehip was regarded as a capable and professional officer, who performed well in both command and staff assignments. After his retirement he travelled to Ethiopia to advise Haile Selassie's troops against the Italians in 1936.

It is evident from the redeployment of Mehmet Ali's I Corps back to the Kum Kale operational area in Asia that the Ottomans were also concerned about their weak flanks, which were now rather exposed as the forces previously stationed there were drawn into the battles on the peninsula. In fact, internal Fifth Army messages in early July indicated an appreciation of the danger to both Asia and Saros Bay.[85] On 4 July, Colonel Fevzi was notified that the exhausted 12th Division would be sent to his Saros Group (XVI Corps) for reconstitution and coastal defence duty. Liman von Sanders also planned to redeploy the 5th Division to Esat's Northern Group as well.[86] Taken together, these changes rebalanced the operational posture of the Fifth Army by reinforcing the wings (Asia and Saros Bay), while at the same time cleaning up the messy and overlapping command arrangements in the Southern Group. In point of fact, by 5 July 1915, Weber (a German colonel and commander of XV Corps) was in command of two Ottoman general officers, who were also fellow corps commanders (Faik of II Corps and Mehmet Ali of I Corps). Although the working relationships between these officers seems to have been cordial, there must have been turf battles and conflicting opinions. Whether these relationships negatively affected the unsuccessful operations in late June and early July 1915 is unclear. In any case, the relief of Weber and his replacement by a senior Ottoman army level general supports the idea that the dynamics of human behavior may have influenced operations. In his memoirs, Liman von Sanders, related that by 16 July rumors of an impending allied landing were rift and that on 22 July he received word from the chief of the German general staff that landings could be expected in Asia or Saros Bay.[87] In light of the actual allied landings at Suvla Bay in early August 1915, it seems evident that Enver and Liman von Sanders exercised prescient and prudent strategic and operational direction.

The Ottoman 8th Division and the XIV Corps, which was commanded by German Colonel Bruno Trommer, began to arrive in the operational area on 8 and 11 July respectively. Mirliva (Brigadier General) Mehmet Vehip arrived at Fifth Army headquarters on 8 July and the next morning accompanied by Staff Colonel Nihat went to Southern Group headquarters. Vehip issued his first orders in command at 5.30 pm, 9 July by sending warm greetings to his troops, who numbered about 45,000 men. That day the first battalions of the 14th Division began to arrive as well, while the V Corps headquarters reached the rail terminus at Uzunköprü. On 11 July, Vehip issued his operational plan and map overlays, which organized the defensive area into the First Area (on the right flank) and the Second Area (on the left flank).[88] Trommer's XIV Corps was assigned the First Area and disposed the 1st and 11th Divisions in line from the right. Brigadier General Fevzi's V Corps headquarters had not arrived but the Second Area disposed the 7th and 4th Divisions in line from the right and was backstopped by the 6th Division in group reserve. Vehip noted that, for the moment, the Second Area divisions would remain under Southern Group Command. Vehip alerted his group on 11 July with orders giving them three days to finalize their defensive preparaions as increased British artillery fires indicated that an enemy offensive was in the making.

The action of Achi Baba Nullah or Second Kereves Dere (12–13 July)
The allies launched a major multi-national attack in mid-July aimed at seizing the Ottoman trenches on the peninsula's eastern flank using the British 52nd Division and both French divisions. A shortage of artillery forced the British division into a split attack in sector using two brigades attacking abreast but 9 hours apart.

The Ottoman trenches were described by Aspinall-Oglander as 'haphazard', 'irregular' and 'confusing' and were defended by the men of the 4th and 7th Divisions.[89] The allied plan was poorly conceived and relied on an intelligence appreciation that Ottoman morale was very low and likely to collapse. Making things worse, updated accurate trench diagrams of the enemy positions were made available but failed to find their way down the British chain of command to the men who would use them. Naval gunfire and aerial bombing began at 4.30 am, 12 July and the artillery preparation started 30 minutes after (which was scheduled to drop some 60,000 shells on the Turks over a 3-hour period). The allied infantry went over the top at 7.30 am into the face of fierce machine-gun fire, which caused very heavy casualties. A major problem for the British evolved as their reporting system broke down as battalion and company officers were killed causing a loss of situational awareness at division and brigade headquarters respectively. Such confusion reigned that by midday, Hunter-Weston was unsure as to whether he should continue with the scheduled second attack.

On the left flank of the 7th Divison, Major Halit, commander of the 20 Regt, reported at 8.55 am that he had blown apart the attacking enemy units and had retaken the trenches lost in the initial assault. Halit's regiment had been in reserve and had been committed earlier in a counterattack. In the adjacent 4th Division sector, the French had done somewhat better and the situation there was regarded as 'dangerous'. As a result the division commander committed his reserve, the 12th Infantry Regiment (12 Regt), to stabilize the situation. About 4 pm Ottoman artillery units began to pound the exposed allied infantry. The second wave of British attacks went in reinforced by a Royal Naval Division brigade, but these units foundered on inaccurate trench maps and incomplete intelligence as well. As night approached the allied attacks were all but finished with Hunter-Weston relieving the 52nd Division commander and replacing him with the 13th Division commander, who was inexperienced and new to the peninsula.

The allied attack caught the Southern Group in the middle of an incomplete reorganization and the Ottoman divisions in contact were still directly under Vehip's command. As the battle developed Vehip left the fighting to his subordinate division commanders, whose reports indicated that the situation was in hand. This was a sound decision and left Vehip free to manage the reinforcement flow. At 9.15 am, he ordered the acceleration of two regiments of the incoming 6th Division into a staging area in the left flank rear of the 4th Division (near Domuz Dere).[90] The deployment was conducted with stealth and the incoming regiments were ordered to camouflage themselves immediately upon arival in their staging areas. The first companies began to arrive at Domuz Dere soon after 1 pm. Sometime that afternoon, Fevzi Pasha and the V Corps staff arrived at Vehip's Salimbey Çiftliği headquarters and prepared to take control of the tactical battle. As night fell on 12/13 July 1915, Vehip and Fevzi co-ordinated the battle handover of the left sector of the front. Group orders were issued that night formally transfering the Second Area to V Corps control and also assigning the 4th, 6th and 7th Division's to Fevzi's command.[91] Vehip's staff also coordinated artillery support with the First Area and began to plan for a night counterattack using Fevzi's troops.[92] Orders to the Second Area to this effect were sent early on the morning of 13 July. Throughout the day, Fevzi shifted units and gave the 6th Division command of the 12 Regt, which was in the line. Fighting was dulsatory and he made preparations with his division commanders for a night attack. A complete copy of Suleyman Sakir's 6th Division attack order may be found in his memoirs and involved a joint attack by the 4th and 6th Divisions.[93] However, as the day progressed it was apparent that the allied will to continue the battle was finished and they withdrew from most of the Ottoman trenches that they retained. In turn the necessity for a counterattack evaporated and Vehip cancelled the operation entirely, thus bringing the battle to an end by night-fall on 13 July.

Ottoman losses were heavy, with a total of 9,462 casualties reported.[94] Of this total (and very strangely) the returns listed 7 officers and 4,561 men as missing in action, which seems unusually high for a defensive battle of such short duration. Allied casualties were listed as around 4,000 in total and, realistically, the Ottoman casualties should have been about the same. The Turkish histories and documents available do not explain this apparent discrepancy and the author is at a loss to explain it. It is possible that the casualties returns presented are the initial numbers unadjusted for missing men who later returned.

Fifth Army operations, 14 July–6 August

Esat's Northern Group conducted divisional attacks on 29 June and 12 July with small results. Minor fighting then continued around the ANZAC perimeter throughout the month of July, which was characterized by trench raids and mining operations. Neither Esat or Birdwood had either the capability or the desire to renew the heavy fighting that had previously depleted their strength. Esat chaffed at the lack of reinforcements and replacements, which mostly went to the Southern Group.

Enver Pasha dispatched a telegram to Liman von Sanders on the night of 15/16 July expressing the idea that although Fifth Army had been sent new divisions the difficulty of executing successful offensives grew with each passing moment.[95] He directed that the new divisions be integrated quickly with the experienced divisions in order to learn the tactical conditions more rapidly. This would assist them in preparing for new offensive operations. For his part, Liman von Sanders was more concerned with the physical and psychological reconstitution of his army. The following day, Enver fired off another alarming telegram to Liman von Sanders asserting that he knew conclusively from intelligence sources that the British were about to execute an amphibious landing in Saros Bay.[96] He demanded an update on the status of Fifth Army units in that area and directed that all replacement soldiers then going to Fifth Army be sent to the divisions guarding the Saros Bay region. Moreover, he indicated that he considered an adequate garrison for the area to be two full army corps and he wanted the Ottoman XVII Corps to be sent there. A follow-up message on 18 July from Enver asserted that he now knew that the British intended to strike at Bolayır (Bulair). In spite of these two messages, Liman von Sanders did not think the narrow neck of Bulair was a viable landing site and that the invasion might come either in Saros Bay or nearer the middle of the peninsula. Nevertheless, he put the troops at Bulair and Saros Bay on high alert and ordered them to rehearse their plans throughly and as secretly as possible. On 25 July, the Asia Group began to send Fifth Army messages warning that the commander believed a landing was imminent there as well and that he was coordinating with the German artillery commander, Colonel Wehrle, for heavy artillery support against ships. Following up on this news, Liman von Sanders coordinated with Admiral von Usedom in the strait fortresses to conduct execises to determine how fast the ferry and road system could support the reinforcement of the Asian side of the strait.[97] Adding to the array of opinions, Esat Pasha sent messages to Fifth Army that he believed an enemy attack was building oriented on the Çonkbayırı-Kocaçimen plateau (Sari Bair ridge), while his brother, Vehip, agreed with Enver.[98] On 28 July 1915, Enver Pasha came to the peninsula for briefings and to see the situation for himself. As July ended there was clearly a variety of conflicting opinions about where the actual blow would fall.

By early August there were also a number of indications that the allies intended to attempt a naval attack to force the strait. On 4 August Liman von Sanders alerted Faik's II Corps (4th and 8th Divisons) to be ready to deploy to the Asian side. To the north of Willmer's detachment, the Fifth Army formed a cavalry screening force called the Tayfur Detachment to screen the coast up to the Bulair lines. On the northwestern shoulder of the ANZAC perimeter Mustafa Kemal expressed concern over the weakness of the Willmer Group, which lay to the immediate rear of his sector. Kemal later claimed to have accurately predicted that the assault would come by way of Sari Bair and Suvla Bay.[99] However, this did not square with the III Corps staff's appraisal and, apparently fooled by the ANZAC deception measures, Esat sent a revised secret appreciation of the situation to Liman von Sanders on 5 August that identified enemy activity aimed at the area between Gaba Tepe and Kanlısırt (Lone Pine). Moreover, he outlined the positions of the battalions that he had set in place to prevent any breakthrough in this area. After discussions with Liman von Sanders, Esat also moved Kannengiesser's 9th Division to an area along the coast between Gaba Tepe and Krithia.

The ending of the Third Phase of the Ottoman campaign

In spite of Enver's determination to continue the attacks the realization that an imminent second allied invasion approached caused the Ottoman Fifth Army to shift its strategic and operational posture from the offensive to the defensive. This shift brought to an end Ottoman attempts to seize the initiative through vigorous large-scale offensive operations and thus identifies the end of the third phase of the Ottoman campaign for Gallipoli. By early August 1915, the Fifth Army readied itself and tried to recover the strength that would allow it to absorb the expected blow. Three divisions guarded each flank at Saros Bay and Kum Kale in Asia. Esat's four divisions contained Birdwood's three-plus division ANZAC and Vehip's six divisions were ranged against four British and two French divisions at Cape Helles. Altogether Liman von Sanders held sixteen divisions in various stages of readiness to oppose the roughly ten allied divisions in contact and six additional uncommitted divisions (which the Turks knew were loaded in ships and enroute to the area). With this in mind and with incomplete intelligence and conflicting opinions about where the allies would strike, Liman von Sanders put the Fifth Army in an operational posture designed to create balance and recoverability. As the Fifth Army had done successfully in late April 1915, Liman von Sanders hoped to hold the enemy on the beaches long enough to allow the rapid lateral movement of reserves necessary to contain the attack.

Fevzi's Saros Group comprised the 6th, 7th and 12th Infantry Divisions, an independent cavalry brigade and two heavy artillery battalions. Facing the ANZAC, Esat's Northern Group held the 5th, 9th, 16th and 19th Infantry Divisions. Facing the Anglo-French, Vehip's powerful Southern Group contained the II Corps (4th and 8th Divisions), the V Corps (13th and 14th Divisions) and the XIV Corps (1st and 10th Divisions), and a heavy artillery regiment. At Kum Kale, Mehmet Ali's Asia Group was composed of the 2nd, 3rd and 11th Infantry Divisions. There were two small independent commands as well, the Tayfur Sector garrisoned by the 4th Cavalry Regiment and the Anafarta Sector held by the Willmer Group. The composition of Willmer's small forces bears elaboration as it bore the full weight of the Suvla Bay amphibious landing on 6 August 1915. Willmer was assigned the 2/31 Regt and the 1/32 Regt. He was also assigned the Bursa and the Gallipoli Jandarma Battalions; the 6th Company, 1st Engineer Regiment; the 1st Battalion, 9th Artillery Regiment; three independent batteries of artillery (4th and 5th Batteries, 15th Artillery and the 7th Battery, 11th Artillery); and a small cavalry squadron. Altogether Willmer probably fielded somewhere in the region of 4,000 men out of a Fifth Army total of approximately 250,000 soldiers.

As this phase ended the Fifth Army had suffered very heavy casualties with almost no positive outcomes. The massive Ottoman attacks in June on the ANZAC and the equally massive attacks on the Anglo-French corps at Cape Helles were catastrophic failures. Such successes as had been achieved were defensive and owed as much to poor allied planning and co-ordination as anything else. The reasons for failure were clear – mass attacks over no-man's-land against strongly held enemy positions that had not been subjected to heavy and sustained artillery preparation were suicidal. The Turks knew this from their Balkan War experience and all of the senior Ottoman officers present were veterans of that war. Thus the question begs to be asked and answered regarding why they continued these seemingly futile repetitive operations.

First, the Ottoman officer corps remained firmly wedded to the concept of the offensive as the decisive arbiter in war. This was, of course, a legacy of the 'German way of war' that had been imbedded in their strategic, operational and tactical doctrines by way of the Ottoman War Academy curriculum and the influence of a generation of German military advisors. In this phase there appeared to be consensus by both Ottoman and German commanders at all levels regarding the imperative to seize the initiative through offensive action. Secondly, the lack of positional depth of the allied beachheads meant that the Turks did not have to develop complex plans involving deep penetrations or pursuits. The simple act of punching through and driving forward 2 or 3 kilometers would have put them on the landing beaches themselves. Unlike the allies they did not have to plan for follow-on objectives and multi-phase attacks. The very simplicity of objective was itself decisively seductive. Thirdly, the

Ottoman commanders clearly understood the tactical dynamics involved in offensive operations and their consequent vulnerability to massed fires. They attempted to compensate for this by planning night operations that mitigated some of the effects of allied firepower, especially that of naval gunfire support. All of the major offensive operations were planned to begin just before dawn broke. Fourthly, the Ottoman army excelled in rapid movement at the operational level. This allowed them to concentrate their fresh reinforcing units at points of their choosing. Combined with their ability to cross-attach battalions within the triangular division architecture and their effective reporting system, this capability gave the Ottoman army on the peninsula a significant advantage. Finally, at this stage of the war the army maintained high morale and fighting spirit, which made it possible to generate combat power reliably. Ottoman regiments and divisions committed to the campaign were well trained and cohesive and these factors gave commanders at all levels a high degree of confidence in the ability of the army to land powerful blows on the enemy. Taken together, these factors seemed to promise an achievable decisive victory but instead, the Fifth Army almost destroyed itself as an effective fighting organization and barely recovered its strength and balance in time for Hamilton's Suvla Bay operation.

Chapter 4

Anafarta,
7 August 1915–8 January 1916

Introduction

The allied attempt to break the deadlock in August 1915 was a comprehensive series of battles that ranged from Cape Helles up the peninsula to Suvla Bay, which lay just to the northwest of Anzac beach. In the western world this phase of the campaign is simply and most frequently referred to as 'Suvla Bay'. However, Hamilton's principal objective was not Suvla Bay at all but was actually the high ground dominating the ANZAC perimeter known as Sari Bair ridge (from Koja Chemen Tepe or 'Hill 971' to Battleship Hill), the possession of which meant that 'the Turkish defences at Anzac would at once become untenable.'[1] Suvla Bay, although an important component of the operation, was merely a secondary attack designed to widen and deepen the beachhead. Unfortunately, the abysmal performance of the British commander at Suvla Bay made it the signature failure of an already blighted campaign and the phrase 'Suvla Bay' perhaps invokes the greatest 'if only' of the entire Gallipoli campaign.

From the Ottoman perspective Ian Hamilton's long-awaited offensive marked the beginning of the fourth and final phase of the Ottoman campaign for control of the Gallipoli peninsula. Hamilton's August attacks returned the Turks to a reactive posture as they lost control of the operational initiative. In Turkey today the Ottoman side of this phase of the campaign is most commonly known as *Anafarta Muharebeler*, or the Anafarta Battles, and these are particularly famous because of their connection with Mustafa Kemal. In fact, there were heavy battles fought at Cape Helles and on Sari Bair ridge that were equally important in the successful conduct of this phase of the campaign. Nevertheless, it is Mustafa Kemal's performance that the Turks remember and as 'Suvla Bay' has come to represent defeat snatched from the jaws of victory *Anafarta Muharebeler* has come to represent victory against impossible odds. In truth, both views are flawed visions of what actually happened.

Hamilton's offensive began on the afternoon of 6 August 1915, with attacks at Cape Helles and Lone Pine at Anzac. These were only diversionary attacks and the main effort began after dark with a daring night *coup de main* assault on Sari Bair ridge. At the same time that night Lieutenant General the Honourable Sir Fredrick Stopford's IX Corps began landing at Suvla Bay, a complementary operation that would guard the flank of Birdwood's 'left hook' sweeping up and over Sari Bair ridge. Unfortunately for Hamilton, the 61-year-old Stopford was spectacularly passive and his divisions famously stalled after landing. Hamilton's subsequent failure to push him into action or promptly relieve him destroyed the reputations of both generals as competent professional commanders.

Cape Helles, 6–13 August 1915

By early August Vehip had solidified the defense of the Southern Group using three operational corps commands. Trommer's XIV Corps held the right flank with the 1st and 10th Divisions, while Fevzi's V Corps held the left flank with the 13th and 14th Divisions. Each division in line put two regiments forward and held one in reserve. Supporting them was Major Rıfat's artillery group. Behind Alçı Tepe and along the Soğanlıdere line lay Faik's II Corps with the 4th Division to the north of Soğanlıdere and the 8th Division on the western shore. It was a well-balanced posture characterized by defense in depth and reserve capability (almost half of Vehip's combat power was in reserve).

British artillery began firing at 2 pm on 6 August and Rıfat's artillery group returned fire immediately and effectively. And 2 hours later the infantry of the British 29th Division attacked the strongly held lines of the 10th Division. The British attack was a massive failure (with 2,000 casualties out of 3,000 men involved). Vehip's first report to Fifth Army at 4.30 pm noted that the 10th and 13th Divisions had been attacked but that the enemy failed to gain a foothold.[2] Moreover, Vehip reported that the morale of his soldiers was good. The next morning a Fifth Army telegraph message relayed Vehip's report to Enver with the additional news that a major, two lieutenants and sixty-two soldiers had been captured. At 9.40 am, 7 August, the British 42nd Division launched a similar attack, which resulted in a similar repulse with the exception of a vineyard seized in the 46th Infantry Regiment's (46 Regt) sector. British casualties that day were listed as about 1,500 altogether. A supporting French attack on the 14th Division began at 10 am that day and met with the same result. According to the Turkish histories the French attack was supported more effectively with machine-gun and artillery fire, which allowed them to get into the Ottoman trenches with bayonets and hand grenades. Nevertheless, with great difficulty the French were forced back by Ottoman counterattacks as well. Vehip's evening report that night outlined the defensive success and mentioned that the 14th Division had captured thirty-eight men.[3] He finished the report by an assessment that his front and his men were in splendid shape. The XIV and V Corps formations were so successful that on neither day did Vehip have to commit his general reserve (II Corps) to the fight. His reports reflected confidence and control and these reports would have a decisive impact on the outcome of the campaign.

Early in the evening of 6 August Liman von Sanders began to receive reports from Suvla Bay and the ANZAC perimeter alerting him to Hamilton's attacks. He prompted his chief of staff, Colonel Kazım, to order the Southern Group, which according to Vehip appeared to have things well in hand, to send two regiments from the 4th Division to reinforce the Northern Group. By 10.45 pm the Southern Group chief of staff, Colonel Nihat, had alerted Lieutenant Colonel Cemil, the 4th Division commander, who soon put the regiments on the road to the north. This left Vehip with one regiment in reserve to cover the Soğanlıdere line and on 7 August, he was ordered to put an 8th Division regiment on the road north as well.[4] Further instructions from Liman von Sanders followed later that day pointing out that as II Corps commander Faik was not urgently needed at Cape Helles and to send him north to join four regiments coming south from Saros Bay.[5] It is clear from this exchange of messages that the allied attacks at Cape Helles on 6/7 August 1915 did not fix Ottoman reserves in place nor fool either Vehip or Liman von Sanders into believing them to be a major effort. Indeed, the rapidity of the Fifth Army reaction indicates a well-developed sense of situational awareness that enabled a coherent tactical response. By 9 August, Colonel Nihat recorded in the Southern Group war diary that the critical fighting was then occurring at Conkbayırı (Chunuk Bair) far to the north. The fighting went on sporadically until 13 August with small-scale attacks at the end of which Vehip expressed great pleasure at the performance of his 13th Division. The fighting was intense, however, and cost the Turks 2,758 dead, 4,180 wounded and 572 missing for the period 6–13 August.[6] Total casualty figures for both the British and French at Cape Helles for this entire period are not available in the published histories, but as they were conducting offensive operations they likely equalled or exceeded those of the Turks.

These were not the only reinforcements that Liman von Sanders deployed to the center of mass of the peninsula. The Fifth Army sent warning orders to the Saros Group on the night of 6 August to be prepared to send the XVI Corps south. This was likely a surprise to Colonel Ahmet Fevzi who believed that a landing at Saros Bay was imminent. In fact, in an almost unknown comic opera incident two Royal Navy ships landed a 300-man detachment of Greco-Thracian volunteers under a Greek lieutenant named Gruparis after dark on 6 August in the Karaçalı area of Saros Bay.[7] Alerted by the coastal posts of the Keşan Jandarma Battalion, the commander of the Independent Cavalry Brigade counterattacked the Greeks at 7 am, 7 August with a cavalry squadron and an artillery platoon. The Greeks withdrew under pressure covered by naval gunfire and by setting two forests on fire with benzene to cover their withdrawal. In total, 28 Greeks were killed and 3 were captured, while the Turks lost 8 killed and 12 wounded in the fight. In the meantime, at 1.45 am, 7 August the XVI Corps was ordered to send a regiment to Anafarta but the regiment did not make it onto the road until 5 am.[8] Then at 6.30 am Liman von Sanders ordered Ahmet Fevzi (Saros Group commander and XVI Corps commander) to bring two 7th Division regiments with an artillery battalion and the 12th Division to Anafarta in order to conduct counterattacks on the morning of 8 August. These forces were on the road shortly

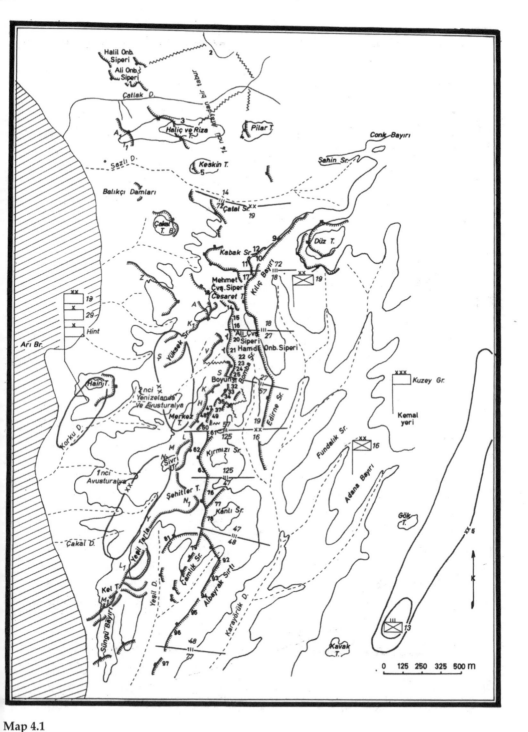

Map 4.1
Northern Group general defensive situation, 6 August 1915. The Ottomans employed a numbering system to identify their trenches as shown on this map. Occasionally, trenches were named for a particular person, for example Mehmet Çvş Siperi (Sergeant Mehmet's trench). An important point is that the Ottoman trenches on the northern shoulder are not continuous.

thereafter and conducted a hard-forced march which lasted all night that brought them nearly to Büyük Anafarta on the morning of 8 August. The 6th Division and the Independent Cavalry Brigade remained at Saros Bay to cover the beaches. Ahmet Fevzi himself reached the Fifth Army headquarters at 2 pm, 7 August where Liman von Sanders oriented him to his plan to conduct a counterattack from the vicinity of Küçük Anafarta.

Realizing that Liman von Sanders was facing a crisis situation, the Ottoman general staff sent warning orders to Field Marshal Colmar von der Goltz and the headquarters of the Ottoman First Army, then in the capital, to prepare to deploy to Saros Bay. In Asia Mehmet Ali was also ordered to dispatch forces across the strait as well. It is clear from the scope of these movements that Liman von Sanders was certain by midnight on 6/7 August that Hamilton's main effort lay to the north of Anzac rather than at Cape Helles, Saros Bay or Asia.

Lone Pine, 6–10 August 1915

Operations at ANZAC began with a brigade-sized attack at Lone Pine on the evening of 6 August 1915, which would be followed by the remainder of the 1st Australian Division seizing Gun Ridge and Scrubby Knoll. While this was a diversion it was also a serious attack designed to take and hold ground in order to relieve pressure on the main axis of advance. The Turks call this the Battle of Kanlısırt. Map 4.1 shows the situation at Anzac on 6 August 1915.

Esat's Northern Group deployed the 16th and 19th Divisions northward from Gaba Tepe. The right flank of Mustafa Kemal's 19th Division was flanked by a single battalion of the 14 Regt holding a series of strong points in the broken terrain (rather than a continuous trench) along the slopes of Sari Bair ridge. Esat held the 5th Division in close reserve just behind his artillery belt. Despite efforts at secrecy, the Turks noticed increased activity on the ANZAC piers as early as 5.30 am, 6 August, which caused them to increase their artillery firing into the Australian beachhead. Esat and Liman von Sanders remained focused on the area south of Gaba Tepe, where they had positioned the 9th Division earlier as well as alerting Admiral von Usedom and requesting artillery support from the Asian side in the event of a landing.[9]

Ottoman soldiers at a temporary rest halt on the march. This platoon is likely moving forward to the front because their packs appear to be full. The well-organized lines of equipment indicate a high level of discipline and leadership.

An Ottoman artillery crew in a posed photograph preparing a 150mm howitzer for firing. The ammunition is 'separate loading' with a fuzed projectile loaded first followed by bagged powder charges.

Ottoman soldiers moving an unusual pedestal-mounted light artillery gun on a wheeled carriage. The bulb on the muzzle appears to be a wooden block designed to assist in pushing the piece forward.

Ottoman trenches, 1915. These soldiers appear fresh with khaki uniforms complete with puttee leg wrappings and full cartridge belts. They are wearing the distinctive Enveri field cap and have Mauser rifles.

This is a formal portrait of Mustafa Kemal as a Field Marshal during the Turkish War of Independence (1919–1922).

An unknown young Ottoman artillery officer who has been awarded a German Iron Cross.

Lieutenant Colonel Mustafa Kemal shown in a famous pose. This painting is based on an iconic photograph of Kemal at Gallipoli and is part of the Gallipoli mural in the Atatürk Mausoleum in Ankara, Turkey.

Corporal Seyit of the Rumeli Mecidiye Fort carrying a 240mm shell on his back. This famous incident occurred during the 18 March 1915 naval attack and is well known in Turkey today.

Hasan Efendi, a lieutenant in 4 Company, 14th Infantry Regiment. He was killed on 10 August 1915 on Chunuk Bair.

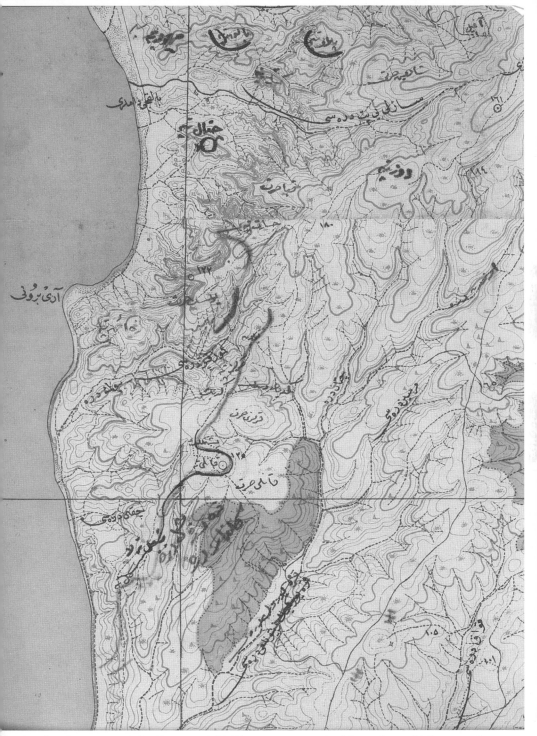

he detail and accuracy of the Ottoman 1:25,000 maps are seen in this section, which covers the area
f the Anzac beachhead. The bold lines indicate Australian positions at the beginning of August
915.

ه.

بكدم يكجی آلای قومانداننه

ما بك ٢٥ كیس بعدالزوال ربغت اوزره ده دكمه بوزره جبه ده سنفی بأتنه أجمید والله بكجی آلای جبهه سنده بو با ايله أجمید
اولیفی كدكلده ١٠ ده دعا قورطلو سیلری اشغال ايله خط اهالیی بارغد موقع الشده ٠٠ الله بكی آلا ی جبه سنه
میله جبا هنده جبا نده جریانه ایله ذخرماته وقف دكل ايسمه بشنك نمرضا ذزنه ١٠ فندرلی سبك صاغ جبا هنده دشنی
خالی محمد النبا ایدم آلنآنز ده د ٢چه دعا بنه كیه كورطلو سبد ودشه بوجهنده طلا یزن ملد جبا هن أتسه آلقه الشده ٠٠
جبه نمانده اآدمه برقوت ٠٠٠ دعا فندرلی سبلر أروستهكی ده ودله بوسیلن ایه سبده ده ٢٢ ٢٢
نورطلو سبلر مد أتیمه برمیارله بوروده كی دشمه فتح ایلشده ٠٠ أره دبرایم بزیا بادكینی حامه ١٠ بكی آلایج
خط اهبلنك با یعبضم اسا نجمسه داونجلو آغا یغذ با شلدكده حقبقت حالك بوتكزده اولیض كوج حال ٩٢
العشیر بیشه ٠٠ ٥٠ فندرله سبكزده قوت وهبم محافظ ايلك بغلمی بوكمبز دشنك شمارده
صاخرسنه خایش نذیر لدنم اتقا ذاولنه دبطرته ١٠ فندرلی سبه آبنه بوك فنها ايه وكاك شام جبم جبته ١٠دد
ايلشده ٠٠ ربغت بدبده سبركلماذ دشنده نظوی ايلسه دلطم عاله بولنده ١٠ بكی آلابه نبم اله دئ برعكمبز
اولاند آئشه ٠٠ دشه سبركی خط موقعی اولیفی نما بالغی دلكمانده بشه فتح طلوبه ری طقپابه بر جبما آبذی
ادبغ نفر ضریا ایلشه ٠٠ برما یه ده ١٠ شبما ايم ٢٨ جروح دبدك ٠ ربغ ایه برعظاطوه ضابه ٠٠ ٢٢ نفنك
ایلم ١٠ خطاطوره سقطلاننه ٥٠٠ جنتم جنا ايم ٥٠٠ جدوبما صعا ايلسه د ٠٠ دشنك مقرد دطروحه ٥
مظلینا نفبه ایم ملك محدثه ٠٠

The Ottoman army used a comprehensive and accurate reporting and orders system. This is an example of a brief combat report from Major Halis to Lieutenant Colonel Şefik, 27th Infantry Regiment commander. It details the Australian attack on Halis' 3rd Battalion trenches by Australians on 5 June 1915. His successful defense cost twelve dead and sixty-eight wounded.

Major Hüseyin Avni, commander of the 57th Infantry Regiment, who was promoted to lieutenant colonel in June. Avni was killed on 13 August 1915 when a howitzer shell landed on his headquarters.

Six Gallipoli veterans of the XV Corps serving in Galicia in 1916. An Ottoman non-commissioned officer and two Austrian officers appear ready to deliver orders. The men appear alert, battle hardened and well equipped.

Decorated veteran soldiers during deployment by rail car after Gallipoli. The stress of combat shows on their faces.

General Otto Liman von Sanders in Germany sometime after the Gallipoli campaign. He is wearing an Ottoman cap and is wearing an Ottoman medal.

General Otto Liman von Sanders with his staff in Palestine in 1918. After Gallipoli, he commanded the Yildirim Army Group at the Battle of Megiddo in September 1918.

Field Marshal Mustafa Kemal (later Atatürk) during the Turkish War of Independence (probably sometime in 1922).

Artillery and naval gunfire began to fall on the Ottoman lines starting at 3 pm, 6 August and at 4.30 pm the bombardment focused on the lines of the 16th Division. The division commander, Colonel Rüştü, deployed the 125 Regt, commanded by Lieutenant Colonel Abdülrezzak, in line on what the ANZAC called Johnston's Jolly and the 47 Regt, commanded by Major Tevfik, on what was known as Lone Pine.[10] The Turks had occupied their trenches for some time and had covered much of the front line with logs and earth as protection against artillery fire. The Australian trenches (which protruded toward the Turks in a bulge called the Pimple) were less than 100m from Tevfik's lines and he put the 1/47 Regt and 2/47 Regt in line (north and south respectively) backed up by his 3rd Battalion in reserve. At 5.30 pm the Australians swarmed out of their trenches and raced into the Ottoman lines. There a bitter hand-to-hand fight using bayonets and hand grenades quickly developed as the Australians struggled to dislodge the Turks from their underground positions. Casualties on both sides were unusually heavy but within 30 minutes the Australians held Tevfik's first line of trenches. Map 4.2 shows the attack on Lone Pine and the Ottoman counterattacks.

Learning of the enemy's success, Northern Group commander Esat's reaction was immediate and predictable. At 6 pm, he ordered Colonel Kannengiesser's 9th Division to move three infantry regiments with artillery into positions behind Gaba Tepe and the 15 Regt (5th Division) to march as quickly as possible to Kanlısırt. By 7 pm, Esat decided to go over to the offensive and launch a counterattack. In addition to the 15 Regt, he ordered the 1/57 Regt from Kemal's 19th Division and the 2/13 Regt (from the 5th Division in reserve) forward to link up with Tevfik's 3rd Battalion. Colonel Rüştü was able to organize these units quickly and launched a powerful counterattack after dark at 11 pm.[11] Again fighting was exceptionally violent but the Turks were only able to recover the 47 Regt's second line of trenches. According to the official history, Major Tevfik and Lieutenant Colonel Ibrahim Şükrü, the 15 Regt commander, were both killed by hand grenades in the attack.[12] Undeterred by this failure, the aggressive Colonel Rüştü wanted to continue the attacks and requested additional reinforcements from the adjacent regiments on his left flank (the 48 Regt and 77 Regt).[13]

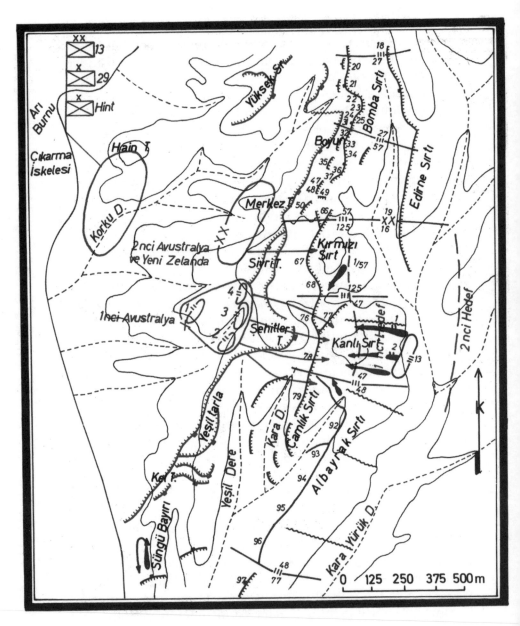

Map 4.2
Anzac Lone Pine attack and Ottoman counterattack, 6 August 1915. The Turks know the Battle of Lone Pine as the Battle of Kanlı Sırt (Bloody Ridge), which is shown clearly on this map. Other points of interest include Kırmızı Sırt (Red Ridge) and Bomba Sırt (Bomb Ridge).

Liman von Sanders' report to Enver on the morning of 7 August noted that 300 men had been killed in the Northern Group's left sector by naval gun fire and artillery prior to the Australian ground attack and that the extreme violence of the assault had pushed back the line at Kanlısırt some 300m.[14] Esat was displeased with the night's failure and telephoned Rüştü from his Kemalyeri headquarters at 5.45 am to insist that the forward line of trenches be retaken. Moreover, Esat promised that the adjacent 19th Division would render assistance. By this time Rüştü had received his regimental reports and he courageously replied 15 minutes later with a special report to the Northern Group that he was unable to comply because in the night attack on Kanlısırt casualties had been very heavy.[15] Rüştü continued by adding that the reports from his regimental commanders indicated that there was not enough strength left to conduct further attacks. Events soon made Esat's demands largely irrelevant as the battles to the north gained momentum. Nevertheless, Esat sent the 16th Division reinforcements in the form of the 4/77 Regt from Gaba Tepe, which Colonel Rüştü launched in an attack on the afternoon of 8 August. Again the fighting was fierce and hand to hand with bayonet and hand grenades. Parts of the Ottoman first line of trenches in the center were retaken and the Turks suffered many killed and missing. But violent Australian counterattacks retook the line soon after. That night Esat sent more reinforcements to the 16th Division – the 4th Battalion, 10th Infantry Regiment (4/10 Regt from the 4th Division) and the 12 Regt (from the 8th Division). Rüştü attacked with these fresh troops at 5 am, 8 August 1915, and the Turks again retook part of their line on the right. Hard fighting continued relentlessly all day, all night and into the next day (10 August). By this date it was apparent that the fight for Kanlısırt was counterproductive and Esat ordered a halt to the attacks. In the end the Australians held on to most of their initial gains made on 6 August. Although sporadic combat continued for the next several days, the Turks marked 10 August as the end of the Battle of Kanlısırt. Casualties were exceptionally heavy: 1,520 killed, 4,750 wounded, 760 missing and 134 taken prisoner (7,164 men altogether).[16] The Australians reported losses of 1,700 and the disparity in loss ratios is hard to explain.

From the British perspective the battle served its purpose, which was to divert Esat and to draw in his available reserves. In fact, the Northern Group committed the 12 Regt, 13 Regt, 15 Regt and one battalion of the 10 Regt to the battle, a force that exceeded the strength of an entire Ottoman army division. From the Ottoman perspective Kanlısırt is remembered as one of the most fiercely contested points of the campaign and the Turks nick-named the ridge Kanlısırt or 'Bloody Ridge'.[17] However, as Aspinall-Oglander also rightly pointed out that when Esat put Kannengiesser's regiments on the move toward Kanlısırt he unintentionally created a powerful and immediately available force, which was diverted to Chunuk Bair in time narrowly to divert disaster.

The Battle of Sari Bair, 6–10 August 1915

The British called the ridge line on the north face of the ANZAC perimeter Sari Bair and in its length nested three hills. The hills grew higher from south to north and were called Battleship Hill (Düz Tepe), Chunuk Bair, which was 262m high (Conkbayırı), and Koca Chemen Tepe, which was 303m high (Kocaçimen Tepe). Hamilton's main effort was an assault that was intended to seize the two highest hills on Sari Bair, which would open the way to seizing the strait. The southern two-thirds of the ANZAC perimeter were mostly continuous trenches but due to the broken terrain the northern third was composed of fortified posts and unconnected pieces of trenches. The Ottomans opposed this with a similar defensive layout and, as a result, there were only a few isolated Ottoman outposts on the ravine-laced slopes of Sari Bair held by small detachments of men. Here the Turks (and the ANZAC as well) depended on the extremely broken terrain as defense against a large-scale assault. Hamilton's plan capitalized on this weakness and he scheduled a surprise assault using columns to penetrate between the Ottoman posts and scale the heights during the hours of darkness. The attack began with covering forces clearing the Ottoman outpost lines to create a secure base. At 10.45 pm, 6 August 1915, a Left Assaulting Column would make its way up to the summit of Hill 971 (Koca Chemen Tepe), while a Right Assaulting Column would take Chunuk Bair and then wheel southwest to capture Battleship

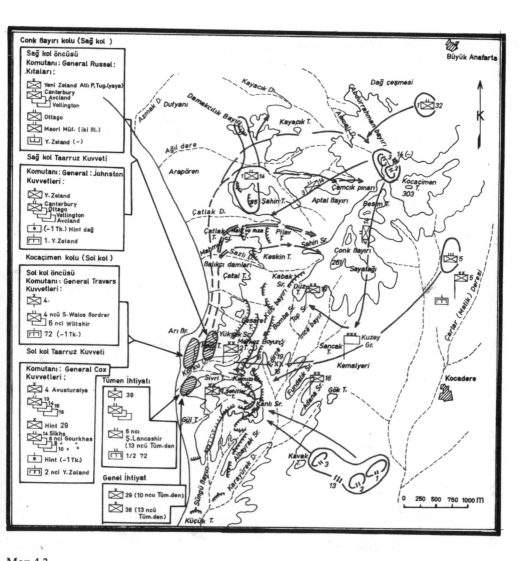

Map 4.3

Ottoman situation, 6/7 and 7 August 1915 and Chunuk Bair envelopment plan. This map shows
the planned allied avenues of advance up the slopes of Chunuk Bair and the Ottoman response
and commitment of the immediate tactical reserves. The three key terrain features are also
shown: Düz Tepe (Battleship Hill), Conkbayırı (Chunuk Bair) and Kocaçımen Tepe (Koca
Chemen Tepe).

Hill. Both columns were to achieve these results by an hour before dawn on 7 August. Then shortly after dawn the Australian Light Horse was to assault the Nek, a thin ribbon of land leading to Baby 700, which in turn was to be hit simultaneously from the rear by friendly troops coming down hill from Battleship Hill. Unfortunately for the allies, not one of the objectives was taken and the story of how this plan went wrong is well told in the extant official and popular British and Australian histories. The British called this series of engagements the Battle of Sari Bair, while the Turks know it as *Conkbayırı Muharberleri*.

With the exception of Tim Travers' work, the entire extant English language historiography asserts that the Koca Chemin Tepe (Hill 971) and Chunuk Bair hill masses were virtually un-defended on 6 August, an idea that is apparently based exclusively on the memoirs of Colonel Kannengiesser. In fact the Ottomans had considerable combat power there well before the ANZAC assault. The first reports of the attack flashed up the Ottoman chain of command at 1.30 am, 7 August from the 1/72 Regt, which held the far right flank of the 19th Division. This report identified a raiding column (*avcı kolu*) of approximately two companies in strength that passed Halit ve Reza Tepe going up Çatlak Dere (Chailak Dere) and another raiding column going up Ağıl Dere (Aghyl Dere).[18] The report estimated an attacking strength of two regiments and noted that firing had been heard in the lines of the adjacent battalion. Unknown to the ANZAC intelligence staff, the Ottoman had positioned strong reserves on the northwestern slopes of Hill 971: the 14 Regt, which deployed its 1st Battalion in the outpost line along what the allies called Table Top and Bauchop's Hill and its remaining two battalions on Abdul Rahman Spur. Additionally, the 1/32 Regt of Major Willmer's Group was positioned nearby (halfway between Hill 971 and the village of Büyük Anafarta). Map 4.3 shows the Ottoman response at Chunuk Bair on 6/7 August 1915.

As his 1st Battalion delayed the assault columns in the early hours of 7 August, the 14 Regt commander, Lieutenant Colonel Ali Rıfat, deployed his 3rd Battalion and two companies of the 2nd Battalion to the forward slopes of Abdul Rahman Spur blocking the 4th Australian Brigade, while the remaining

2nd Battalion companies went south to block the 29th Indian Brigade.[19] At the same time, the 72 Regt commander, Major Mehmet Münir, extended his lines northward to block the New Zealand Brigade. Thus by dawn a coherent Ottoman tactical response emerged to Hamilton's main effort, although over 150 men from the 1/14 Regt had been captured in the Aghyl Dere. For his part, Kannengiesser arrived at the Northern Group's Kemalyeri headquarters at 4.40 am where he was briefed and ordered to take command and form a detachment on Hill 971. Esat also ordered him to move his 64 Regt and 25 Regt, then on the march, to the area near Hill Q (Besim Tepe) for counterattacks. While Kannengiesser was at the Northern Group headquarters, a situation report arrived from Mustafa Kemal that his 18 Regt and 27 Regt had repulsed an attack at 4.30 am and inflicted heavy casualties on the enemy.[20] This was, of course, the disastrous Australian Light Horse attack on the Nek, which went sadly off schedule with its artillery preparation and without a corresponding attack from Chunuk Bair on the Ottoman rear.

Kannengiesser arrived at Hill Q about 6.30 am, August 7 with the advanced elements of his 64 Regt (the 25 Regt was marching about a kilometer behind) where he found some of the survivors of the 14 Regt eager to counterattack and other men eager to retreat. All present agreed that the 'English companies were worrying at Conkbayırı.'[21] He quickly ordered the 64 Regt into the line at Asmalı Dere and the 14 Regt to conduct a counterattack, and the arriving 25 Regt to occupy Chunuk Bair (Conkbayırı). Willmer's 1/32 Regt had also moved forward to a position immediately behind the 14 Regt. At 8 am, Kannengiesser briefed the tactical situation as he knew it to his chief of staff, Major Hulusi, 25 Regt commander, Lieutenant Colonel Nail, and the 2nd Artillery Regiment (2 Artillery Regt) commander, Lieutenant Colonel Izzet. Professor Travers is correct in his analysis that, contrary to Aspinall (and every other western author for that matter) who asserted that Chunuk Bair was poorly defended until about 9 am, 7 August, Kannengiesser had a relatively strong and coherent force at his disposal immediately upon arrival.[22] The enemy attacks on the high ground intensified about 9 am as the Australians attacked the 14 Regt and heavy naval gunfire began to pound the Turks on Chunuk Bair. The Indians and New

Zealanders also joined in the attack, which severely shook the survivors of the 1/14 Regt. Only the direct fire of Lieutenant Besim's quick-firing mountain battery (8th Battery, 5th Artillery Regiment), which had arrived with Kannengiesser, saved the position.[23] Recognizing the danger, Kannengiesser sent in the men of his 25 Regt to reinforce the battered 1/14 Regt, which seemed about to collapse. But then, at this critical moment, Colonel Kannengiesser was seriously wounded in the chest and evacuated.

Fortunately for the Turks, the commander of the 4th Infantry Division, Lieutenant Colonel Cemil, had arrived at Kavak Dere after an all-night march. He went to see Esat at 4.30 am and was ordered to bring on his men as fast as possible. At 6.30 am, Cemil had assembled his division command group at Kemalyeri, where they were continuously updated on the unfolding battle. Northern Group messages reveal that Esat received accurate and timely information from Kannengiesser and Mustafa Kemal that enabled him to react intelligently to the rapidly changing tactical landscape.[24] For example, Cemil received Northern Group orders at 10.10 am to send the incoming 10 Regt to Kuru Dere and the 11th Infantry Regiment (11 Regt) and two machine-guns to Battleship Hill.[25] Cemil's aide-de-camp, Lieutenant Ziya Bey, translated the orders from German into Turkish. About noon, the Northern Group staff telephoned Cemil and told him that Kannengiesser had been wounded and that he (Cemil) and the 10 Regt should go immediately to Conkbayırı where he would receive written orders. At 1.10 pm, Cemil arrived at the 9th Division command post to find that Esat had assigned him to command what was styled the Aghyl Dere Detachment (*Ağıl Dere Müfrezesi*), which was to be composed of the 14 Regt with two batteries of artillery, Kannengiesser's 25 Regt and 64 Regt and his own 10 Regt and 11 Regt.[26] His mission was to take up where the badly wounded Kannengiesser left off and defend the heights and Esat promised to send him twelve machine-guns as re-inforcements from Bigalı. As he had done previously, Esat Pasha created an ad hoc battle group under a single commander tasked to deal with a particular tactical and geographic situation. Cemil struggled to sort out his units and to understand what was happening and he sent his chief of staff, Major Hulusi, out to talk to the regimental commanders. By 3.30 pm, Cemil felt comfortable enough to report that the enemy attacks had apparently been stopped along a line well below the summits and that the troops were digging trenches.[27] He also noted that he was preparing the 64 Regt for a night attack on Şahinsırt.

Cemil's situational awareness increased at 7 pm when cavalry Lieutenant Ekrem Rüştü, a Fifth Army aide-de-camp, arrived with the news that Willmer's group was successfully holding a new enemy landing at Suvla Bay along the Kireç Tepe–Ismailoğlu Tepe line.[28] Better news arrived a half hour later in a report from Willmer's chief of staff, Major Mehmet Haydar, stating that inexplicably the enemy had halted operations for the night. Now alerted to the threat to his north, Cemil cancelled the night bayonet attack and directed the 64 Regt to concentrate on fortifications and creating immediate reserves. Later that night, Colonel Ahmet Fevzi, commander of the Saros Group, who had come down to Anafarta telephoned Cemil and informed him that 'tomorrow the 7th and 12th Infantry Divisions would attack the enemy from Anafarta.'[29] He continued with instructions that Cemil would take command of the incoming 33 Regt and the 11th Artillery Regiment (sent from the 8th Division at Cape Helles) and simultaneously attack from the vicinity of Dağ Ceşme. This was a surprise to Cemil who had not yet been informed that Liman von Sanders was placing the Sari Bair position (and Cemil's detachment) under Colonel Ahmet Fevzi effective at 9 am, 8 August.[30]

In the early hours of 8 August the 3rd and 4th Battalions of Cemil's 11 Regt moved into reserve positions behind the 25 Regt and Ali's battered 14 Regt respectively. Cemil diverted the 1st and 2nd Battalions, 11 Regt into the line between Kemal's 19th Division and the remnants of the 1/14 Regt. As dawn broke, the enemy renewed the offensive toward Chunuk Bair and Hill 971. The New Zealanders caught the tired survivors of the 1/14 Regt, who had been in constant combat since the initial attack on the evening of 6 August, asleep in their trenches and they punched through reaching the summit of Chunuk Bair. For the Turks it was simply a matter of bad luck that most of the survivors of Lieutenant Colonel Ali's 1/14 Regt had been pushed uphill to the southwestern shoulder of Chunuk Bair directly in the path of the New Zealanders. In any event around 4.40 am, Malone's New

Zealanders held the forward and rear crests of Chunuk Bair. But the adjacent attack by the 39th Brigade foundered as it ran into the fresh men of Lieutenant Colonel Nail's 25 Regt. This fight was bitterly contested and marked by hand-to-hand combat during which Nail was seriously wounded and later died. The 64 Regt lay in the line between the two allied attacks and was relatively unengaged but laid down withering fires on the 39th Brigade to support the 25 Regt. When Nail was wounded, Cemil ordered the 64 Regt's commander, Lieutenant Colonel Servet, to take command of the entire line and restore the situation. About this time, the formal reorganization message from Liman von Sanders reached Cemil that placed him under Colonel Ahmet Fevzi.[31] Very shortly thereafter, Ahmet Fevzi arrived on Chunuk Bair to direct the battle.

The battle for control of Chunuk Bair raged through the day as the adjacent Ottoman units on the higher ground of Hill 971 and Hill Q (Besim Tepe) laid down heavy fires on the New Zealanders. Ahmet Fevzi reported that he had talked by telephone with Cemil at 1 pm outlining his plans to conduct a counterattack with the 7th and 12th Infantry Divisions, which were deploying into Dağçeşme and Mesan Tepe respectfully. In turn Cemil went to Dağçeşme to meet with 7th Division commander, Colonel Halil, where a Fifth Army aide-de-camp found him and gave him a message from Liman von Sanders that German Lieutenant Colonel Pötrïh had been appointed to take command of the 9th Division.[32] Meanwhile, the fighting on Chunuk Bair grew to brutal intensity, Malone was killed along with hundreds of his men and at 5.40 pm, Ahmet Fevzi was finally able to send a message outlining the tactical situation. He reported that the 64 Regt had pushed the enemy about 30m down off the crest of Chunuk Bair and that he was personally present at that location. He also reported that he was preparing to counterattack with his divisions, which were just now coming into their assembly areas. Other reinforcements from the Southern Group were also about to arrive in the form of Colonel Ali Reza's 23rd and 24th Infantry Regiments (23 Regt and 24 Regt) as well as a field-artillery battery (from Reza's 8th Infantry Division), the first two battalions of which reached Chunuk Bair at 10.30 pm

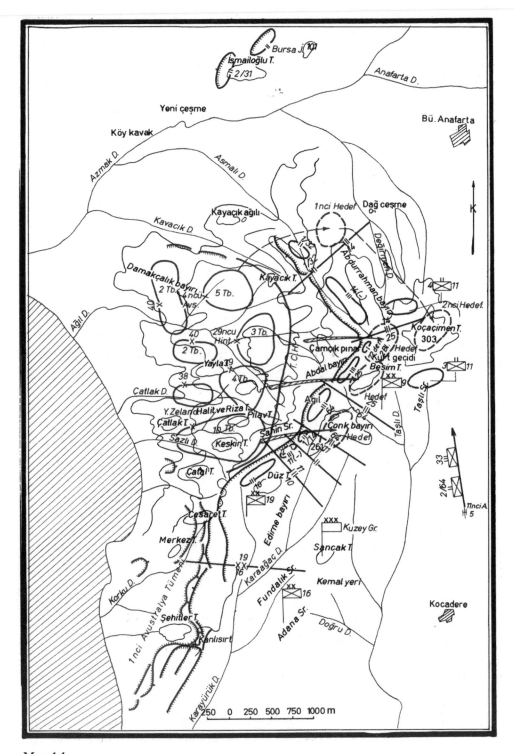

Map 4.4
Morning situation on Chunuk Bair and British attack plan, 8 August 1915. The British avenues of advance are shown along with the associated objectives (Hedef). Note that the New Zealand (Y. Zeland) Brigade's avenue passes directly through the sector of the exhausted Ottoman 1/14 Infantry.

that evening. Map 4.4 shows the Ottoman counterattacks of 8 August 1915.

The specific reasons included in the extant histories regarding the relief of Anafarta Group commander, Colonel Ahmet Fevzi, on the night of 8/9 August 1915 vary. Professor Travers, for example, cites the confusion that reigned on Chunk Bair and the panic of the 8th Division commander (who did not know what to do) as prompting Liman von Sanders.[33] In his memoirs Liman von Sanders noted with great disapproval that Ahmet Fevzi had not carried out his explicit orders to launch a counterattack on the night of 8 August 1915 and for this reason replaced him.[34] However, the evolving Ottoman reorganization on Chunuk Bair as well as Ahmet Fevzi's positive report indicates a clear sense of situational awareness by the Fifth Army. And it is a fact that until late in the day, Ahmet Fevzi's XVI Corps divisions had not reached their assembly positions.[35] A memoir of one of the junior officers marching with the 7th Division's 21 Regt speaks of the difficulty of the forced march south.[36] Except for several half-hour rest stops the regiment marched continuously through the night and the officers had to drive the men who wanted to drop out. The officers had no maps and no idea of where or when the head of the column would arrive at a destination. That said, only fifty men per battalion failed to complete the march (or about 5 percent) but those that did arrive were spent men. It is hard to imagine Liman von Sanders being unaware of the difficulties that the XVI Corps commander faced in mounting a multi-divisional counterattack after such a forced march (the 7th Division travelled 30km and the 12th Division 40km). In any case, at 7 pm Liman von Sanders telephoned Esat Pasha expressing his concern for the situation.[37] Liman von Sanders then telephoned Mustafa Kemal, who was then directing his forces from a position on Battleship Hill, to ask him what he thought about the situation. Although Kemal spoke German fluently, Liman von Sanders put Colonel Kazım directly on the phone to avoid any misunderstanding. According to Kazım, because of the nature and quantity of the enemy forces that had landed Mustafa Kemal thought it necessary to ensure command and control by uniting the entire effort under a single commander.[38] Liman von Sanders had a deep sense of respect for the soldierly qualities of Mustafa Kemal as well as an understanding of his talents as an aggressive leader of men and he ordered Kemal to take command of the Anafarta Group effective at 9.45 pm, 8 August. Kemal's 19th Division was at the same time placed in the capable hands of the veteran 27 Regt commander, Lieutenant Colonel Şefik.

In actuality, the decision to relieve Ahmet Fevzi and replace him with Mustafa Kemal likely rested on more pragmatic grounds. First, Kemal was intimately familiar with the ground and the units involved in the fight for Sari Bair. He had been in action on the ANZAC perimeter since 25 April and since early May commanded the northern shoulder of Esat's Northern Group. As such, the Sari Bair ridge line fell in Kemal's 'tactical backyard'. Secondly, there is evidence that Kemal expressed concern to Esat over the vulnerability of Sazlıdere to the north of the Arıburnu sector in what Turkish historians call the 'Sazlıdere Discussion'. It began as a result of a lengthy correspondence between Kemal and the Northern Group staff over this issue, which irritated Esat so much that he personally came to the 19th Division headquarters with his chief of staff Colonel Fahrettin in mid-June.[39] From there they proceeded to Battleship Hill where Kemal pointed out to Esat the vulnerability of the unguarded territory to the north of Hill 971. According to an Ottoman officer who was present, Fahrettin said 'only a gang of guerrillas could advance there!', whereupon Kemal then indicated where and how the enemy might successfully advance.[40] Esat remained unconvinced patting Kemal on his shoulder and minding him not to worry. Another critical factor was Kemal's experience on the peninsula itself in the Balkan Wars of 1912/1913 during which he had served as the chief operations officer of the Gallipoli Army. Taking these facts altogether, the unfortunate Ahmet Fevzi was a poor choice to command an ad hoc grouping of forces on unfamiliar ground compared to the experienced Mustafa Kemal, who was intimately familiar with the key terrain of Anafarta.

Suvla Bay, 6–9 August 1915

Stopford's 11th Division came ashore at Suvla Bay at 9.30 pm, 6 August on undefended beaches. These troops were from Kitchener's New Army and they were the first New Army troops committed to combat in the war. The bluffs known as Soffa Tepe (Hill 10) and Lalababa Tepe overlooking the beaches were held by posts from the 3 Coy and 4 Coy of the Bursa Jandarma Battalion. These posts shot up flares and fired on the British. Lalababa was taken almost immediately but Hill 10 held out all night as the British piled battalions into the cramped beachhead. Willmer's troops put up a spirited defense that held the 11th Division to small gains. As dawn broke on 7 August confusion reigned in the small beachhead. About 8 am the 10th Division began to land as well with orders to capture Mestan Tepe or Chocolate Hill. Unfortunately for the British, the Bursa Jandarma commander, Major Tahsin, who was on Hill 10 all night, continually furnished Willmer with accurate situation reports, which enabled Willmer to deploy the 1 Coy and 2 Coy of the Bursa Jandarma Battalion as well as the entire 2/31 Regt to blocking positions on the hill.[41] At the same time, he sent the 1 Coy and 4 Coy of the Gelibolu Jandarma Battalion to reinforce the 2 Coy, 1/32 Regt which was holding the Karakol Dağı or Kiretch Tepe. Each group was well supported by Willmer's small number of artillery pieces. His situation report to Liman von Sanders that morning accurately reflected the situation with confidence as well as urgently requesting reinforcements. At this point Willmer had about 3,000 men to hold approximately 27,000 British and Irish troops. However, in a muddled day of chaotic orders and counterorders (a heartbreaking story that is well told in the English-language histories), the British failed to push forward. Moreover, the torrid sun and water shortages rapidly drained the strength of the British officers and men, most of whom had no clear idea about what they were supposed to accomplish.

Aspinall-Oglander rightly asserts that the 24 hours lost on 7 August were critical because during that time Liman von Sanders ordered Ahmet Fevzi's XVI Corps south from Saros Bay. Not only did this enable the XVI Corps to arrive in time to influence decisively the battle but the additional time allowed Willmer's accurate reports to flow through Fifth Army to Ahmet Fevzi.[42] His first orders as Anafarta Group commander, issued enroute from Saros Bay to his divisions, outlined with great clarity the front-line trace as well as identifying the exact locations of the divisional assembly areas (the 7th Division's to the west of

Büyük Anafarta and the 12th Division's to the north of Küçük Anafarta).[43] It is clear from Ahmet Fevzi's orders that the Ottoman reporting system was, once again, creating an enhanced situational awareness for the Turks in comparison to the chaotic reporting of the British. Making things worse, the muddle continued all day on 8 August and Stopford's corps again failed to advance much to the consternation of Hamilton and his staff. Another vital 24 hours passed during which the XVI Corps divisions arrived. This failure destroyed the reputation of Stopford and several of his division commanders and all were relieved in short order. However, did Stopford's failure doom the campaign? In truth, Hamilton's main effort, the fight for Sari Bair, was lost concurrently. Might Stopford have out flanked Hill 971 and retrieved the failed main effort? In the author's opinion, it is likely that Willmer would have used his 1/32 Regt against Stopford instead of sending it on 7 August to assist the 14 Regt on Abdul Rahman Spur. This would have added a thousand well-trained infantry to the defense of Chocolate Hill and it is likely that, even if pushed off the hill, Willmer would have fought a delaying action back to the lower slopes of Sari Bair. By mid-morning 8 August battalions of the 11 Regt had arrived on the northern approaches of Hill 971 and that afternoon battalions of the XVI Corps were arriving in Büyük Anafarta. It is fair to conclude that had Stopford aggressively pushed forward his progress would not have been rapid and, moreover, the ever increasing flow of Ottoman reinforcements could have been diverted to slow him further. It is unlikely, therefore, that Stopford, even under the best of circumstances, could have penetrated beyond Büyük Anafarta and Küçük Anafarta before the two divisions of the XVI Corps arrived on the field. Once these divisions were present, as well as the 4th, 8th and 9th Divisions on Chunuk Bair, Hamlton's plan was doomed to fail.

First Anafarta and Conkbayırı, 9 August 1915

The Turks now occupied a continuous front from Kiretch Tepe on the Aegean Sea to Chunuk Bair. The newly appointed commander, Mustafa Kemal, was determined to launch a co-ordinated counterattack early on the morning of 9 August. The 12th Division, commanded by Lieutenant Colonel Selahattin

Adil, occupied hilltop assembly areas running on a north–south line from Kidney Hill to Tekke Tepe. Adil had his 34 Regt, 35th and 36th Infantry Regiments (35 Regt and 36 Regt) as well as the 1st Battalion, 12th Artillery Regiment (10,471 men). Willmer's group remained steadfast at Chocolate Hill supported by part of the 9 Artillery Regt and Colonel Halil's 7th Division now occupied the ground in between Willmer and Cemil's 4th Division on the Abdul Rahman Spur. Halil had only two regiments, the 20 Regt and 21 Regt (5,982 men), but Adil's 2nd Battalion 12th Artillery (2/12 Arty Regt) was split off to support Halil's infantry.

The 12th Division's advance began at 4 am and can be characterized as a movement to contact rather than an attack as the British lines were over 2,000m distant. Its mission was simply to gain and maintain contact as far forward as possible. However, the 35 Regt (minus its 1st Battalion, which was deployed on the right flank) quickly ran up against the British 32nd Brigade, which was itself advancing on Tekke Tepe. A meeting engagement ensued in which the experienced Turks coming down hill and well supported by artillery crushed the inexperienced British causing a disorderly retreat. In addition to killing and wounding numbers of the enemy, the victorious 35 Regt captured 3 officers, 41 men, 3 machine-guns and a large quantity of rifles.[44] The 34 Regt's advance ran into the British 33rd Brigade, which was attempting to seize the northern shoulder of Chocolate Hill, in the area of Scimitar Hill where a desperate meeting engagement ensued. Fighting was heavy, Turkish losses were high and, adding to the confusion, the artillery fires caught the scrub brush on fire which was fanned by brisk winds. In the end the 35 Regt pushed the British back to their start lines. To the north, the British 10th Division attempted to push east on the Kiretch Tepe ridge but, despite impressive naval gunfire support, these attacks failed. Altogether the 12th Division lost 1,085 officers and men on 9 August. Map 4.5 shows the attacks of 9 August at Suvla Bay.

Under the cover of heavy friendly artillery and machine-gun fires the 7th Division's attacks began at 4.30 am, 9 August. The division's objective was to seize the enemy positions on Damakjelik Bair (Damakçılık Bayrı) and unlike its sister division's advance, these positions were strongly held by

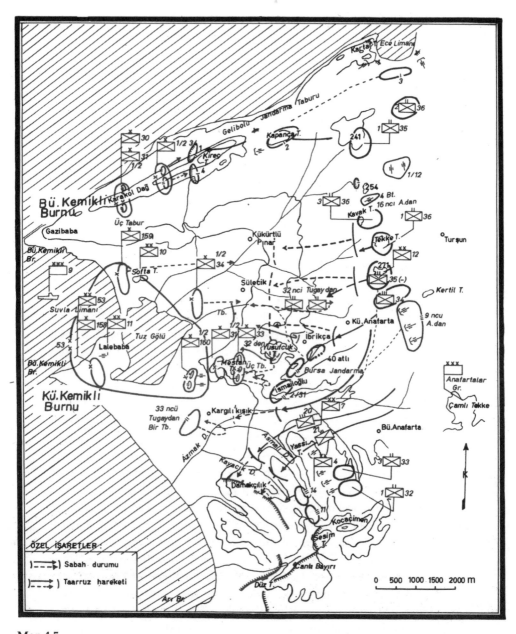

Map 4.5
Morning situation at Suvla, 9 August 1915 and the attacks of that day. This is essentially a movement to contact where the Ottomans are pushing forward to fix the enemy front line. The 7th Division headquarters is located on Yassı Tepe and the 12th Division headquarters is located on Hill 271. Mustafa Kemal's Anafarta Group headquarters is centrally positioned on Çamlı Tekke.

the 4th Australian Brigade and the 40th Brigade. Cemil's adjacent 4th Division artillery attempted to assist the attack by firing on the enemy machine-guns and he had the machine-guns of the 14 Regt assist as well. In this case, the Turks went downhill from Bomba Tepe into the ravine of Kayaçık Dere and then assaulted uphill. Fighting was hard with severe losses and a British counterattack at 10 am pushed the two regiments back down into the Kayaçık Dere. Both commanders, Lieutenant Colonel Halit of the 20 Regt and Lieutenant Colonel Yusuf Ziya of the 21 Regt, were badly wounded and both died two days later.[45] Most of the officers in the battalions were killed or wounded as well. Altogether the two regiments lost 978 officers and men that day.[46] The Turks know these battles involving the XVI Corps divisions as First Anafarta.

The final British attack on the Chunuk Bair ridge began about 5.15 pm against Hill Q (Besi Tepe) after a heavy bombardment. The attack went wrong from the start when several assaulting columns were delayed by the difficult terrain and only Allanson's Gurkhas and South Lancs made it to the summit. They punched through the lines of the newly arrived 24 Regt, which had taken over the 64 Regt's lines on the night of 8/9 August, to occupy Hill Q. Many of the regiment's officers and men were killed and wounded in the struggle. When the commander attempted to conduct a counterattack he found it impossible due to collapsed morale.[47] The sector commander, Colonel Ali Reza of the newly arrived 8th Infantry Division, appealed to Esat Pasha for the release of the Northern Group's reserve (Reza's own 23 Regt). It is difficult to understand why Ali Reza notified Esat rather than Mustafa Kemal (as his division was then assigned to the Anafarta Group) but this gives credence to Professor Traver's assertion that the 8th Division commander did not know what was going on. Esat Pasha, on his part, took the initiative to release the 23 Regt and to send a battalion from the 26 Regt, which was then under his control at Kemalyeri, as well. These reserves proved unnecessary as Ali Reza was able to push Allanson off Hill Q within several hours using his local forces. In a related vignette, while the Hill Q attacks were proceeding, the newly appointed 9th Division commander, in whose sector the bulk of Hill Q actually lay, was trying to reach his new headquarters. This was

German Lieutenant Colonel Pötrih (Kannengiessier's replacement), who did not speak Ottoman Turkish and could not seem to find any Turks who could show him the way. Frustrated and unable to find his new divisional command post he returned to the Northern Group headquarters.[48] Esat then assigned a staff officer who spoke fluent German, Staff Major Kemal, to assist Pötrih and finally together they made it to Pötrih's new command.

The incidents at Hill Q on 9 August serve to show the high levels of confusion on the Ottoman side as Mustafa Kemal attempted to take control of his new command. Now aware of these problems, Liman von Sanders issued orders to the 8th Division that afternoon, which clarified the command arrangements by stating 'The 8th Division and all units assigned to it, at 3.14 pm, are ordered to the Anafatra Group. You are authorized to abandon attacks.'[49] Nevertheless, at 7 pm, Liman von Sanders was able to send his first situation report to Enver Pasha stating that, as of 3 pm that day, the British attacks were very uncoordinated and unsuccessful. His second report to Enver was more favorable and followed at 11.45 pm, 9 August stating that the enemy attacks on Anafarta and Sari Bair had ended and that he felt that his forces could deal with any renewed attacks.[50] However, Liman von Sanders caveated the report by noting that reinforcements and replacements were needed to restore Fifth Army's reserves so that counterattacks could be launched. The irrepressible Enver immediately returned a message to Fifth Army noting that the Ottoman general staff had ordered the 24th Infantry Division to entrain immediately for the railway station at Uzunköprü for deployment into the peninsula![51]

Meanwhile, Mustafa Kemal went to the headquarters of the 8th Division at Chunuk Bair with his aide-de-camp, cavalry Lieutenant Zeki. From there Kemal and Zeki went forward to conduct a personal reconnaissance and to survey the condition of the men in the forward positions. He determined that conditions for a multi-divisional counterattack were favorable due to the presence of relatively fresh Ottoman troops. Kemal was especially pleased with the fact that the enemy trenches were a mere 20–25m over the crest of the ridgeline from his own lines and he believed that his men might even recapture the lost ground on Rhododendron Spur (Şahınsırt). He began to make preparations for what became one of the most successful local attacks made by the Turks during the campaign. Kemal sent orders to Colonel Ali Reza informing him that the 8th Division would make the main effort in an attack that would begin at 4.30 am, 10 August.[52] These orders also contained instructions to conduct a vigorous pursuit after breaking through the enemy lines with a bayonet assault. Pötrih's 9th Division was ordered to conduct a supporting attack. The tireless Kemal worked through the night to coordinate the counterattack and ordered the 7th and 12th Divisions to support by an advance as well.

Mustafa Kemal crept forward with his scouting screen in order personally to give the order to attack at the critical moment when a brief artillery bombardment ended. Kemal hugged the ground while the Ottoman artillery and machine-gun raked the enemy positions over his head and then, at the exact moment when the firing ceased, he raised himself up and pointed to the enemy line with his riding crop (his own prearranged signal to attack).[53] Ali Reza's 23 Regt and 24 Regt swept forward on the right (this was actually the center of the main effort), while on the division's left flank the 16 Regt and 28th Infantry Regiment (28 Regt) went forward as well. On the 8th Division's right flank Pötrih's 1/33 Regt and his 25 Regt attacked simultaneously. The allied histories speak of a six-battalion attack, and against the Pinnacle area this was true, but Kemal actually employed about sixteen battalions altogether. It was a massive blow and the Turks achieved almost complete surprise with what amounted to a human-wave attack.[54] Aspinall-Oglander wrote that 'dense waves of Turks came pouring over the skyline.'[55] The Ottoman infantry hardly fired their rifles and relied on the shock power of the bayonet to sweep into the British and New Zealand lines. The 1/23 Regt was able to sweep down from the heights into the small table-like area called the Farm Plateau (Sarı tarla) where a brigade headquarters and a large number of men were resting. The surprised British died in large numbers and some units were entirely eliminated (perhaps as many as a thousand British and Irish soldiers were killed in a matter of minutes[56]). The Turks, for their part, suffered greatly and were too spent to exploit their success. Kemal's attack frittered into stasis by midday but,

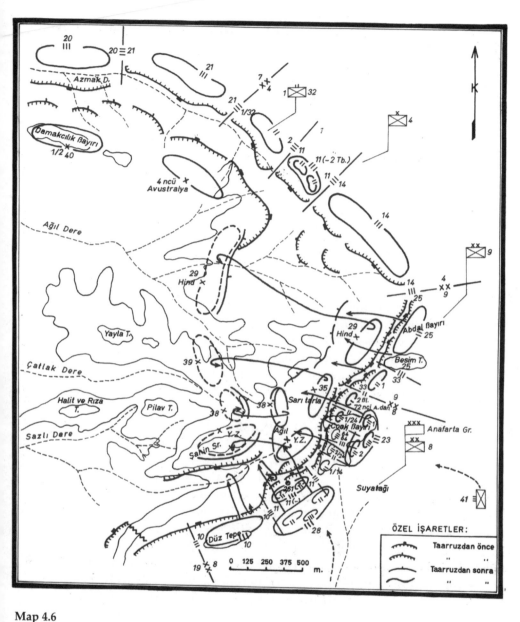

Map 4.6
Morning situation at Chunuk Bair, 10 August 1915 and Ottoman counterattack. This map
illustrates the massive surprise attack, led by Mustafa Kemal, that swept over the Farm plateau
(Sarı tarla). The Anafarta Group headquarters relocated to Conkbayırı on the evening of
9 August and then relocated again to Suyatağı to support the attack.

nevertheless, the Turks managed to push the New Zealand Brigade and the 38th Brigade back about 500m. The 39th Brigade withdrew 1,000m and the 29th Indian Brigade pulled back almost 1,500m thus ending the threat to Sari Bair ridge. The Turks refer to these battles for Sari Bair ridge as the Conkbayırı battles. To the north the 7th and 12th Divisions found themselves under British attacks that began about 5 am and continued throughout the day. Unable to attack themselves they successfully held their ground against the assaults of the British 11th Division. Map 4.6 shows the Ottoman counterattacks of 10 August 1915 at Anzac.

During the counterattack at Chunuk Bair on 10 August an unusual incident happened when Mustafa Kemal, who was present with the leading elements of the 8th Division, was hit in the right side of his chest by a shrapnel ball. He might have been killed right then and there except that the ball hit and shattered his pocket watch. Kemal, ever the cool combat commander, then shouted to his men who had seen him hit 'Silence! Don't let the troops lose their morale.'[57] Turkish sources assert that many soldiers witnessed this incident and it is famously retold in Turkey today.[58] After the battle, Liman von Sanders took the shattered watch as a souvenir and presented Mustafa Kemal with his own watch (decorated with his family crest) as a replacement.

Other operations, 11–20 August

Overall, operations on Sari Bair and at Suvla had been very costly for both sides with the British losing about 25,000 men and the Turks losing about 20,000 men during the period of 6–10 August 1915. The day of 11 August passed uneventfully as both sides paused to recover their cohesion. The offensive operations on Sari Bair on 10 August had exhausted the 8th Division and casualties from the day's defensive operations of the 7th and 12th Divisions were 687 and 413 men respectfully. The British, however, planned to continue offensive operations on the next day.

Under intense pressure from Hamilton, Stopford launched the 54th Infantry Division's 163rd Brigade, supported by a half-brigade of the 11th Division, at 4 pm, 12 August in an attempt to seize the Tekke Tepe hill mass. The attack was poorly planned with no reconnaissance or rehearsals. Moreover, the maps were inaccurate, the officers had no idea of exactly where the enemy positions were or in what strength they were held, and the supporting artillery was employed ineffectively. The inexperienced British Territorials rushed forward into the well-laid defensive fires of the 1/36 Regt and the 3/35 Regt and were mown down. The Ottoman battalions conducted immediate counterattacks that pushed the survivors back. About 6.30 pm, the Turks unleashed the 9 Coy and 11 Coy of the 3/36 Regt, which had been in immediate tactical reserve. These two companies delivered a slashing bayonet pursuit of the 1/5 Norfolks during which the Turks reported killing 15 officers and 250 men.[59] Part of the Norfolk's losses were from the Sandringham Company, which seemed to disappear entirely in the fighting and was made famous in the film *All the King's Men*. The Turks refer to this battle as Küçük Anafarta Ovası Muharebesi.

Stopford ordered another attack to be launched on Kiretch Tepe ridge on 15 August by the 10th Infantry Division. Like the attack of 12 August, this attack was badly managed. The British expected to attack the jandarma, which had held the ridge since the landings, and they expected to break through and drive on to occupy Kidney Hill. In their favor they held a wonderful flanking position on the hill and a near perfect opportunity to use naval gunfire support to suppress the Turks. Unfortunately, the Turks had brought up significant reinforcements in the week prior to replace the jandarma.

In the ongoing Ottoman tactical reorganization the 5th Division, in Northern Group reserve, saw its organic infantry regiments reassigned to the Lone Pine and Sari Bair fights. As a result the division headquarters element was sent to join Major Willmer, who formed and took command of an ad hoc 5th Division. He established his division headquarters, not at Tursuhn Keui as noted by Aspinall-Oglander, but on the Kapanca Hill (near Jephson's Post) and he had five additional infantry battalions assigned to him as well as the Gelibolu Jandarma Battalion and the two companies of the 127 Regt already in defensive positions on Kiretch Tepe.[60] Willmer also had two batteries of guns from the 11 Artillery Regt supporting his positions. Major-General Mahon wanted to begin his attack at 8.40 am, 15 August by launching a multi-directional attack from the west and north simultaneously. Unfortunately, the orders were late in passing and the attack did not begin until 2.15 pm. The attacks gained some ground against moderate Turkish resistance but as darkness fell, the British were unable to consolidate their gains and were left in a vulnerable position. In the meantime Willmer came to Kiretch Tepe about 8.30 pm to examine personally the situation. He was very encouraged and ordered the 1/19 Regt and the 1/39 Regt to march forward from Tekke Tepe for a counter-attack.[61] They arrived at the front about midnight and Willmer rapidly organized a counterattack using these two battalions plus the 2/19 Regt, which was lying in close reserve just 500m behind the front. He wanted to launch a night attack at 2 am but last-minute adjustments in positioning delayed the attack until 4 am, 16 August. The attack tore into the 30th Brigade's left flank causing heavy casualties. Willmer then brought up the fresh 2/17 Regt from Tursuhn Keui (Türşunköy) for a follow-on counterattack about 8 am with hand grenades. The battle raged all day as the Turks tried to push the Irish off the ridge. At midday Mustafa Kemal diverted incoming reinforcement battalions to reinforce Willmer. These were the 2/1 Regt and 3/1 Regt from the Asia Group, which began to arrive in Tursuhn Keui about 4 pm. Liman von Sanders was also concerned about the situation on Kiretch Tepe and directed that the 9th Division's 126 Regt be deployed to the Anafarta Group as a reserve. From these move-ments it is clear that neither Kemal nor Liman von Sanders possessed an accurate understanding of what was happening on Kiretch Tepe on 16 August. This is perhaps because Willmer became personally involved in the fighting and was unable to render timely reports as he had done so effectively on 6/7 August. In any case, Mahon decided to recall his battered brigades about 7 pm that evening and the Irish pulled back to their start lines ending the battle.

On 17 August, Willmer's men reoccupied all of their original positions and restored their outposts. The 5th Division then rein-forced the defensive position by garrisoning the lines with the 1/19 Regt and 2/19 Regt. Willmer also sent 2 artillery batteries and 2 medical companies to the ridge as well as 4,000 sand bags for the restoration of the trenches. Casualties were evenly distributed with the Irish reportedly losing about 2,000 men, while the Turks lost 3 officers and 315 men killed, 8 officers and 1,238 men wounded and 2 officers and 85 men missing (1,651 men altogether).[62]

As the Ottoman VI Corps arrived at Saros Bay with the 24th and 26th Infantry Divisions, Liman von Sanders was able to bring the 6th Infantry Division south to the Anafarta front.[63] Two infantry regiments (the 16 Regt and 17 Regt) and two field-artillery batteries of this division marched down through Tursuhn Keui and began to arrive at an assembly area behind Tekke Tepe at 6 am, 17 August 1915. Accompanying the 6th Division was the 11th Cavalry Regiment (11 Cavalry Regt). As active operations on Sari Bair seemed to subside, Mustafa Kemal pulled out most of Pötrih's 9th Division out of the line (the 25 Regt and 64 Regt and one artillery battery) and redeployed them to a reserve position just north of Tursuhn Keui. Thus by 20 August, Kemal's Anafarta Group had the following divisions in contact running from Kiretch Tepe in the north to Battleship Hill in the south: 5th, 12th, 7th, 4th, 28 Regt (from 9th Division) and 8th Division. Lying just behind the Tekke Tepe ridge, Kemal had the 9th Division (-) and the 6th Division. The bulk of the Anafarta Group's artillery lay in the W Hills directly supporting the 12th Division's 34 Regt and 35 Regt. Mustafa Kemal's group headquarters was positioned behind the center on Camlı Tekke, which was the southern hill of the Anafarta Saddle.

Aspinall-Oglander wrote that with the departure of the 6th Division from Saros Bay 'this vital point had been completely denuded of troops.'[64] This is not at all true; in fact, the lead elements of the 24th Division began to arrive by foot in the Saros Bay sector on 16 August followed by the 26th Division two days later. The VI Corps headquarters, with German Colonel Ulrich Back as its chief of staff, moved to houses in the town of Gallipoli, where it melded with the headquarters of General Faik. Previously, 14 August, Lieutenant Colonel Freze, a Fifth Army staff officer, had gone to Istanbul to discuss revisions in the operational control of the upper peninsula.[65] The outcome of the discussions was that von der Goltz's First Army would extend its area of responsibility south to cover not only Saros Bay but the isthmus of Bulair to a line running east from Despot Bay to a point on the strait just south of Gallipoli. This change relieved Liman von Sanders of the worrisome amphibious threat to his north and left him free to focus on the ongoing battles and orders to this effect went out on the evening of 17 August.[66] Altogether on 21 August 1915, the Ottoman army now had seventeen infantry divisions, one infantry detachment of brigade strength and an independent cavalry brigade (counting all First and Fifth Army assets) committed to the campaign.

Scimitar Hill and Hill 60 (Second Anafarta), 21–28 August 1915

While the Turks were busy reinforcing and rearranging their forces, Hamilton relieved Stopford and replaced him with Major General de Lisle, the commander of the 29th Division and ordered the new commander to attack once again. De Lisle issued orders on 20 August tasking the 29th Division to attack Scimitar Hill (Yusufçuk Tepe) and the 11th Division to attack the W Hills (Ismailoğlu Tepe). Coming just behind the 29th Division to Chocolate Hill was the just-arrived 2nd Mounted Division (2nd Yeomanry Division). In support of de Lisle's IX Corps offensive Birdwood's ANZAC would launch Cox's Force to attack Hill 60 (Bomba Tepe). This was a limited scope offensive and the British hoped simply to get a better position on the W Hills from which they might then assault the Anafarta Spur. The Turks call this series of battles the Second Anafarta Battles (*Ikinci Anafartalar Muharebesi*). The Turks lay in lines that they had occupied for about 10 days and they had 99 artillery pieces (not the 84 that Aspinall-Oglander thought).[67] Supporting the Kiretch Tepe sector were 16 field-artillery guns, 14 mountain howitzers and 2 howitzers (32 pieces). Supporting the 12th Division sector were 20 field-artillery guns and 8 mountain howitzers. Importantly this sector had an additional 11 heavy guns in the 120mm to 150mm calibre range (39 pieces including most of the Anafarta Group's heavy artillery). Supporting the 7th, 4th and 8th Divisions on Sari Bair ridge were 8 field-artillery guns, 16 mountain howitzers and 2 150mm howitzers (28 pieces in all).

Enemy shells began to rain on Scimitar Hill and the W Hills starting at 2.30 pm, 21 August, which started the scrub brush on fire. The British artillery preparation in this battle was particularly ineffective and scarcely touched the Turkish trenches causing almost no damage and few casualties. The Ottoman artillery began to fire in return on well-registered and easily observed targets causing many casualties in the 29th Division and in the follow-on yeomanry. The 11th Division kicked off the attack at 3 pm pitting two brigades against a single Ottoman battalion, the 1/34 Regt on the southern slopes of the W Hills. The unshaken Turks stopped them cold. At 3.30 pm the 87th Brigade attacked the 2/35 Regt on Scimitar Hill while its sister 86th Brigade in the 29th Division hit two Ottoman battalions, the 2/34 Regt and the 2/31 Regt (which had been put under the command of Lieutenant Colonel Mehmet Ali, the 34 Regt commander) on the northern slope of Scimitar Hill. These brigades also attempted to cross no-man's-land in front of trenches manned by an alert and unshaken enemy. The 29th Division was seasoned and the most effective British division on the peninsula but its brigades fared no better than the 11th Division's brigades. Cox's force (roughly nine under strength battalions of Indians, Australians and New Zealanders) also attacked at 3.30 pm against the 1/20 Regt, 3/20 Regt, 1/21 Regt and 3/21 Regt (7th Division) with similar results. Nevertheless, Colonel Halil, the 7th Division commander, immediately requested reinforcements from the Anafarta Group. The British and ANZAC attacks continued fitfully until about 6 pm by which time vigorous Ottoman bayonet counterattacks had restored the entire line.

When the British attack began Mustafa Kemal reacted with his usual alacrity by immediately ordering his reserves into action. He ordered the 11 Cavalry Regt and the 9th Division (-) to reinforce the 12th Division and the 6th Division to move forward to Küçük Anafarta. The cavalry arrived in the 34 Regt's sector at 5.30 pm, while the more-distant 9th Division (-) arrived at the W Hills at 7.30 pm.[68] Pötrih's 64 Regt was then deployed to reinforce Scimitar Hill, while the 25 Regt remained in immediate tactical reserve. Finally, Kemal ordered the unengaged 8th Division to dispatch two infantry battalions to reinforce the 7th Division. These battalions arrived in Halil's sector at 7.40 pm, while the 11 Cavalry Regt was sent to secure the 7th Division's right flank.

To the surprise of the Turks the entire 2nd Mounted Division, which consisted of dismounted yeomanry troopers used as

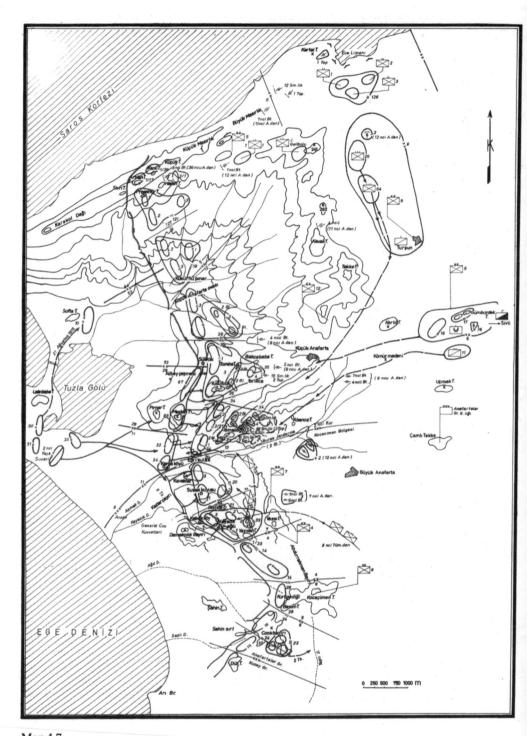

Map 4.7
General situation Scimitar Hill and Hill 60, 21 August 1915. The failed British attacks are clearly shown on this map along with the avenue of attack taken by the British 2nd Mounted Division (2nci Yaya Suvari). The Ottoman have two entire infantry divisions in reserve and Mustafa Kemal's Anafarta Group headquarters has returned to Çamlı Tekke to better control the battle.

infantry, set in motion a second major attack from Chocolate Hill on the hard-pressed 34 Regt. The attacks began about 6 pm and lasted into the night. Unfortunately for the British, the yeomanry commanders, division and brigade, possessed almost no situational or spatial awareness and they simply went forward through the lines of the defeated 29th Division. This famously futile attack destroyed the division and with it the lives of a number of well-known British officers (including Colonel Sir Johnnie Milbanke VC, Lord Longford and Brigadier General Kenna, VC). Fire and smoke from the burning brush obscured the yeomanry advance and gave the dug-in Turks an advantage with their pre-ranged rifles and machine-guns. The fighting was so intense that the 12th Division commander, Lieutenant Colonel Selahattin, had to launch a dawn counterattack at 4.30 am, 22 August in the 34 Regt sector with bayonets and hand grenades to clear completely and secure the area.[69] Cox's men would continue the fight for Hill 60 for another two days against the 7th Division and, at the end, held a small salient in the center of the 21 Regt's sector. Map 4.7 shows these battles around Scimitar Hill.

Cox advocated renewing the attacks on Hill 60 as it dominated his hard-won ground. After consultations with Birdwood it was approved to attack again with a force of about 1,000 men on 27 August. The Turks call this the Kayacıkağılı or Bomba Tepe Muhareberleri. Colonel Halil, the 7th Division commander, strongly held Hill 60 with the 3/21 Regt and had reinforced the position with two companies of the 4th Battalion, 41st Infantry Regiment (4/41 Regt). Cox attacked at 4 pm with heavy artillery fire support and his men made some progress capturing several lines of Turkish trenches, as well as forty-six men and three machine-guns.[70] Fighting raged throughout the night and Halil launched a powerful counterattack with the 1/33 Regt and the 2/33 Regt, which recaptured all but several sections of the forward trenches. In the meantime, the 2/126 Regt was sent over to the 7th Division sector from the adjacent 9th Division as a reserve. At the strategic level, Liman von Sanders sent the 59th Infantry Regiment (from the 26th Division) south on the night of 27/28 August and the remaining regiments (the 76th and 78th Infantry Regiments) and the artillery followed the next morning. This division closed on assembly areas in the vicinity of

Tursuhn Keui on 28–30 August. Additionally, on 27 August four infantry battalions and three artillery batteries from the 3rd Division in Asia were staged in Erenkoy and put on alert for deployment to the European side.

The fight for Scimitar Hill and Hill 60 proved to be the last major battles of the Gallipoli campaign. British losses were extremely heavy. The Turks claim that the British IX Corps lost 6,558 men and Cox's force lost around 1,300 men for almost no gain at all.[71] Ottoman losses are recorded as 1,192 men in the 12th Division (350 killed, 561 wounded, and 281 missing) and 1,406 men in the 7th Division (including the fight on Hill 60 on 27 August).[72] On the evening of 22 August, Mustafa Kemal pulled the 12th Division back from Scimitar Hill and the W Hills and replaced it with the fresh 9th Division. His after action report to Liman von Sanders recapped the victory, exuded confidence, and noted that 'with his own eyes he had observed English casualties in excessive numbers.'[73] Kemal also requested that Vehip's Southern Group chief of engineers be sent up to Scimitar Hill to advise him on the construction of strong points (*direnek noktalari*).

Ottoman operational reorganization, 29 August–November 1915

On the night of 28/29 August, Mustafa Kemal pulled the exhausted 7th Division out of the line and replaced it with the fresh 6th Division. The 7th Division then moved back into a reserve area just east of Büyük Anafarta for rest and reconstitution. The equally tired 12th Division remained in the line but it shifted to the north, compressing the length of its sector and allowing the 9th Division to move forward into the Scimitar Hill area. To the south, Esat Pasha's Northern Group took advantage of the lull in fighting to rearrange its command arrangements. Esat divided his front in half. He established a Right Wing Sector under Colonel Yakub Şevki, which controlled Mehmet Şefik's reinforced 19th Division (18 Regt, 27 Regt, 57 Regt and 72 Regt) and the detached 10 Regt and 12 Regt. Esat also established a Left Wing Sector with Colonel Rıfat in command of Lieutenant Colonel Abdürrezzak's 11th Division and Colonel Rüstü's 16th Division.

Recognizing that Mustafa Kemal might be experiencing

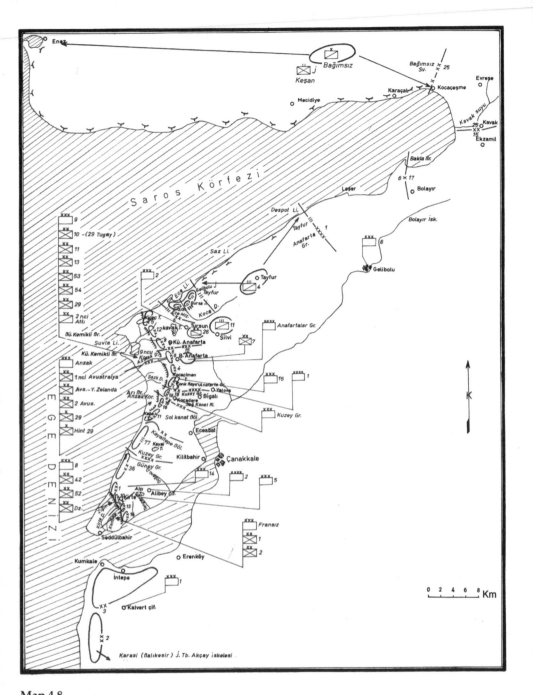

Map 4.8
Fifth Army forces general situation, 31 August 1915. The operational shrinkage of the Fifth
Army's area of responsibility is evident on this map as the First Army has assumed control of
the upper peninsula. The Fifth Army headquarters, located in Yalova, has been incorrectly
labeled as the First Army headquarters.

difficulty in command and control of an operational group containing over seven infantry divisions, Enver Pasha and Liman von Sanders decided to construct a conventional command architecture to assist him.[74] On 29 August, Colonel Nicolai was ordered to reform the II Corps headquarters and take command of the 5th, 9th and 12th Divisions and Colonel Ali Reza was ordered to reform the XV Corps headquarters and take command of the 4th, 6th and 8th Divisions.[75] The refitting 7th Division would remain as the Anafarta Group reserve along with the 26th Division and the battalions from the 3rd Division. This arrangement gave Kemal a group of two corps rather than a group of seven divisions. Brigadier General Fevzi was also assigned as Kemal's chief of staff. Additional strategic reinforcements were also arriving in the combat area. On 17 August Enver Pasha put the XVII Corps, comprising the 15th and 25th Infantry Divisions, on movement orders for the rail terminus at Uzunköprü. After detraining the 15th Division marched toward Saros Bay and began to arrive on 25 August and the 25th Division began to arrive four days later. As August ended the Ottoman army had over nineteen infantry divisions committed to the Gallipoli Campaign or about 40 percent of its forty-eight organized infantry divisions on strength as of 1 September 1915.[76] Map 4.8 shows the deployment of Ottoman forces in the combat zone at the end of August 1915.

On 4 September Enver advised the Fifth Army that he had intelligence that over 77,000 Italian soldiers were poised at Brindisi, Naples and Rhodes to invade the Gallipoli Peninsula. This set off another round of movements in which the 2nd Division was moved to Erenkoy and the 20th Infantry Division from Izmir (Smyrna) ordered north to reinforce the XVII Corps at Saros Bay. Two cavalry brigades and three independent cavalry regiments were deployed to the area from the capital as well. The campaign seemed to have no limits on the demands it placed on the Ottoman force structure. On the plus side for the Turks, the imminent collapse of Serbia offered the prospect of reopening the rail lines between Germany and the Ottoman Empire. In anticipation of this event enabling artillery and ammunition to be sent to the hard-pressed Turks, the German general staff sent Colonel Gressman, an artillery specialist from the

Western Front, to the Fifth Army to advise Liman von Sanders on the most current artillery tactics.[77] Ottoman casualties also dropped significantly in September as combat operations slowed to an overall combat death rate of 300 men per month; however, the number of men admitted to hospital for sickness was increasing. Overall Ottoman strength committed to the campaign in September 1915 stood at 5,282 officers and 255,728 men.[78]

No invasion materialized and, moreover, rumors began circulating that the British intended to evacuate the peninsula or draw down their forces there. Thus, as winter approached, Enver Pasha decided to pull significant forces back into Thrace where they could be more easily sustained. On 6 October he notified the Fifth Army that he intended to reconstitute the Second Army in Constantinople and assign three infantry corps to it.[79] Vehip was ordered to return to the capital with part of his Southern Group staff to begin the process of reconstitution. The infantry corps would be removed from the peninsula in three groups and sent north. The first group included the I Corps headquarters and the 3rd and 2nd Divisions, which departed for Uzunköprü on 8 and 11 October respectively. The II Corps headquarters departed on 16 October with the 4th Division for Keşan and the 13th Division followed on 21 October. The V Corps headquarters with the 5th and 10th Divisions left the following week. Enver remained concerned about the possibility of an allied offensive and he sent more fresh forces to the area alerting the 42nd Infantry Division in Smyrna (Izmir) and the 136th Infantry Regiment in Constantinople for service on the peninsula.

At Cape Helles on 9 October, Vehip Pasha departed and was replaced by XIV Corps commander, Brigadier General Cevat, as the Southern Group commander. On the Anafarta front, Kemal's men spent the month reinforcing their trenches and building strong points with overhead cover. A number of individual replacements arrived from Aleppo and it became possible to pull men out of the front lines to conduct much-needed training on weapons and tactics. On 21 October the 15th Division went into the line at Cape Helles to relieve the 13th Division, which went to Keşan for rest and reconstitution. Because of tactical disasters occurring in far away Mesopotamia, the Ottoman general staff asked Field Marshal von der Goltz to take over that theater. As he departed, Enver Pasha appointed Northern Group commander, Esat Pasha, as the new First Army commander. Replacing Esat in the Northern Group was XV Corps commander, Colonel Ali Reza from the Anafarta Group. The incoming 42nd Division went by train from Smyrna to Bandirma then by ferry to Gallipoli, arriving on 22 October. Replacing the II Corps in the Anafarta Group, Colonel Kannengiesser returned and reformed the XVI Corps headquarters on 27 October. Finally, the 11th Division was reformed to take the place in line of the departing 5th Division and, for the first and only time in the Gallipoli campaign, the Turks formed a provisional infantry division. This was a common tactical practice for the Ottoman army in the Balkan Wars and in other theaters in the First World War but was hitherto not seen on the peninsula. This unit was made up of miscellaneous infantry regiments and was activated as the 5th Provisional Division. It was assigned to the southern-most part of the Northern Group's area near Gaba Tepe.[80] Combat in October remained stable and light and was characterized by bombing raids and sniping. As a possible way to break the dead-lock, the Ottoman general staff organized the 254th Tunnelling Company and sent it to the peninsula.[81] Ottoman strength committed to the campaign peaked in October 1915 at 5,500 officers and 310,000 men.[82]

Important reinforcements arrived at the Uzunköprü rail terminus from northern Europe on 9 and 10 November. These were a motorized battery of Austrian 240mm mortars and a battery of 150m howitzers. The heavy mortars went to the Anafarta Group, while the howitzers went to the Southern Group.[83] They were in action around 20 November and were used to pound Chocolate Hill. The long-expected arrival of heavy artillery from Germany and Austria caused allied morale to plummet immediately. By the end of the month two additional 210mm heavy mortar batteries and six heavy howitzer batteries arrived from Germany.[84] This gave the Turks a total of twenty heavy artillery batteries on the peninsula and, equally important, large quantities of ammunition began to arrive as well. The results were immediate and powerful as Colonel Gressman and the German artillery specialists began to organize Turkish gunners using the latest gunnery techniques from the

Western Front. The Germans also sent down several staff officers as technical advisors to assist the Turks on the employment of the newset combat methods in use on the Western Front as well. These officers were also specialists on the latest tactics utilized by the British Army in France. These officers were Colonel von Bercut, Lieutenant Colonel Klemet and Major Kutes and they were followed quickly by engineering specialists. The appearance of German heavy artillery, ammunition and technical specialists on the Gallipoli Peninsula signalled the end of the campaign for the British. With winter fast approaching and the Turks still in possession of the high ground the opportunity to conclude the campaign successfully had passed.

In fact, the British had already decided (on 7 December) to withdraw from Suvla Bay and Anzac but retain the Cape Helles position for the time being. This difficult decision was the result of not only the German heavy artillery and the abysmal position but also other factors such as the severe Mediterranean storms in November that had destroyed many of the landing piers and an unseasonably severe snow blizzard that produced frost bite and hypothermia injuries in the hundreds. The Australian and British evacuation was exceptionally well planned and completed on the night of 19/20 December. The Turks were surprised by the evacuation and were in no condition to exploit the situation. The first news of it reached the Fifth Army headquarters at 4 am, 20 December when Staff Captain Ali Remzi, a staff officer in the operations division, received a call from the Northern group's staff duty officer.[85] An excited Ali Remzi notified the army chief of staff, Lieutenant Colonel Kazım, who cautiously instructed the captain to double check the reports. Finally they woke up Liman von Sanders, who immediately authorized an advance to the beaches. One individual who was not on hand to witness the victory was the tireless Colonel Mustafa Kemal, who had become exhausted and sick and had been evacuated to hospital in Constantinople on 10 December (he was replaced as Anafarta Group commander by V Corps commander, Colonel Fevzi Pasha). It is very possible that had Kemal remained active in his position that the evacuation might have been discovered and exploited.[86]

Encouraged by the success of the evacuation the British

decided on 24 December to evacuate the Cape Helles position as well. The well-conceived evacuation plan that had worked so well at Suvla and Anzac was tailored and reworked for conditions at Cape Helles. Now alert to what the allies might try, Liman von Sanders instructed his staff to begin work on an attack plan to wipe out the evacuation as it began to unfold. The plan involved an attack employing four to eight divisions using the latest tactical methods from the Western Front.[87] German officers were sent down from the Second Army headquarters in Thrace to assist the Fifth Army planners. Liman von Sanders briefed Enver Pasha on the plan as it evolved and received approval to carry it out. The story of the final battle is told well in English by both Aspinall-Oglander and Liman von Sanders. The Turks worked hard to draw the plan together quickly and brought the 12th Division from Anafarta to the Cape Helles front where it began intensive assault training. On 7 January 1916, the Southern Group launched the 12th Division, now lavishly supported by artillery, against the British 13th Division on Gully Spur. Two mines were exploded under the British trenches immediately followed by a violent artillery bombardment starting at 4 pm that shook the British. But they fought back hard and handily repulsed the Turks, who appeared to not be particularly enthusiastic about the attack.[88] The Turks attributed the failure to the existence of strong points in the trench system and also the effectiveness of naval gunfire support. The stalwart British defense served to convince the Southern Group that the enemy was still active defending the Cape Helles lines. As a result they almost missed the second evacuation, which took place the very next night (8/9 January 1916). In places the Turks pushed forward when their fire was not returned and there were some minor skirmishes as the British conducted an evacuation partly under fire. Nevertheless, the last man got off successfully at 3.45 am completing the evacuation. The campaign was over.

The withdrawal of the Ottoman Fifth Army, 9–20 January 1916

Liman von Sanders notified Enver Pasha by telegraph at 8.45 am, 9 January that 'God be thanked, the entire Gallipoli peninsula has been cleansed of the enemy.'[89] The Fifth Army commander immediately followed this with a congratulatory order to his troops lauding their achievements and promising to get them off the peninsula as soon as possible.[90] The orders also specified the units that would remain behind to guard the peninsula against any future allied invasions. And, in fact, Liman von Sanders was as good as his word and began to redeploy his divisions immediately.

Table 4.1
Redeployment of Fifth Army Units, 9–20 January 1916

Unit	*Departure from the Peninsula*
III Corps (Brigadier General Ali Reza)	
7th Division	15 January 1916
8th Division	13 January 1916
9th Division	14 January 1916
XV Corps (Colonel Şevki)	
19th Division	19 January 1916
20th Division	20 January 1916
XVI Corps (Colonel Kannengiesser)	
11th Division	9 January 1916
12th Division	16 January 1916
XVII Corps (Colonel Back)	
15th Division	18 January 1916
16th Division	17 January 1916
Unassigned to a corps	
1st Division	12 January 1916
14th Division	11 January 1916

Source: T.C. Genelkurmay Başkanlığı, *Çanakkale Cephesi Harekati (Haziran 1915–Ocak 1916)*, p. 502.

Most of these divisions were sent up into Thrace to such pre-war garrison towns as Edirne (Adrianople), Çorlu and Pinarhisar where they could be easily resupplied and refitted. Liman von Sanders himself and his chief of staff, Colonel Kazım, left their headquarters at Yalova at 9.30 pm, 15 January 1916 by road to

Uzunköprü to catch the train to Constantinople. The Fifth Army headquarters and staff moved to Akbaş Pier where they took a steamer named the *Akdeniz* to Constantinople at 8 pm, 18 January 1916. Remaining behind to garrison the peninsula was a truncated army named the Gallipoli Group Command (*Çanakkale Grubu Komutanlığı*) commanded by Brigadier General Cevat Pasha. The new command was composed of the VI Corps (24th and 26th Divisions) and the XIV Corps (25th and 42nd Divisions) as well as a cavalry regiment, an independent infantry regiment, four Jandarma battalions and two independent artillery battalions. The heavy artillery was left in place and then moved out later to active theaters of war. The peninsula was never attacked again.

After action considerations

The fourth phase of the Ottoman campaign for Gallipoli was defensive and can be characterized as reactive in nature. The Turks were poised and ready to receive Hamilton's second amphibious assault and reacted coherently and violently. Once again the Ottoman army's superb reporting system enabled Liman von Sanders rapidly to release his reserves and to shift forces from sectors that were not under attack. The army's resilient command structure, which was built around common institutional doctrines and the flexible regimental structure, was again able to build ad hoc combat groups rapidly at decisive points. Ottoman and German commanders seemed to be essentially interchangable parts in an effective machine. On the defensive, the Fifth Army proved to be almost an immovable object that could not be ejected from ground that it chose to hold.

The crippling losses aside, there were several important outcomes of the Gallipoli campaign for the Ottoman Empire. Most importantly a cadre of seasoned commanders emerged, who would go on to bedevil the British for the next three years in Palestine and Mesopoamia. These men continued to serve and later, in the Turkish War of Independence (1919–1922), the majority of the nationalist army's senior commanders had served in command assignments on the peninsula. In fact, in that army led by Mustafa Kemal, except for Lieutenant General

Nurettin Pasha, every senior army and corps commander had served personally with Kemal at Gallipoli (see Appendix E: Gallipoli Commanders in the War of Independence). Likewise, a body of seasoned combat divisions also emerged from the campaign that would act as a sort of fire brigade for Enver Pasha's strategic projects and the British would meet many of the Gallipoli divisions again in Palestine and Mesopotamia. Finally, the victory at Gallipoli in January 1916, combined with the victory at Kut al Amara in April 1916, renewed the commitment of the Young Turk triumvirate to maintaining the Ottoman Empire's commitment to the war. It may be said that rather than shorten the war, in the end, the Gallipoli campaign prolonged it.

Chapter 5
The Fifth Army Rear Area

Introduction

An important combat multiplier for the 1Fifth Army in the Gallipoli campaign was the geographic location of the peninsula in southern Thrace and its proximity to Constantinople. The empire's capital region was densely populated, had excellent communications networks and highly productive industry and agriculture (at least in comparison with the more distant theaters of Palestine, Mesopotamia and Caucasia). This endowed the Ottoman general staff with the capability to replenish and reinforce the Fifth Army on a scale unseen in any of the Turkish theaters in the First World War. Moreover, the mobilization and concentration plan of 1914 delivered the bulk of the field army to Thrace for operations against Bulgaria and Greece. In fact the plans sent seven of thirteen army corps on strength in September 1914 to Thrace. This was because the Ottoman Empire expected the 'next war' to be a repeat of the Balkan Wars. Instead, it found itself at war with the Entente in places like Basra, the Sinai Peninsula and the Caucasian mountains where it was terribly mismatched against its opponents. Meanwhile, the forces in Thrace sat idle but trained constantly and achieved higher degrees of combat effectiveness. While this imposed great penalties on the commanders fighting on the active fronts, the concentration plan served to create a strategic reserve that was ideally placed to reinforce the Gallipoli front in the spring of 1915.

Very little is known in the western world of the Ottoman army's twentieth-century logistics and administration doctrines and procedures. This chapter attempts to correct that by examining the Fifth Army's Rear Area and its service-support architecture and structure. Unlike nineteenth-century armies, twentieth-century armies did not have a discrete rear edge (for wont of a better term) of the organization and the rear parts of the combat forces merged into a large zone that was full of field hospitals and veterinary stations, magazines and ammunition dumps, food and supply depots, field bakeries and postal companies and all manner of service-support facilities needed to keep the combat troops supplied and fighting. This part of the Fifth Army was called its Rear Area and was organized on rational principles laid down by the German army in its doctrines and procedures.

The Fifth Army staff and doctrinal standardization

When Liman von Sanders arrived on the Gallipoli peninsula, he brought part of the Ottoman First Army staff with him to form the nucleus of the new Fifth Army staff. His new staff grew quickly and he must have been comfortable with its operations since the Ottoman army staff system was nearly an exact copy of the German staff system and employed numbered staff sections that mirrored the staff divisions of the higher level Ottoman general staff (itself modelled on the German general staff).[1] The Fifth Army staff was administered by a chief of staff, Staff Lieutenant Colonel Kazım (later Kazım Inanç, 1880–1938), who remained in this position for the duration of the campaign. Lieutenant Colonel Kazım was ideally suited for this critical staff appointment under Liman von Sanders partly because he spoke fluent German.[2] More importantly, Kazım graduated from the Ottoman War Academy in 1902 and was appointed to the elite general staff officer corps. He served immediately thereafter in the general staff's operations directorate. This was followed by two command tours in infantry battalions. On 20 March 1911, Kazım was sent to Germany for a one-year training tour with the German army. When he returned he served as a corps chief of operations, a field army chief of logistics in the Balkan Wars and as the general staff chief of intelligence. When war broke out he was serving as the First Army chief of operations but moved up to chief of staff on 12 February 1915. It is hard to imagine a more-qualified or experienced general staff officer to fill the critical post of Fifth Army chief of staff.

Of the Fifth Army staff directorates, the first among equals (as it was also in the German army) was Operations (1st Section) followed by Intelligence (2nd Section). The other sections were:

Lines of communications and supply (3rd section), Personnel (4th Section), Medical services (5th Section), Veterinary services (6th section), Munitions (7th Section), Telegraph and telephone services (8th section), Postal services (9th section), Judge Advocate (10th Section) and the Documents and records services (11th section). Additionally, there were two unnumbered offices that had tactical functions dealing with the fielding, maintenance and operations of combats arms; these were: the chief of artillery and the chief of engineers. The entire physical overhead of the headquarters was the responsibility of a headquarters commandant, who in addition to billeting and messing the staff, had an infantry company for protection and a cavalry troop for escorts. The Ottoman army staffs appeared German because they were directly copied from the German army, which had a military mission in the empire since 1882. The Ottoman conscription and reserve system in use until late 1913 was also patterned after the German model that had been so successful against the French in 1870–1871. The Ottoman general staff was a duplicate of the German general staff, as were the selection criteria and curriculum of the Ottoman War Academy. Moreover, the War Academy, as well as the tactical and branch schools of the army, used German Army manuals (translated into Ottoman Turkish) in its instruction.[3] The Ottoman army also conducted annual maneuvres and exercises using German methods and procedures.

Doctrines and the orders process were also based on direct translations of German originals, which made operations in the Ottoman army remarkably standardized. The Ottoman general staff moved off this model somewhat as a result of reform efforts after the disastrous Balkan Wars. The army's tactical posture hinged on General Orders Number 1 issued by Enver Pasha on 14 March 1914, which contained detailed guidance for the conduct of army troop and unit training at the tactical level.[4] The first section of the order dealt with the imperative to exercise direct leadership from the front. Section two dealt with tactical instructions for moving from march columns rapidly into combat formations, offensive operations and immediate counterattacks, defensive operations including rapid entrenching, integration of machine-guns and the development of effective artillery fire support. These measures were integrated immediately into the training of the army and demonstrated an institutional willingness to address problems in a meaningful way.[5] Significantly, General Orders Number 1 showcased a newly found awareness by the Ottoman army of the importance of firepower by stressing the imperative of quickly establishing combined arms fire superiority over the enemy. The army's operational posture continued to rest on German doctrines that focused on offensive operations aimed at the destruction of the enemy (ideally by campaigns of encirclement).

The tactical operations orders used by the army continued in the German five-paragraph format that was a model of clarity (situation, mission, execution, coordination and service support). This was supplemented on 24 May 1914 by additional general orders that contained comprehensive instructions for the writing and formatting of war diaries (*Harp Ceridesi*).[6] The orders also contained a list of the units required to maintain war diaries. The format was standardized into seven sections covering organization and signals; orders, reports and operations; missions; logistics; personnel and animals; special trials and experiments; and special instructions. The war diaries were classified as secret documents, and were opened and closed for operations or at the end of each calendar quarter. Completed war diaries were sent quarterly to the Ottoman General Staff.[7] At the same time, the formats of written battle reports and situation reports were standardized in the Ottoman Army's Instructions for Field Service (*Hidemati-ı Seferiye Talimnamesine*).[8] Spot reports also followed a specified format but could be either oral or written.

The Ottoman army's maps of the peninsula were generally accurate and had been surveyed by the army's ordnance-survey section and printed in the general staff's printing house. The maps used in the opening phase of the Gallipoli campaign were pre-war products that were updated in the spring of 1915. In early May 1915, new maps were issued using the scale of 1:25,000.[9] The maps were issued as sets composed of seven individual map sheets and were initially issued only down to battalion-commander level. Mustafa Kemal's instructions to his regimental and battalion commanders concerning the issue of the new maps specified that they were not to fall into enemy hands and that officers travelling near the front should only carry the map section of the area they were located in (rather than the entire set of seven map sheets).[10] Kemal further specified that the new maps were not to be taken forward during attacks. However, it did not take very long for the new Ottoman maps to fall into enemy hands. C.E.W. Bean reported that on 19 May a map of Baby 700 was recovered from a mortally wounded Ottoman officer lying in a trench near the Nek. The captured Ottoman maps were sent to the Survey Office in Egypt and enlarged to a scale of 1:20,000, overprinted with grid squares and then issued to Australian and British units. On 7 August, Şefik's 27 Regt recaptured a trench with some dead enemy soldiers in it and recovered some of the British 1:20,000 maps.[11] According to Şefik the Turks were especially impressed by the system of grid lines that divided the British maps into squares that facilitated the targeting of artillery.

Organizational standardization also came in the form of the Ottoman army's unique triangular infantry division.[12] In 1911, the Turks decided to reduce their standard square infantry division comprising two brigades of two infantry regiments each down to a triangular division of three infantry regiments. The new triangular structure mirrored their new corps structure and was a dramatic breakthrough in tactical organization. Under this arrangement the number of infantry battalions in an infantry division was reduced from sixteen to nine. This was a remarkably prescient decision. In the static trench-warfare environment of the First World War the large four-regiment infantry division proved to be extremely unwieldy and organizationally unsuited to tactical requirements. The German army would be the first European army to begin converting its four-regiment divisions to the Turkish model in 1915. The Turkish model enabled an infantry division to maintain two regiments 'up front' and one regiment 'back' (in reserve), which proved to be the ideal organizational solution to the tactical requirements of trench warfare. Every major combatant European army would change its organizational structure to this model by 1918. This organizational model enabled the Turks to cross-attach regiments at will to task organize their forces for combat operations, a process that was greatly enhanced by commanders and staffs at all levels who thought in the same doctrinal framework.

Fifth Army logistics

The Ottoman army of 1914 patterned itself, its doctrines, its operational thought and its approach to war on the German army, which had a military assistance mission in the empire since 1882. Logistically the Ottomans mirrored the German army in separating their operational field armies from supporting logistics infrastructure by creating lines of communications inspectorates (LoCIs) upon mobilization.[13] These 'formed the conveyor of the army' and were 'the middleman between home and army'.[14] In doctrinal terms, the LoCIs were a service-support organization (as opposed to a combat or combat-support formation) and had no intrinsic combat capabilities. This system enabled combat commanders at the front to focus their energy on operational and tactical matters while logisticians handled supply matters. This was all done according to the doctrines and procedures set forth in the army's Lines of Communications and Services Regulations (*Menzil Hidematı Nizamnamesi*) published in 1911. As its capstone logistics command element the Ottoman general staff activated the General Lines of Communications Inspectorate (*Menzil Genel Müfettisliği*) on 5 August 1914 in Constantinople. This organization exercised command authority over the logistical lifelines of the empire at the strategic level.[15] High-level logistical planning and coordination remained a function of the general staff's Fourth Division, while the GLC Inspectorate coordinated daily movements and logistical functions through lower level subordinate numbered army inspectorate commands.[16] In the Gallipoli campaign, the Fifth Army Lines of Communications Inspectorate (*5nci Ordu Menzil Müfettisliği*, hereafter referred to as 5 LoCI) supported Liman von Sanders' army on the peninsula. The 5 LoCI headquarters became operational on 27 March 1915 in the town of Gallipoli using officers brought down from the Ottoman First Army and general staff. Map 5.1 shows the logistical and administrative establishment in the strait area and on the peninsula at the end of August 1915.

The 5 LoCI had an array of subordinate units that provided for the needs of the army and distributed the supplies necessary for continued combat operations.[17] These subordanate units were consolidated into the hands of commanders called post or node

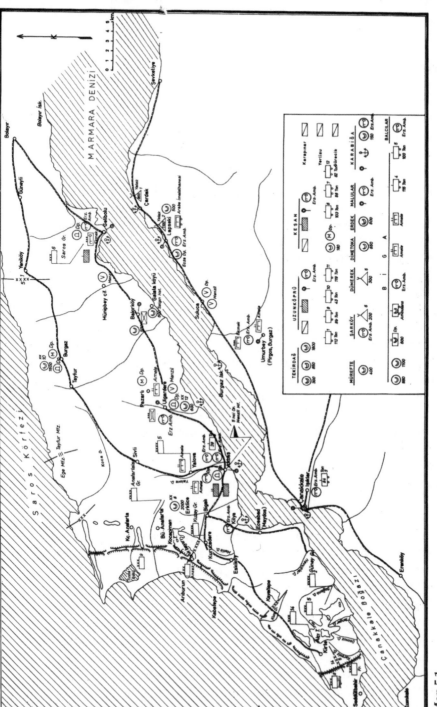

Map 5.1
Fifth Army area lines of communications, 31 August 1915. The Ottoman logistical complex mirrored contemporary German doctrines and moved supplies and ammunition forward while moving casualties back. The field hospital symbols (a circle with a crescent inside) show bed capacity. Facilities in towns not on the map are shown in the inset box (Tekirdağ, for example, has three hospitals with bed capacities of 300, 850 and 1,600 respectively).

commanders (*nokta komutanlıkları*), who were located in Uzunköprü, Keşan, Gallipoli, Bayırkoy, Ilgardere, Akbaş, Biga, Karabiga, Malular, Lapseki, Burgaz and Çanakkale. Because of the importance of sea transport in supplying the peninsula, a unique additional command post was created known as pier commander (*iskele komutanlıkları*), responsible for the port operations at the critical piers and docks servicing the army. These were located at Çardak, Gallipoli, Ilgardere, Akbaş, Kilya, Karabiga, Lapseki, Burgaz and Çanakkale. These commanders controlled twelve distribution centers to move supplies from grainery and food warehouses in Gallipoli aand Burgaz. Bread was baked by bakery platoons in five central locations and similarly distributed. The supplies were moved to the forward infantry divisions by ten transport columns. Aditionally there were two specialist ammunition columns which delivered shells and other munitions. There was even a bridging company on hand if needed. By September 1915, the 5 LoCI had 765 officers, 27,378 men and 12,851 animals (including oxen, draft horses, camels, mules and donkeys) assigned to its rolls.[18]

Because of its proximity to the large peacetime garrison cities of Edirne (Adrianople), Luleburgaz and Constantinople, the 5 LoCI did not have to keep large amounts of supplies on hand (as did, for example, the Ottoman Third Army in remote Caucasia). During the course of the campaign the lines of communications structure mainained about thirteen days of fresh food products and about forty days of non-perishables on hand in its systems of depots.[19] Fresh fruit and vegetables were available on a seasonal basis but proved difficult to get up to the troops in the trenches on a regular schedule. Ottoman soldiers were authorized daily rations totalling 3,149 calories in the amount of, or equivalent to, 900g bread, 250g meat, 150g bulgar, 20g olive oil and 20g salt (as well as 9g of soap).[20] Animals were, likewise, authorized a daily combination of fodder, feed and grains in the average amount of 10–11kg depending on the type and size of the animal.[21] Although the animals could be pastured, they quickly consumed such natural fodder as existed on the peninsula and thus their rations had to be brought in like the soldier's rations. All of this came by rail to Uzunköprü or by ship to the piers on the strait and then loaded by men into animal-drawn carts and wagons and moved forward. As the men and animals consumed a daily ration at a fixed rate the amounts required were tallied by staff officers to a matrixed requirements schedule, in effect, while the movement itself was difficult to accomplish the planning was highly predictable. Ammunition, on the other hand, was highly unpredictable and requirements were based on consumption which could vary wildly during periods of quiet or raging battle. The main problem for the Ottoman army in munitions was overall scarcity rather than delivery.

The Ottoman army replacement system

The Ottoman army's replacement system was modeled on the German wehrkreis system of peacetime corps areas that conscripted men twice annually. In wartime the corps headquarters and divisions deployed to their wartime stations leaving numbered corps military districts (*kolordu askeralma bölgesi*) behind to manage conscription. The annual input of fit Ottoman men available ran to about 100,000, of which about 35,000 came from the corps areas that normally serviced western parts of the empire. The corps military districts that fed the Fifth Army during the campaign were: I Corps Military District in Ankara, II Corps Military District in Constantinople, III Corps Military District in Bandirma and the IV Corps Military District in Smyrna. At the beginning of the Gallipoli Campaign the infantry divisions of the Fifth Army were maintained at full strength; likewise, reinforcements sent to the peninsula were at full strength. But as trench warfare ground down these Ottoman formations, they were worn down to shells of their original strength. To compensate for this, the Ottoman army had a replacement and training system that periodically infused the combat divisions with freshly trained officers and men.

The Ottoman army's training and replacement system functioned well at this point in the war and in this locale.[22] Recruits and draftees were sent to training centers (*Eğitim Merkezleri*) for six weeks of basic training. There they were organized and received training classes (*sınıf eğitim*) under the supervision of sergeants. The Fifth Army received its replacements from the 3rd Training Center in Davutpaşa, the 7th Training Center in Konya, the 8th Training Center in Eskişehir and the 9th Training

Center in Adapazara. After the completion of training, the men were shipped to depot regiments (*depo alay*) for the fitting of uniforms, medical checks and treatment and a further fifteen days of tactical training. The Ottoman army's depot regiments were branch specific and servicing the Fifth Army there were six infantry depot regiments in Ankara, Manisa, Konya, Bursa, Smyrna and Yeşilköy (San Stefano), and two cavalry depot regiments at Yildiz and Bandirma. Additionally, there was an engineer depot battalion at Haskoy, two heavy artillery depot battalions at Hadimkoy and Taksim, three infantry depot battalions at Tekirdağ, Eskişehir and Erenkoy and a cavalry depot battalion at Bandirma. The number of men in a depot battalion could reach 1,000 (or 3,000 in a depot regiment) but rarely reached several hundred at any given time. Once the men were certified as fully trained the corps military districts made arrangements to ship them to the combat zone. Many of the replacements for the peninsula were shipped by sea to either Gallipoli or Tekirdağ by way of the II and IV Corps Military Districts. Others came by way of the Uzunköprü–Keşan road.

Training in the depot regiments was physically harsh and very demanding. The American army attaché in Constantinople was a frequent observer of the local training centers. He noted that corporal punishment was common and observed instances of Turkish officers and NCOs slapping and punching recruits who were sloppy in drills.[23] He also observed that the recruits were pressed hard, training hours were long, included much physical exercise and that 'it is really surprising what a great difference is made in a short time in these slouchy peasant recruits.'[24] Running was an integral part of the training regime and recruits who could not keep up were sometimes struck with leather belts to spur them on.[25] Otherwise, 'the school of the soldier' training in the Ottoman army was similar to that of other armies and included bayonet drill, first aid and rifle marksmanship.[26]

The Ottoman replacement system was originally designed to provide regimentally trained men to specific army regiments but in the First World War it rapidly became a 'pipeline system'. In this sense, the Ottoman army's wartime system functioned more like the American army system used during the Second World War rather than the British system of regimentally trained men, who were sent to regiments from their home counties and towns. In the Ottoman and American systems the system provided a stream of trained men to the units that needed them the most. During the Gallipoli campaign the system worked efficiently and provided men where they were needed on a real time basis. Casualties at battalion level frequently ran into the hundreds of killed and wounded, especially during offensive operations. The army's replacement system then responded by filling the vacant ranks. The case of the 48 Regt is illustrative of this. In a night attack on 18/19 May 1915, the regiment lost 311 men killed, 477 men wounded and 319 men missing (out of total assigned strength of about 3,500 soldiers).[27] The regiment continued to take casualties from artillery fire during the following weeks as well. On 28 June 1915, the regiment received 331 trained and 84 untrained replacements, for a net loss of some 700 men.[28] In a letter to his father after the early May night attacks, Staff Lieutenant Colonel Fahrettin, the III Corps chief of staff, noted that some battalions were reduced to 2 officers and 200 men. However, he noted that replacements were on the way to bring the battalions back up to strength.[29] Fahrettin also wrote that without the timely arrival of replacements within three days of the initial landings (25 April) the strait would have been lost.

For more effective examples of the success of the Ottoman army's replacement system it is necessary to examine some of the combat divisions that took very heavy casualties in the battles of April–June 1915 and were physically pulled back for formal reconstitution. One of the original Fifth Army infantry divisions was the 3rd Division, which fought the French at Kum Kale on 25 April and then was transferred by regiments to the peninsula. By early June 1915, the 3rd Divison was pulled out of the line to reconstitute behind Achi Baba and was then sent back to Kum Kale on the Asian side on 10 June.[30] After a period of training the division returned to the peninsula with two regiments to participate in the attack on Cape Helles scheduled for 5 July. Strength returns from the 3rd Division show it returned to combat with its infantry at full authorized strength with six infantry battalions fielding an average of 1,050 officers and men each.[31] The 5th Infantry Division, which also participated in the 5 July attack, had been reconstituted by the replacement system to nearly full strength as well. The 5th Division, which had not had quite as long a period out of the line, averaged 11 officers and 973 men per infantry battalion (the 3rd Division averaged 13 officers and 1,038 men per infantry battalion).[32]

The 5 July attack was a bloody failure and the 3rd Division lost 8 officers and 1,393 men killed, 26 officers and 1,555 men wounded and had 226 men missing for a total butcher's bill of 3,208 casualties (or a casualty rate of almost 50 percent).[33] The 5th Division lost a total of 1,843 killed, wounded and missing in the attack as well. Additionally, the Southern Group incurred another 10,858 casualties during the period 28 June through 5 July 1915, making overall casualties in excess of 16,000 for a single week (this does not include any casualties from the Northern Group at Anzac).[34] Needless to say, casualties on this scale far exceeded the normal replacement system capacity needed to reconstitute these formations and the divisions involved in the attacks of early July 1915 took months to be rebuilt.

Medical support and morale

The Ottoman army maintained a surprisingly robust medical system in the Fifth Army Rear Area.[35] Each infantry division had an organic medical company as well as a field hospital. Every Ottoman army corps also had an assigned field hospital. Behind these forward facilities, there were 22 area hospitals in the towns of southern Thrace, the capacity of which was an astonishing 11,080 beds (manned by 4,006 doctors, nurses and orderlies).[36] Moreover, there were 4 Constantinople ferryboats (Numbers 60, 61, 63 and 70) converted for casualty evacuation as well as 2 hospital ships (the *Akdeniz* and the *Gülnihal*) with an additional 1,600 beds altogether. Medical supply depots completed the system of support for the army's wounded and sick by providing supplies and medicines. Backing up these assets were the civilian and military hospitals in Constantinople, which had an additional capacity of over 10,000 beds. While medical care was, by British standards, somewhat primitive it was comprehensive and hygienic. The American army attaché estimated that by 3 May 1915 about 7,000 wounded men had been brought to the capital city's hospitals and were being adequately cared for.[37]

Getting into the medical evacuation system and off the peninsula could be difficult. The memoirs of Lieutenant Colonel Cemil
(later Cemil Conk, commander of the 4th Division at Sari Bair),
the commander of the 36 Regt, describe the procedures.[38] He was
seriously wounded in the mid-afternoon of 24 June 1915 and he
was taken from the trenches to his regimental headquarters at
4 pm where his wounds were treated by a doctor. He was able to
telephone his own divison headquarters and transferred
command of his regiment to the 34 Regt commander, Major
Yümnü. At 9 pm, Cemil was taken to the 12th Medical Company
operating in a covered position in the Soğanlıdere (a valley
behind the lines) where about 12.30 am (25 June) he was examined by the medical company commander, Captain Hamdi, and
the 2nd Division's chief surgeon, Ziya Bey. They decided that the
correct course of action was to evacuate the patient. Cemil's
memoirs note that he 'was treated like a guest.' At 11 am he left
the medical company by ambulance and was taken to the Field
Hospital for the Wounded (*Seyyar Yaralılar Hastahanesi*), which
was the 2nd Division's organic hospital. At the field hospital
Cemil was examined by the 71 Regt chief medical officer, Doctor
Moiz Bey (Moishe Bey) and several Jewish orderlies and logged
into the Ottoman medical system.[39] Since he had not eaten in
24 hours he was given some yogurt and conserves for lunch. In
the early afternoon, his belongings, which had been forwarded
from his regimental headquarters, arrived. At 3 pm, the hospital
staff told him he would be taken to Akbaş pier for transport to
Constantinople.

Cemil was taken down the Değirmendere Spur to await Ferry
Number 60 from Çanakkale but because of allied naval gunfire
from Saros Bay that routinely fell on the pier the loading of
260 wounded men was halted at 5.45 pm. Nevertheless, the ship
was loaded at 6.30 pm. The volunteer orderlies then fed every
soldier aboard a large hot meal that consisted of chicken soup,
bread, meat and beans, pilav and baklava, after which pistachio
nuts were given out as treats. There were two doctors on board
to tend to the wounded men. At 4 am, 26 June 1915, the ship left
the pier bound for Karabiga, at which they arrived at 11 am and
where they received more food. The voyage across the Sea of
Marmara was harrowing because, in spite of flying a large Red

Crescent flag, the sailors were fearful of being torpedoed by British submarines. The ship then departed for Ereğli, arriving there at 8.15 am on 27 June, and from there Cemil was taken to Silivri where he waited less than 2 hours for a train. During this brief time two of the wounded men died. At 4.45 pm Cemil arrived at Sirkeci station where a waiting ambulance took him to the Etfal Hospital in Şişli (a Constantinople neighborhood just north of Taksım Square). Cemil's recovery from his wounds took eighteen days and on July 15 the doctors pronounced him fit for duty. Several days later he reported to the Ministry of War where he was told that he was to be assigned as the commander of the 4th Division on the Gallipoli peninsula. In a subsequent meeting, Enver Pasha told him of his secret plans to wipe out the allied lodgement on Cape Helles. Cemil spent another week recovering his strength in the capital and departed for the peninsula on 28 July.

While Cemil's status as an officer and regimental commander likely got him a more rapid exit from the combat zone it is clear from his memoirs that the soldiers accompanying him also received excellent and compassionate care. Another officer, Lieutenant Colonel Abil, wrote in a letter to his father that the medical services were excellent and that no wounded were over-looked.[40] He described a system that took the wounded by stretcher to ambulances and thence to hospitals. The army reported the number of wounded men as 56,394 for the months of April, May and June 1915.[41] While the tempo of combat varied, during the first four months of the campaign the Fifth Army Army averaged about 300 men per day being sent back into the medical system.[42] On 28 July 1915, about 5 percent of the 250,818 soldiers of the Fifth Army were in hospital (11,788 men). Taking these numbers together about half of the wounded men must have been treated at divisional or corps medical companies and then returned to duty on the front. Unlike the British, who were affected by the unhygienic conditions of being compressed into overcrowded beachheads, the Turks did not seem to suffer excessively from sickness. According to the Turkish official history of the campaign, in operations from 25 April through 1 July 1915, the ratio of wounded to sick men in the Ottoman hospital system was about 24:1 (only 2,358 for the period April,

May and June 1915).[43] It is unclear why the ratio of wounded to sick was so lopsided, except to note that the Turks had abundant supplies of fresh water, adequate food and rest camps well beind the lines out of enemy artillery firing range. However, over the course of the campaign as the peninsula became very crowded, sanitary conditions deteriorated and the Turks ran short of imported medicines. The cold and wet winter accelerated the rates of men going sick. A modern Turkish scholar recently asserted that 28,009 men died from diseases in the Fifth Army hospitals in the calendar year 1915.[44] Although this seems like an unusually high number, the empire had lost over 100,000 men to diseases by January 1916 and, as the Fifth Army was the largest army fielded in that period, it would have also sustained proportionate deaths.[45] Overall, however, it appears that the Ottoman medical system, as it existed in close proximity to Constantinople, was able to provide (given the limitations of a largely primitive unindustrialized society) acceptable levels of medical care.

The idea is sometimes advanced that the Ottomans were poor record keepers. Nothing could be farther from the truth and, in fact, the Ottoman army maintained extensive and exhaustively complete records. Every soldier had a *kuniye,* or individual records and pay book, in which his important personal data was maintained, such as place of birth, next of kin, promotions, assignments and locations, training and pay matters. Most of these are kept today in the general staff's archives in Ankara, although the Turkish military academy archives maintain the registers and *kuniye* of their graduates. Much of the data was maintained also in regimental registers maintained by full-time clerks. So complete was the system of property accountability that in the absence of a *kuniye* it was possible to identify a dead body by tracking the serial number of the dead man's bayonet. During the Gallipoli campaign, the Ottoman army's reporting system accurately recorded a man's status and at the end of the campaign the army had a very accurate accounting of its casualties. Altogether the 128 war diaries from units that fought in the campaign held by the Fifth Army operations section recorded 213,882 casualties during the period 3 November 1914 through 9 January 1916. Unfortunately, the statistics listed in the Turkish official history only show Ottoman army casualties in the period

3 November 1914 through 19 December 1915, and do not record forty-nine days of naval casualties or the final twenty-one days of the campaign.

Table 5.1

Ottoman Army Casualties, Gallipoli Campaign

Period	——— Officers ———				——————— Men ———————					
	Dead	Wounded	Missing	Total	Dead	Wounded	Missing	Died Hospital	Weather Related	Total
3.11.1914 8.3.1915	8	2	0	10	97	125				222
25.4.1915 19.12.1915	587	1,016	27	1,630	56,048	95,989	11,151	18,746	8,307	190,241
Total	595	1,018	27	1,640	56,145	96,114	11,151	18,746	8,307	190,463

Source: T.C. Genelkurmay Başkanlığı, *Çanakkale Cephesi Harekati (Haziran 1915–Ocak 1916)*, Çizelge (Table) 4, p. 500.

Caring for the 80,000 animals on the peninsula was also a huge job requiring a system of veterinary detachments, animal hospitals and remount depots that mirrored its human counterpart. Very early in April 1915, the 5 LoCI opened its Fifth Army Animal Hospital in Rodosto for sick and wounded animals at Münipbeyçiftliği (Münip Bey's Farm).[46] As the campaign began and Fifth Army acquired more units and then more animal casualties, the 5 LoCI opened the 2nd Animal Hospital at Suluca and the 3rd Animal Hospital at Ilgardere. To provide service support for the animal force, the 5 LoCI opened an animal medicines depot at Suluca and three wagon and animal depots at Pazarlı, Burgaz and Keşan. It must also be noted that the animals required a huge amount of fodder and grains (in excess of 800,000kg per day).

In spite of the heavy casualties, the morale of the Turkish soldiers, in this time and place, was extremely high. Many Ottoman soldiers prayed with their regimental Imams before going into battle and the Imams then went forward with the men.[47] One Ottoman diary speaks of the visit of a *Hodja* (a wise and learned religious teacher) visiting the trenches of 7 Coy, 47 Regt where he delivered a sermon.[48] The *Hodja* returned two days later, while the trenches were under enemy artillery fire, to inspire the men by his personal example of touring the trenches. The importance of religion as a central aspect of Ottoman combat effectiveness is a unifying factor in the Turkish interviews of the Liddle Collection.[49] There were other factors at work as well. In the III Corps area, there was abundant fresh water, adequate rations and the divisional bands played every day. The small pleasures of tobacco, coffee and tea were easily available on the peninsula. Important to the morale of any soldier, Colonel Fahrettin noted that regular mail enabled families to send packets of supplies to soldiers at the front.[50] The diary of an Ottoman officer, who spent months in the trenches opposite the Australians at Lone Pine, mentions the same as well as the boost caused by the receipt of newspapers containing news of the war and home.[51] Living conditions for the Turks exceeded those of the Australians and British and many soldiers lived in roomy dug outs, roofed with planks and earth which included such amenities as shelves, tables, field telephones, cupboards and sometimes electric lights. Moreover, on a periodic basis units were pulled out of the line and sent back to rest camps some 10–15km out of the range of enemy artillery fire.[52]

Although problems with morale at Gallipoli were not mentioned as an issue in the modern Turkish official histories, there is a vignette from Colonel Fahrettin concerning the crew of the famous minelayer *Nuseyret*, which had been sent to the front to assist the army.[53] These sailors were posted to an Arab battalion and threatened to flee to the rear. Fahrettin claimed that 'three of them were shot which brought the others to their senses.'[54] The diary of Lieutenant Mehmed Fasih noted that several cases of desertion in an adjacent regiment were reported in the corps order of the day on 3 December 1915 and on the same day a man in Fasih's company went missing as well.[55] This incident caused great distress for the lieutenant and for his battalion commander, who launched a thorough investigation. The voice and tenor of Fasih's diary indicates that this was a great embarrassment to the battalion. It appears that desertion, at least in the controlled geographic conditions of a peninsula, does not appear to have been a significant problem for the Ottoman army at this point in the war.

Official communiqués

The Ottoman general headquarters released official communiqués on a frequent basis as the campaign increased in intensity. These were numbered sequentially and were typically short and written in a terse style. The official communiqué that announced the landings on the peninsula was number 6533, dated 27 April 1915, which described the allied lodgements at Ariburnu and Tekkeburnu (Anzac and Cape Helles).[56] This was followed by number 6534 the following day which outlined the fights at Gaba Tepe, Gully Ravine and the allied naval bombardments. Individual Royal Navy ships were often identified in the official communiqués (for example, HMS *Majestic* in number 6534). Of course, the civilian newspapers often carried the news earlier than the official communiqués and the communiqués real purpose was to serve the propagandistic interests of the Ottoman government by showcasing the army and navy's successes. The official communiqués were based on the Fifth Army's reports that flowed constantly into the Ottoman Ministry of War and general staff.

In June 1915, the intelligence section of the army headquarters sent a circular invitation to about thirty literati to visit the Gallipoli battlefields, including writers, poets and artists.[57] The invitation formed the Literary Delegation, whose task it would be to tour the battlefields and record their impressions in a variety of forms. The delegation met in Constantinople and departed for the peninsula on 11 July 1915. After a stop at Bulair the group went to Fifth Army headquarters where a group photograph was taken showing the delegation dressed in conventional khaki uniforms and the standard Ottoman army kabalak cap.[58] They were identified by a white brassard worn on their left arm with a double laurel-leaf symbol. The delegation spent twelve days in the headquarters, trenches, hospitals and cemeteries of the Fifth Army. On 16 July the group visited Esat Pasha's Northern Group headquarters. One of the delegation, poet Ibraham Alaettin (Gövsa), published his impressions in 1922 in book form which contained his famous poem *At the Tomb of Süleyman Pasha.*

Summary

Liman von Sanders' Fifth Army was, comparatively, the best-fed and best-supplied Ottoman field army in the First World War. This was a result of the army's proximity to the capital and its rich wealth of human and material resources. Adding to this was the huge pool of idle infantry divisons that had accumulated in Thrace as a result of the mobilization and concentration plan. As the Fifth Army went toe to toe with Ian Hamilton's Mediterranean Expeditionary Force it was able to maintain and increase its strength as the campaign evolved. For the Ottoman infantry divisions fighting on the peninsula, the Fifth Army's logistics architecture proved to be a combat multiplier that increased combat effectiveness. For their part, the Australians and British were well aware of the advantages that the Turks held in this regard and this hurt their morale. Reciprocally, the Turks knew that the allies lived and fought under worse conditions than they endured and this boosted their morale. Thus, in many ways, the Fifth Lines of Communications Inspectorate emerges from the campaign as a significant asset in the overall ability of the Ottomans to wage a successful campaign.

Appendix A
Ammunition Reports,
14 August 1914–18 March 1915

**Çanakkale Commander's Magazine Situation of the
2nd Artillery Brigade's Regiments, 14 August 1914**

| Formation | | *Total* | | | |
| | *Number* | *shells* | | *Selected types* | |
Weapon	*of guns*	*on hand*	*AP*	*HE*	*Capped*
3rd Regiment					
240/35 coastal	7	518	57	42	103
355/35 coastal	3	172	20	16	36
210/6.4 mortar	6	193			118
Heavy coastal	19	1,739			
Light	25	3,386			
4th Regiment					
240/35 coastal	6	474	51	36	88
355/35 coastal	2	117	14	11	24
210/6.4 mortar	8	308			
Heavy coastal	23	2,895			
Light	22	4,403			
5th Regiment					
240/35 coastal	4	456	41	22	59
Heavy coastal	13	1,223			
Light	6	2,635			
Fortress Command					
Depot magazines		5,616			

Notes
1. Weapons: shell diameter in mm/length of barrel in caliber, ex:
355/35 is a 355mm gun with a barrel 35 caliber in length.

Generally, higher caliber means longer barrels, which result in higher muzzle velocities (or more powerful guns). 240mm and 355mm guns of 35 caliber are listed separately. The category 'Heavy coastal' includes guns of 210/20, 210/22, 240/22, 260/22, 280/22 and 355/22. The category 'Light' includes guns of 150/46, 150/40, 87/24 and 57/40.

2. HE (High Explosive), AP (Armor Piercing) and Capped (Steel Capped) are shown by quantity since the official histories indicate that these types of shells were particularly effective against battleships. The remaining shell types were: solid shot, shrapnel, timed fuze and delayed fuze.

3. The types and quantities of shells in the depot magazines were unreported.

Source: T.C. Genelkurmay Başkanlığı, *Birinci Dünya Harbinde Türk Harbi, Vnci Cilt, Çanakkale Cephesi Harekati, Inci Kitap (Haziran 1914–25 Nisan 1915* (Ankara: Genelkurmay Başimevi, 1993), Chart 13.

Table A.2
Artillery Weapon Situation, 26 February 1915

Formation Weapon	Number of guns	Total shells on hand	Selected types HE	AP	Capped
8th Regiment					
150/108 howitzer	32	7,627	7,627		
210/6.4 mortar	10	602		86	171
3rd Regiment					
150/40 ship	5	462			
Smaller guns	18	2,076			
4th Regiment					
150/45 ship	12	147			
150/26 fixed	6	969			
210/6.4 mortar	4	20			
Smaller guns	18	6,737			

Notes
1. Ammunition for the 120/11.6 howitzers was not included in this report.

2. None of the cannon and ammunition quantities in this report were included in the 14 August 1914 ammunition report.

Source: T.C. Genelkurmay Başkanlığı, *Birinci Dünya Harbinde Türk Harbi, Vnci Cilt, Çanakkale Cephesi Harekati, Inci Kitap (Haziran 1914–25 Nisan 1915* (Ankara: Genelkurmay Başimevi, 1993), Chart 14.

Table A.3

Magazine Expenditures: Çanakkale Fortress Commander's Report, 18 March 1915

Formation				Types of shells expended					
Weapon	*No.*	*Solid*	*Shrapnel*	*Time Fuze*	*HE*	*AP*	*Delay Fuze*	*Steel Cap*	*Total*
8th Regiment									
150/10.8 howitzer	31								1,602
210/6.4 mortar	10		17						17
120/30 howitzer	12								142
120/11.6 howitzer	6	13	13		33				59
3rd Regiment									
355/35 coastal	2				15				15
240/35 coastal	7				7	53			60
150/40 ship	5	4			36	12		63	115
4th Regiment									
240/35 coastal	6			12	22	25	67		126
150/45 ship	3								114
Total									**2,250**

Note: 'No.' refers to the number of guns or howitzers that fired shells on 18 March 1915.

Source: T.C. Genelkurmay Başkanlığı, *Birinci Dünya Harbinde Türk Harbi, Vnci Cilt, Çanakkale Cephesi Harekati, Inci Kitap (Haziran 1914–25 Nisan 1915)* (Ankara: Genelkurmay Başimevi, 1993), pp. 184, 210.

Table A.4
Special Mine Fields – Dardanelles Strait

Serial Number	Date of emplacement	Number of mines
1	4/8/1914	39
2	5/8/1914	47
3	15/8/1914	47
4	24/8/1914	29
5	1/10/1914	29
6	9/11/1914	15
7	17/12/1914	50
8	17/12/1914	28
9	30/12/1914	39
10	26/2/1915	53
11	5/3/1915	26
Total		**402**

Source: T.C. Genelkurmay Başkanlığı, *Birinci Dünya Harbinde Türk Harbi, Vnci Cilt, Çanakkale Cephesi Harekati, Inci Kitap (Haziran 1914–25 Nisan 1915)* (Ankara: Genelkurmay Başimevi, 1993), Kroki (Map) 13.

Appendix B
Ottoman Orders of Battle, Gallipoli Campaign, 25 April–1 May 1915

Order of Battle, The Landings, 25 April 1915

Fifth Army	commander	Marshal Liman von Sanders
	chief of staff	Lt Col Kazım
	chief of operations	Capt Mümtaz
	chief of admin	Maj H. Hüsnü
	aide-de-camp	Lt Ekrem Rüştü
III Corps	commander	Brig Esat Pasha
	chief of staff	Lt Col Fahrettin
	chief of operations	Maj Ohrili Kemal
	chief of engineers	Maj Ziya
	staff officer	Capt Burhatettin
	aide-de-camp	Lt Baki
7 Div	commander	Col Ahmet Remzi
	chief of staff	Maj Şükrü Naili
19 Regt	commander	Lt Col Sabri
20 Regt	commander	Maj Halit
21 Regt	commander	Lt Col Halil
7 Art Regt	commander	Lt Col Salih Ulvi
9 Div	commander	Col Halil Sami
	chief of staff	Maj Hulusi
25 Regt	commander	Lt Col Irfan
26 Regt	commander	Lt Col Hafız Kadri
3/26	commander	Maj Mahmut Sabri
27 Regt	commander	Lt Col Mehmet Şefık
1/27	commander	Capt Malatyalı Ibrahim
2/27	commander	Maj Ismet
3/27	commander	Capt Halis

9 Art Regt	commander	Lt Col Mehmet Ali
Bursa Bn	commander	Major Tahsin (jandarma)
19 Div	commander	Lt Col Mustafa Kemal
	chief of staff	Maj Izettin
57 Regt	commander	Maj Avni
1/57	commander	Capt Ahmet Zeki
2/57	commander	Capt Ata
3/57	commander	Capt Hayri
72 Regt	commander	Maj Mehmet Münir
77 Regt	commander	Capt Saip
39 Art Regt	commander	Maj Halil Kemal

XV Corps	commander	Col Weber
	chief of staff	Maj Thauvenay
	chief of operations	Capt Nihat
3 Div	commander	Col Nicolai
	chief of staff	Capt Suphi
31 Regt	commander	Lt Col Ismail Hakkı
32 Regt	commander	Lt Col Hasan Basri
39 Regt	commander	Lt Col H. Nurettin
3 Art Regt	commander	Lt Col Binhold
11 Div	commander	Col Rafet
	chief of staff	Maj Ali Fehmi
33 Regt	commander	Lt Col Şevki
128 Regt	commander	Lt Col Mustafa Şevki
127 Regt	commander	Lt Col Hasan Lüftü
11 Art Regt	commander	Maj Emin

Assigned to Fifth Army (Saros Bay)

5 Div	commander	Col Hasan Basri
	chief of staff	Maj Mehmet Arif
13 Regt	commander	Lt Col Ali Reza
14 Regt	commander	Lt Col Ali Rıfat
15 Regt	commander	Maj Ibrahim Şükrü
5 Art Regt	commander	Lt Col Reza
Ind Cav Bde	commander	Lt Col Hamdi
7 Cav Regt	commander	Maj Avni
13 Cav Regt	commander	Maj Sami Sabit

Order of Battle, Arıburnu Attack, 27 April 1915

Arıburnu Frt	commander	Lt Col Mustafa Kemal (19 Div)
	chief of staff	Maj Izzettin
27 Regt	commander	Lt Col Mehmet Şefik
33 Regt	commander	Lt Col Ahmet Şevki
57 Regt	commander	Maj Avni
64 Regt	commander	Maj Servet
72 Regt	commander	Maj Mehmet Münir
77 Regt	commander	Capt Saip
39 Art Regt	commander	Maj Halil Kemal

Order of Battle, First Krithia, 28 April 1915

9 Div	commander	Col Halil Sami
	chief of staff	Maj Hulusi
25 Regt	commander	Lt Col Irfan
26 Regt	commander	Lt Col Hafız Kadri
19 Regt	commander	Lt Col Alman Sabri (7 Div)
20 Regt	commander	Maj Halit (7 Div)
9 Art Regt	commander	Lt Col Mehmet Ali
Bursa Bn	commander	Major Tahsin (jandarma)

Order of Battle, Arıburnu Attack, 1 May 1915

Arıburnu Frt	commander	Lt Col Mustafa Kemal (19 Div)
	chief of staff	Maj Izzettin
	staff officer	Capt Arif
Rt Wing Gp	commander	Maj Avni
57 Regt	commander	Maj Avni
64 Regt	commander	Maj Servet
3/72 Regt	commander	Maj Mahmut
3/77 Regt	commander	Capt Fehmi
Center Gp	commander	Lt Col Ali Rıfat
14 Regt	commander	Lt Col Ali Rıfat
15 Regt	commander	Maj Ibrahim Şükrü
Left Wing Gp	commander	Lt Col Mehmet Şefik

27 Regt	commander	Lt Col Mehmet Şefik
33 Regt	commander	Maj Rüştü
72 Regt	commander	Maj Mehmet Münir
2/125 Regt	commander	Maj Yahya Kazım

Reserve

125 Regt	commander	Lt Col Abdürrezzak
13 Regt	commander	Lt Col Ali Reza
Arıburnu Arty	commander	Maj Ali Galip

Appendix C

Ottoman Orders of Battle, Gallipoli Campaign, 1 May–5 August 1915

Order of Battle, Night Attacks, 1/2–3/4 May 1915

Southern Gp	commander	Col von Sodernstern
	chief of staff	Maj Mühlmann
	staff officer	Capt Bursalı Mehmet Nihat
	staff advisor	Col Kannengiesser
7 Div	commander	Col Ahmet Remzi
	chief of staff	Maj Şükrü Naili
21 Regt	commander	Lt Col Halil
1/21	commander	Capt Hasan
2/21	commander	Maj Ahmet Muhtar
3/21	commander	Capt Ahmet Niyazi
7 Art Regt	commander	Lt Col Salih Ulvi
9 Div	commander	Col Halil Sami
	chief of staff	Maj Hulusi
25 Regt	commander	Lt Col Irfan
26 Regt	commander	Lt Col Hafız Kadri
19 Regt	commander	Lt Col Alman Sabri (7 Div)
20 Regt	commander	Maj Halit (7 Div)
9 Art Regt	commander	Lt Col Mehmet Ali
Bursa Bn	commander	Major Tahsin (jandarma)
15 Div	commander	Col Mehmet Şükrü
	chief of staff	Capt Veccihi
56 Regt	commander	Lt Col Mahmut
39 Regt	commander	Lt Col H. Nurettin (3 Div)
1/32 Regt	commander	Maj Kazım (3 Div)

Order of Battle, Second Krithia, 6–8 May 1915 and 9–24 May Battles

Southern Gp	commander	Col Weber
	chief of staff	Lt Col von Thauvenay
	chief of operations	Capt Bursalı Mehmet Nihat
7 Div	commander	Col Ahmet Remzi
	chief of staff	Maj Şükrü Naili
19 Regt	commander	Lt Col Alman Sabri
21 Regt	commander	Lt Col Halil
45 Regt	commander	Lt Col Refık (15 Div)
46 Regt	commander	Lt Col Mahmut (15 Div)
127 Regt	commander	Lt Col Hasan (11 Div
7 Art Regt	commander	Lt Col Salih Ulvi
9 Div	commander	Col Halil Sami
	chief of staff	Maj Hulusi
25 Regt	commander	Lt Col Irfan
26 Regt	commander	Lt Col Hafız Kadri
20 Regt	commander	Maj Halit (7 Div)
9 Art Regt	commander	Lt Col Mehmet Ali
15 Div	commander	Col Mehmet Şükrü
	chief of staff	Capt Veccihi
39 Regt	commander	Maj Kazım
11 Div (2 bns)	commander	Col Rafet
12 Div	commander	Lt Col Selahattin Adil (arriving 23/24 May)

Order of Battle, Northern Group Attack, 19 May 1915

Northern Gp	commander	Brig Esat Pasha
	chief of staff	Lt Col Fahrettin
2 Div	commander	Lt Col Hasan Askeri
	chief of staff	Capt Kemal
1 Regt	commander	Lt Col Talat
5 Regt	commander	Lt Col Nazif

6 Regt	commander	Maj Rıfat
5 Div	commander	Lt Col Hasan Basri
	chief of staff	Maj Mehmet Arif
13 Regt	commander	Lt Col Ali Reza
14 Regt	commander	Lt Col Ali Rıfat
15 Regt	commander	Maj Ibrahim Şükrü
16 Div	commander	Col Rüştü
	chief of staff	Capt Mehmet Nazım
47 Regt	commander	Maj Tevfik
48 Regt	commander	Maj Hüseyin Ilhami
125 Regt	commander	Lt Col Abdürrezzak
1/77 Regt	commander	Maj Mehmet Emin
19 Div	commander	Lt Col Mustafa Kemal (19 Div)
	chief of staff	Maj Izzettin
27 Regt	commander	Lt Col Mehmet Şefik
57 Regt	commander	Maj Avni
64 Regt	commander	Maj Servet
72 Regt	commander	Maj Mehmet Münir

Order of Battle, Third Krithia, 4–6 June 1915

Southern Gp	commander	Col Weber
	chief of staff	Lt Col von Thauvenay
	chief of operations	Capt Bursalı Mehmet Nihat
	staff officer	Lt Arif
2 Div	commander	Lt Col Hasan Askeri
	chief of staff	Capt Kemal
7 Div	commander	Col Ahmet Remzi
	chief of staff	Maj Şükrü Naili
Gp Reserve (5 bns)	commander	Lt Col Halil
9 Div	commander	Col Halil Sami
	chief of staff	Maj Hulusi
Right Wing	commander	Maj Adil
Left Wing	commander	Maj Ismail Hakkı (WIA 4 June)

Left Wing	commander	Maj Kazım
Reserve	commander	Maj Mehmet Ali
25 Regt	commander	Maj Mehmet Ali
11 Div	acting commander	Maj Şükrü Naili
	chief of staff	Capt Şemsi
4 Regt	commander	Lt Col Nazif
127 Regt	commander	Lt Col Hasan Lüfti
12 Div	commander	Lt Col Selahattin Adil (arriving 23/24 May)
	chief of staff	Major Süleyman Ilhami
22 Regt	commander	Lt Col Ibrahim
34 Regt	commander	Lt Col Mehmet Ali
36 Regt	commander	Lt Col Cemil
15 Div	commander	Col Mehmet Şükrü
	chief of staff	Capt Veccihi

Order of Battle, Saros Bay, 10 June 1915

Saros Gp	commander	Col Ahmet Fevzi
	chief of staff	Maj M. Hayri
6 Div	commander	Lt Col M. Şakir
16 Regt	commander	Lt Col Hakkı
17 Regt	commander	Lt Col Hasan
Prov Regt	commander	Maj Yusuf Ziya
Ind Cav Bde	commander	Lt Col Hamdi
	chief of staff	Capt Kenan
7 Cav Regt	commander	Maj Avni
13 Cav Regt	commander	Maj Sami Sabit
Bulair Arty	commander	Maj Neşet (heavy arty bn)

Order of Battle, Saros Bay, 21 June 1915

Saros Gp	commander	Col Ahmet Fevzi
	chief of staff	Maj M. Hayri
8 Div	commander	Col Ali Reza
23 Regt	commander	Maj Recai

24 Regt	commander	Maj Nuri
Ind Cav Bde	commander	Lt Col Hamdi
	chief of staff	Capt Kenan
7 Cav Regt	commander	Maj Avni
13 Cav Regt	commander	Maj Sami Sabit
Bulair Arty	commander	Maj Neşet (heavy arty bn)

Order of Battle, First Kereves Dere, 21–22 June 1915

Southern Gp	commander	Col Weber
	chief of staff	Lt Col Çolak H. Selahattin
	chief of operations	Capt Bursalı Mehmet Nihat
	staff officer	Lt Arif
2 Div	commander	Lt Col Hasan Askeri
	chief of staff	Capt Kemal (KIA)
	chief of staff	Capt Mümtaz
	staff officer	Lt Celal
1 Regt	commander	Maj Memduh
5 Regt	commander	Lt Col Nazif
6 Regt	commander	Maj Rıfat
71 Regt	commander	— (1 Div)
7 Div	commander	Col Halil
	chief of staff	Capt Şemsettin
19 Regt	commander	Lt Col Sabri
20 Regt	commander	Lt Col Halit
21 Regt	commander	Lt Col Nurettin
11 Div	commander	Col Rafet
	chief of staff	Lt Col Şükrü Naili
33 Regt	commander	Lt Col Şevki
126 Regt	commander	Lt Col Mustafa Şevki
127 Regt	commander	Lt Col Hasan Lüftü
11 Art Regt	commander	Maj Emin
12 Div	commander	Lt Col Selahattin Adil
	chief of staff	Major Süleyman Ilhami
22 Regt	commander	Lt Col Ibrahim
34 Regt	commander	Maj Yümnü

36 Regt	commander	Lt Col Cemil
1/12 Art Rt	commander	Lt Cemal
15 Div	commander	Col Mehmet Şükrü
	chief of staff	Capt Veccihi

Order of Battle, Gully Ravine, 28 June–3 July 1915

Southern Gp	commander	Col Weber
	chief of staff	Lt Col Çolak H. Selahattin
Right Wing	commander	Brig Çolak Faik Pasha
(II Corps)	chief of staff	Lt Col M. Selahattin
1 Div	commander	Lt Col Cafer Tayyar
70 Regt	commander	Lt Col Vasıf
3/70	commander	Major Reşat
71 Regt	commander	Lt Col Hasan
17 Regt (P)	commander	Col Halil (provisional regt)
6 Div	commander	Lt Col Süleyman Şakir
	chief of staff	Maj Hayri
11 Div	commander	Col Rafet
	chief of staff	Lt Col Şükrü Naili
16 Regt	commander	Lt Col Hakkı (6 Div)
33 Regt	commander	Lt Col Sabri
124 Regt	commander	— (1 Div)
126 Regt	commander	Lt Col Mustafa Şevki
127 Regt	commander	Lt Col Hasan Lüftü

Central Area
| 7 Div | commander | Col Halil |

Left Wing Area
| 12 Div | commander | Lt Col Selahattin Adil |

Order of Battle, Gully Ravine, Ottoman Attack, 5 July 1915

Southern Gp	commander	Col Weber
	chief of staff	Lt Col Çolak H. Selahattin
	asst chief of staff	Capt Tevfık
	staff officer	Lt Arif

Right Wing	commander	Brig Mehmet Ali Pasha
(I Corps)	chief of staff	Maj Eggert
1 Div	commander	Lt Col Cafer Tayyar
	chief of staff	Capt Ibrahim
3 Div	commander	Col Nicolai
	chief of staff	Capt Ahmet Suphi
31 Regt	commander	Lt Col Ismail Hakkı
32 Regt	commander	Lt Col Hasan Basri
39 Regt	commander	Lt Col H. Nurettin
5 Div	commander	Col Hasan Basri
	chief of staff	Maj Arif
13 Regt	commander	Lt Col Ali Reza
15 Regt	commander	Maj Ibrahim Şükrü
5 Art Regt	commander	Lt Col Reza
Engr Coy	commander	Lt Fevzi
6 Div	commander	Lt Col Süleyman Şakir
	chief of staff	Lt Col Selahattin
16 Regt	commander	Lt Col Hakkı
17 Regt	commander	Lt Col Hasan
Prov Regt	commander	Maj Yusuf Ziya
6 Art Regt	commander	Maj Ali Kemal
7 Div	commander	Col Halil
	chief of staff	Capt Şemsettin
19 Regt	commander	Lt Col Irfan
20 Regt	commander	Maj Halit
21 Regt	commander	Lt Col Nurettin

Left Wing Area

12 Div	commander	Lt Col Selahattin Adil
	chief of staff	Maj Süleyman Ilhami
4 Div	commander	Lt Col Cemil
	chief of staff	Maj Alaaddin
10 Regt	commander	Lt Col Kemalettin
11 Regt	commander	Maj Mehmet Emin
12 Regt	commander	Lt Col Servet

Frnt Artillery	commander	Lt Col Binholt
Rt Wing Art	commander	Lt Col Asım
1 Group	commander	Maj Mehmet Ali
Central Gp	commander	Maj Avni
Lft Wing Art	commander	Lt Col Adil
Corps Arty	commander	Maj Rıfat

Order of Battle, Second Kereves Dere (Achi Baba Nullah), 12–13 July 1915

Southern Gp	commander	Brig Mehmet Vehip Pasha
	chief of staff	Col Nihat
	chief of operations	Capt Salih
	aide-de-camp	Lt Arif
XIV Corps	commander	Col Trommer (Right Wing cmdr)
	chief of staff	Lt Col Şefik
1 Div	commander	Lt Col Cafer Tayyar
	chief of staff	Capt Ibrahim Rahmi
8 Div	commander	Col Ali Reza
	chief of staff	Capt Ali Gelip
10 Div	commander	Lt Col Çolak H. Selahattin
	chief of staff	Capt Rüştü
11 Div	commander	Col Rafet
	chief of staff	Lt Col Şükrü Naili
V Corps	commander	Brig Fevzi Pasha (Left Wing cmdr)
	chief of staff	Lt Col Albrecht
4 Div	commander	Lt Col Cemil
	chief of staff	Maj Alaaddin
6 Div	commander	Lt Col Şakir
	chief of staff	Lt Col Selahattin
7 Div	commander	Col Halil
	chief of staff	Capt Şemsettin

13 Div	commander	Col Hovik
	chief of staff	Maj Naci
14 Div	commander	Lt Col Kazım
	chief of staff	Capt Saffet

Order of Battle, Saros Bay, 30 July 1915

Saros Gp	commander	Col Ahmet Fevzi
	chief of staff	Maj M. Hayri
6 Div	commander	Col Nazif
	chief of staff	Maj Bursalı Mehmet Nihat
16 Regt	commander	Lt Col Hakkı
17 Regt	commander	Lt Col H. Nurettin
7 Div	commander	Col Halil
	chief of staff	Capt Şemsettin
19 Regt	commander	Lt Col Irfan
20 Regt	commander	Maj Halit
21 Regt	commander	Lt Col Yusuf Ziya
12 Div	commander	Lt Col Selahattin Adil
	chief of staff	Maj Süleyman Ilhami
34 Regt	commander	Lt Col Mehmet Ali
35 Regt	commander	Lt Col Ali Abbas
36 Regt	commander	Lt Col Münip
Ind Cav Bde	commander	Lt Col Hamdi
	chief of staff	Capt Kenan
7 Cav Regt	commander	Maj Avni
11 Cav Regt	commander	Lt Col Esat
13 Cav Regt	commander	Maj Sami Sabit
Bulair Arty	commander	Maj Neşet

Appendix D

Ottoman Orders of Battle, Gallipoli Campaign, 6 August 1915–9 January 1916

Order of Battle, Cape Helles, Battles of 6–13 August 1915

Southern Gp	commander	Brig Mehmet Vehip Pasha
	chief of staff	Col Nihat
	chief of operations	Capt Salih
	aide-de-camp	Lt Arif
II Corps	commander	Brig Çolak Faik Pasha
	chief of staff	Lt Col M. Selahattin
4 Div	commander	Lt Col Cemil
	chief of staff	Maj Alaaddin
8 Div	commander	Col Ali Reza
	chief of staff	Capt Ali Gelip
V Corps	commander	Brig Fevzi Pasha
	chief of staff	Lt Col Albrecht
	staff officer	Maj H. Hüsnü
13 Div	commander	Col Hovik
	chief of staff	Maj Naci
14 Div	commander	Lt Col Kazım
	chief of staff	Capt Saffet
XIV Corps	commander	Col Trommer
	chief of staff	Lt Col Şefik
1 Div	commander	Lt Col Cafer Tayyar
	chief of staff	Capt Ibrahim Rahmi

10 Div	commander	Lt Col Çolak H. Selahattin
	chief of staff	Capt Rüştü
S. Gp Arty	commander	Maj Rıfat

Order of Battle, Chunuk Bair and Suvla Bay, 6–10 August 1915

Northern Gp	commander	Brig Esat Pasha
	chief of staff	Lt Col Fahrettin
	chief of operations	Maj Çolak Kemalettin Sami
	staff officer	Maj Ohrili Kemal
	staff officer	Capt Burhatettin
5 Div	commander	Lt Col Hasan Basri
	chief of staff	Maj Mehmet Arif
13 Regt	commander	Lt Col Ali Reza
14 Regt	commander	Lt Col Ali Rıfat (died 10 Aug 1915)
14 Regt	commander	Maj Ismail Hakkı
15 Regt	commander	Maj Ibrahim Şükrü (KIA 6/7 Aug 1915)
15 Regt	commander	Maj Veysel
16 Div	commander	Col Rüştü
	chief of staff	Capt Mehmet Nazım
47 Regt	commander	Maj Tevfik (KIA 6/7 Aug 1915)
48 Regt	commander	Maj Hüseyin Ilhami
77 Regt	commander	Lt Col Saip
125 Regt	commander	Lt Col Abdürrezzak
19 Div	commander	Lt Col Mustafa Kemal (to 7 Aug 1915)
	commander	Lt Col Mehmet Şefik
	chief of staff	Maj Izzettin
	staff officer	Capt Hayri
18 Regt	commander	Maj Mustafa (KIA)
27 Regt	commander	Lt Col Mehmet Şefik
27 Regt	commander	Maj Halis
2/27 Regt	commander	Capt Mustafa
57 Regt	commander	Maj Avni
72 Regt	commander	Maj Mehmet Münir

Anafarta Gp	commander	Col Ahmet Fevzi (relieved at 10.10 pm, 7 Aug 1915)
	commander	Col Mustafa Kemal
	chief of staff	Maj Hayri (to 7 Aug 1915)
	chief of staff	Maj Izzettin
4 Div	commander	Lt Col Cemil
	chief of staff	Maj Alaaddin
10 Regt	commander	Lt Col Kemalettin
11 Regt	commander	Maj Memmet Emin
Arty Gp	commander	Maj Ahmet Azmi
8 Div	commander	Col Ali Reza
	chief of staff	Capt Ali Gelip
12 Regt	commander	Maj Bayatlı Arif
23 Regt	commander	Lt Col Recai
24 Regt	commander	Maj Nuri
1/24 Regt	commander	Lt Fahri
28 Regt	commander	Maj Hunker
1/28	commander	Maj Reşat
41 Regt	commander	Lt Col Fuat
33 Regt	commander	Lt Col Sabri (11 Div)
8 Art Regt	commander	Mj Saffet
9 Div	commander	Col Kannengiesser (WIA 7 Aug 1915)
	commander	Lt Col Pötrih (from 8 Aug 1915)
	chief of staff	Maj Hulusi
	staff officer	Capt Refik
25 Regt	commander	Lt Col Nail
26 Regt	commander	Lt Col Hafız Kadri
64 Regt	commander	Lt Col Servet
2 Art Regt	commander	Lt Col Izzet
7 Div	commander	Col Halil
	chief of staff	Capt Şemsettin
19 Regt	commander	Lt Col Irfan
20 Regt	commander	Maj Halit
21 Regt	commander	Lt Col Yusuf Ziya

12 Div	commander	Lt Col Selahattin Adil
	chief of staff	Maj Süleyman Ilhami
34 Regt	commander	Lt Col Mehmet Ali
35 Regt	commander	Lt Col Ali Abbas
36 Regt	commander	Lt Col Münip
Willmer Gp	commander	Maj Willmer
	chief of staff	Maj Hayder
2/31 Regt	commander	Capt M. Şevki
1/32 Regt	commander	Maj Kazım
Gallipoli Bn	commander	Capt Kadri (jandarma)
Bursa Bn	commander	Maj Tahsin (jandarma)
Tayfur Det	commander	Lt Col Hamdi
4 Cav Regt	commander	Lt Col Hamdi

Order of Battle, Saros Bay, 17 August 1915

First Army	commander	Marshal von der Goltz
VI Corps	commander	Brig Hilmi Pasha
	chief of staff	Lt Col Süleyman Ilhami
24 Div	commander	Col Ali Remzi
	chief of staff	Capt Ibrahim
26 Div	commander	Lt Col Esat
	chief of staff	Maj Abdurrahman Nafiz
Ind Cav Bde	commander	Lt Col Hamdi
	chief of staff	Maj Kenan

Order of Battle, Second Anafarta (Scimitar Hill and Hill 60), 21 August 1915

Anafarta Gp	commander	Col Mustafa Kemal
	chief of staff	Maj Izzettin
4 Div	commander	Lt Col Cemil
	chief of staff	Maj Alaaddin
11 Regt	commander	Maj Memmet Emin
14 Regt	commander	Maj Reşit
1/32 Regt	commander	Maj Kazım
1/33 Regt	commander	—

5 Div	commander	Lt Col Willmer
	chief of staff	Maj Mehmet Arif
1 Regt	commander	Lt Col Talat
19 Regt	commander	Lt Col Irfan
127 Regt	commander	Lt Col Hasan Lüftü
1/17 Regt	commander	—
1/39 Regt	commander	—
6 Div	commander	Col Nazif
	chief of staff	Capt Nihat
16 Regt	commander	Lt Col Hakkı
17 Regt	commander	Lt Col H. Nurettin
7 Div	commander	Col Halil
	chief of staff	Capt Şemsettin
20 Regt	commander	Lt Col Ali
21 Regt	commander	Maj Ahmet Zeki
33 Regt	commander	Lt Col Sabri
8 Div	commander	Col Ali Reza
	chief of staff	Capt Ali Gelip
23 Regt	commander	Maj Ahmet Fuat
24 Regt	commander	Maj Nuri
28 Regt	commander	Maj Hunker
41 Regt	commander	Lt Col Fuat
3/70 Regt	commander	Maj Reşat
9 Div	commander	Lt Col Sabri
	chief of staff	Capt Suat
25 Regt	commander	Maj Mehmet Ali
64 Regt	commander	Lt Col Servet
126 Regt	commander	Lt Col Mustafa Şevki
12 Div	commander	Lt Col Selahattin Adil
	chief of staff	Maj Süleyman Ilhami
34 Regt	commander	Lt Col Mehmet Ali
35 Regt	commander	Lt Col Ali Abbas
36 Regt	commander	Lt Col Münip
2/31 Regt	commander	—
Bursa Bn	commander	Maj Tahsin (jandarma)
11 Cav Regt	commander	Lt Col Esat

Order of Battle, Anzac Positional Battles, September–20 December 1915

Northern Gp	commander	Brig Esat Pasha
	chief of staff	Lt Col Fahrettin
	chief of operations	Maj Kemalettin Sami
Right Wing	commander	Col Yakub Şevki
19 Div	commander	Lt Col Mehmet Şefik
	chief of staff	Maj Lüftü
18 Regt	commander	Lt Col Abdülkadir
27 Regt	commander	Maj Halis
57 Regt	commander	Maj Murat
72 Regt	commander	Maj Mehmet Münir
10 Regt	commander	Lt Col Kemalettin
12 Regt	commander	Maj Bayatlı Arif
Left Wing	commander	Col Rıfat
	chief of staff	Lt Col Şükrü
11 Div	commander	Lt Col Abdürrezzak
	chief of staff	Capt Hidayet
13 Regt	commander	Maj Fehmi
15 Regt	commander	Lt Col Veysel
77 Regt	commander	Lt Col Saip
16 Div	commander	Col Rüştü
	chief of staff	Capt Mehmet Nazım
47 Regt	commander	—
48 Regt	commander	Maj Hüseyin Ilhami
125 Regt	commander	Lt Col Abdürrezzak
Kayal Tepe	commander	Lt Col Şükrü
26 Regt	commander	Lt Col Şükrü
Anafarta Gp	commander	Col Mustafa Kemal (to 10 Dec 1915)
	commander	Brig Fevzi Pasha
	chief of staff	Maj Izzettin
II Corps	commander	Col Nicolai (departed 16 October 1915)
	chief of staff	Maj Hayri

XVI Corps	commander	Col Kannengiesser
5 Div	commander	Lt Col Willmer
	chief of staff	Maj Mehmet Arif
1 Regt	commander	Lt Col Memduh
19 Regt	commander	Lt Col Irfan
127 Regt	commander	Lt Col Hasan Lüftü
1/17 Regt	commander	—
1/39 Regt	commander	—
9 Div	commander	Lt Col Sabri
	chief of staff	Capt Suat
25 Regt	commander	Maj Mehmet Ali
64 Regt	commander	Lt Col Servet
126 Regt	commander	Lt Col Mustafa Şevki
12 Div	commander	Lt Col Selahattin Adil (to 12 Sep 1915)
	commander	Col Havik
	chief of staff	Capt Şamlı Cemil
34 Regt	commander	Lt Col Mehmet Ali
35 Regt	commander	Lt Col Ali Abbas
36 Regt	commander	Lt Col Münip
XV Corps	commander	Col Ali Reza
4 Div	commander	Lt Col Cemil (departed 16 Oct 1915)
	chief of staff	Maj Alaaddin
11 Regt	commander	Maj Memmet Emin
14 Regt	commander	Maj Reşit
1/32 Regt	commander	Maj Kazım
1/33 Regt	commander	—
6 Div	commander	Col Nazif
	chief of staff	Capt Nihat
16 Regt	commander	Maj Mehmet Emin
17 Regt	commander	Lt Col H. Nurettin
20 Regt	commander	Lt Col Ali
7 Div	commander	Col Halil
	chief of staff	Capt Şemsettin
21 Regt	commander	Maj Ahmet Zeki

22 Regt	commander	Lt Col Muhittin
8 Div	commander	Lt Col Ali Nuri
	chief of staff	Capt Ali Gelip
23 Regt	commander	Maj Ahmet Fuat
24 Regt	commander	Maj Galip
28 Regt	commander	Maj Hunker
Tayfur Det	commander	Lt Col Hamdi
4 Cav Regt	commander	Lt Col Hamdi
Aegean Det	commander	Maj Tahsin
2/31 Regt	commander	—
Bursa Bn	commander	Maj Tahsin (jandarma)
Hv Arty Gp	commander	Maj Lierau

Order of Battle, Cape Helles Positional Battles, September 1915–9 January 1916

Southern Gp	commander	Brig Mehmet Vehip Pasha (to 9 Sep 1915)
	commander	Brig Cevat Pasha
V Corps	commander	Brig Fevzi Pasha (Second Area)
	chief of staff	Lt Col Albrecht
13 Div	commander	Col Hovik
	chief of staff	Lt Col Selahattin Adil
14 Div	commander	Lt Col Kazım
	chief of staff	Capt Saffet
XIV Corps	commander	Col Trommer (First Area)
	chief of staff	Lt Col Şefik
1 Div	commander	Lt Col Cafer Tayyar
	chief of staff	Capt Ibrahim Rahmi
10 Div	commander	Lt Col Çolak H. Selahattin
	chief of staff	Capt Rüştü
15 Div	commander	Lt Col Hasan Basri
	chief of staff	Maj Vecihi

Appendix E
Gallipoli Commanders in the War of Independence

The Gallipoli campaign proved to be the crucible of the school of command for the Ottoman army and many of the commanders on the peninsula went on to important posts in the remaining years of the war. Later, during what the Turks call the War of Independence (1919–1922), the seasoned Gallipoli commanders emerged as the hard and capable cadre around which Mustafa Kemal built his nationalist army. The personal Gallipoli connection between Mustafa Kemal and his corps commanders in the War of Independence is particularly evident. The table below indicates the officers who rose to division-level command and their assignment in the War of Independence.

Name	*Gallipoli assignment*	*War of Independence assignment (ret. rank)*
Army level commanders		
M. Kemal Atatürk	Anafatra Gp cmdr	National army commander-in-chief (Marshal)
M. Fevzi Çakmak	V Corps/Anafarta Gp cmdr	Chief of general staff (Marshal)
Yakup Şevki Sübaşı	19 Div cmdr	Second Army cmdr (LTG)
Kazım Karabekir	14 Div cmdr	Eastern Front cmdr (LTG)
Corps-level commanders		
Izzettin Çalışlar	19 Div and Anafarta Gp c/s	First Gp and I Corps cmdr (Gen)
M. Selahattin Adil	12 Div and 13 Div cmdr	Second Gp and II Corps cmdr (MG)
Şükrü Naili Gökberk	7 Div chief of staff	III Corps cmdr (LTG)
Mehmet Arif	5 Div and 11 Div ch of staff	III Corps cmdr (Col)
Kemalettin Sami	Northern Gp staff	Fourth Gp and IV Corps cmdr (LTG)
Fahrettin Altay	III Corps chief of staff	V Cavalry Corps cmdr (Gen)
Kaziim Inanç	Fifth Army chief of staff	VI Corps cmdr (LTG)
Çevat Cobanlı	XIV Corps cmdr	Elcezire Front cmdr (LTG)
Nihat Anılmış	Second Army chief of staff	Elcezire Front cmdr (LTG)

Division-level commanders

Nazif Kyacık	5 Regt cmdr	3 Caucasian Div cmdr (MG)
Cemil Conk	4 Div cmdr	11 Div and 18 Div cmdr (MG)
Kazım Sevüktekin	1 Regt cmdr	8 Div and 5 Caucasian Div cmdr (MG)
M. Munip Uzsoy	36 Regt cmdr	24 Div and 61 Div cmdr (Col)
Veysel Özgür	15 Regt cmdr	7 Div and 15 Div cmdr (Col)
M. Emin Yazgan	16 Regt cmdr	7 Div cmdr (MG)
Reşsat Çiğiltepe	1/28 Regt cmdr	11 Cauc Div and 21 Div cmdr (Col)
M. Şefik Aker	27 Regt and 19 Div cmdr	6 Div and 7 Div cmdr (Col)
Ali Sami Sabit	Ind. Cav Bde cmdr (Saros)	13 Div and Urfa Prov Cav Div cmdr (MG)
H. Nurettin Özsu	17 Regt cmdr	17 Div cmdr (MG)
M. Sabri Erçetin	3 Arty Regt cmdr	4 Div and 14 Div cmdr (MG)
Nazmi Solok	1/7 Regt cmdr	6 Div cmdr (LTG)
Mehmet Hayri Tarhan	XVI and II Corps ch of staff	9 Div and Gaziantep area cmdr (MG)
Ismail Hakkı	1/7 Regt and 7 Regt cmdr	11 Caucasian Div and Kars fortress cmdr (Col)
Ahmet Fuat Bulca	3/15 Regt and 3/24 Regt cmdr	1 Div, 29 Div and 11 Div cmdr (Col)
Mehmet Nuri Conker	24 Regt and 8 Div cmdr	41 Div cmdr (Col)
Mehmet Hulusi Conk	9 Div chief of staff	18 Div cmdr (Col)
Alaeddin Koval	II Corps staff officer	41 Div cmdr (MG)
H Hüsnü Emir Erkilet	V and XIV Corps chief of staff	Second Army c/s and 1 Div cmdr (MG)
Ahmet Naci Tinaz	13 Div chief of staff	West Front c/s and 15 Div cmdr (LTG)
Osman Zati Korol	Çanakkale fortress staff off	1 Cav Dic cmdr (MG)
Ahmet Zeki Soydemir	III Corps staff and 1/57 cmdr	2 Cav Div cmdr and general staff (MG)
Mehmet Nazım	16 Div and VI Corps staff	4 Div cmdr (Col)

Miscellaneous commanders

Ali Fuat Cebesoy	25 Div cmdr	Second Army LoCI (LTG)
Cafer Tayyar Eğilmez	1 Div cmdr	Edirne fortress cmdr (MG)
M. Rüstü Sakarya	16 Div cmdr	Konya area cmdr and IV area cmdr (MG)
Nazif Kayacık	6 Div and Saros Grp cmdr	Konya logistics command (MG)
M Muhittin Kurtiş	22 Regt cmdr	Istanbul delegation (MG)

Source: T.C. Genelkurmay Başkanlığı, *Türk Istiklal Harbi'ne Kalilan Tümen ve Daha Ust Kademelerdeki Komutanların Biyografileri* (Ankara: Genelkurmay Basımevi, 1989).

Notes

Introduction

1. George H. Cassar, *Kitchener's War, British Strategy from 1914 to 1918* (Washington, D.C.: Brassey's Inc., 2004), p. 325. The current author cannot verify this assertion.
2. See the bibliography for full citations of these works.
3. Tim Travers, 'The Other Side of the Hill', *Military History Quarterly* 12 (3) (Spring 2000): 2–20, 2.
4. Tim Travers, *Gallipoli 1915* (Charleston, SC: Tempus Publishing, 2001), pp. 222–228.
5. Nigel Steel and Peter Hart, *Defeat at Gallipoli* (London: Macmillan, 1994), p. 420.
6. Field Marshal Lord Carver, *The Turkish Front 1914–1918, The Campaigns at Gallipoli, in Mesopotamia and in Palestine* (London: Sidgwick & Jackson, 2003), p. 246.
7. See C.F. Aspinall-Oglander, *History of the Great War, based on Official Documents: Military Operations Gallipoli, vol. 1 and 2* (London: HMSO, 1924–1930) and C.E.W. Bean, *Official History of Australia in the War of 1914–1918: The Story of ANZAC, vol. 1–2* (Queensland: University of Queensland Press, 1981) (reprint of 1942 edition).
8. In this regard, the English-language historiography of Gallipoli is much like the American historiography of the Battle of Gettysburg (1863), which obsessively dwells on why Confederate general Robert E. Lee lost the battle rather than why Union general George Meade won the battle.
9. Winston Churchill appears to have established Mustafa Kemal as an almost mythic figure, who was personally responsible for the failed landings on 25 April 1915 (and referred to as the 'Man of Destiny'). See Winston S. Churchill, *The World Crisis* (New York: Macmillan abridgement, 1992), pp. 441–442. In fact, Churchill's account of the ANZAC landing is the most inaccurate of any of the western histories.
10. Beginning in the late 1990s, Tim Travers (Canada) and Edward Erickson (United States) have enjoyed access to the Turkish General Staff Archives and have published several books and articles about the Turks in the First World War and the Gallipoli Campaign. They are the first western historians to make use of the archives.

Chapter 1

1. T.C. Genelkurmay Başkanlığı, hereafter TCGB, *Türk Silahli Kuvvetleri*

Tarihi, Balkan Harbi (1912–1913), II Cilt, 2nci Kısım, 1nci Kitap, Şark Ordusu, Ikinci Çatalca Muharebesi ve Şarkoy Çikmarmasi (Ankara: Genelkurmay Başimevi, 1993), pp. 66–67. Hereafter, *Şark Ordusu, Ikinci Çatalca Muharebesi ve Şarkoy Çikarmasi.*

2. TCGB, *Birinci Dünya Harbinde Türk Harbi, Vnci Cilt, Çanakkale Cephesi Harekati, Inci Kitap (Haziran 1914–25 Nisan 1915)* (Ankara: Genelkurmay Başimevi, 1993), p. 79. Hereafter, *Çanakkale Cephesi Harekati Inci Kitap.* The larger defensive area included both sides of the strait, the Gallipoli peninsula and the Saros Bay sector.

3. The material for this paragraph comes from Edward J. Erickson, 'Strength Against Weakness, Ottoman Military Effectiveness at Gallipoli, 1915', *Journal of Military History* 65 (October 2001), 981–1012.

4. TCGB, *Çanakkale Cephesi Harekati Inci Kitap*, pp. 80–91.

5. TCGB, *Şark Ordusu, Ikinci Çatalca Muharebesi ve Şarkoy Çikarmasi*, pp. 66–67. See also Erickson, 'Strength Against Weakness', 981–1012 for a description and comparative maps of the 1912, February 1915 and April 1915 defenses.

6. TCGB, *Şark Ordusu, Ikinci Çatalca Muharebesi ve Şarkoy Çikarmasi*, pp. 66–67.

7. Ibid., Kroki (Map) 79.

8. The late modern-day Gallipoli enthusiast Jul Snelders (from Belgium) uncovered these pits in 1998.

9. TCGB, *Şark Ordusu, Ikinci Çatalca Muharebesi ve Şarkoy Çikarmasi*, Kroki (Map) 19.

10. Ibid., pp. 251, 262. It is sometimes forgotten that Mustafa Kemal served in a combat role during the Balkan Wars and generally unknown that he served as a corps-level operations officer on the Gallipoli Peninsula in 1913.

11. See Edward J. Erickson, *Defeat in Detail, The Ottoman Army in the Balkans 1912–1913* (Westport, CT: Praeger, 2003), pp. 153–156, 252–259 and 325–328 for details of these operations.

12. Richard C. Hall, *The Balkan Wars 1912–1913: Prelude to the First World War* (London: Routledge, 2000), p. 81.

13. The material for this paragraph comes from Erickson, 'Strength Against Weakness', 981–1012.

14. TCGB, *Çanakkale Cephesi Harekati Inci Kitap*, pp. 51–52.

15. Ibid., pp. 49–51.

16. Ibid., pp. 49–51.

17. Ibid., p. 79.

18. ATASE Archive 121, Record 573, File 10-3, Enver Pasha to Çanakkale Fortress commander, 12 August 1914 reproduced in TCGB, *Askeri Tarih Belgeleri Dergisi*, Yıl 38, Sayı 88, Augustos 1989 (Ankara: Genelkurmay Basımevi, 1989), pp. 7–8.

19. TCGB, *Çanakkale Cephesi Harekati Inci Kitap*, p. 52.
20. Ibid., pp. 61–62.
21. Ibid., p. 54.
22. ATASE Archive 4669, Record H-3, File 1-107, III Corps report to First Army, 22 November 1914, quoted in TCGB, *Çanakkale Cephesi Harekati Inci Kitap*, p. 103.
23. ATASE, 19ncu Tümen Tarihçesi, 1970, 9, unpublished staff study (Mekki Erertem), Genelkurmay Askeri Tarih ve Stratejik Etut, ATASE Library, Record 26-834.
24. Ibid., pp. 38–40.
25. Ibid., Kroki (Map) 4.
26. Ibid., pp. 85–88.
27. Ibid., p. 89.
28. Ibid., pp. 85–86.
29. Ibid., pp. 44–45.
30. Ibid., p. 45.
31. Ibid., Chart 9.
32. TCGB, *Çanakkale Cephesi Harekati Inci Kitap*, pp. 97–99, 106–107, 217.
33. Arthur J. Marder, *From The Dreadnought to Scapa Flow*, vol. 2 (London: Oxford University Press, 1965), p. 231. Carden was actually the second choice to command the fleet. The leading contender, Admiral Arthur H. Limpus, had been the chief of the British Naval Mission to the Ottoman Empire until it was withdrawn in September 1914. Not wanting to offend the Ottomans, then not at war with Britain, Limpus was made Superintendent of the Malta Dockyard instead.
34. TCGB, *Çanakkale Cephesi Harekati Inci Kitap*, p. 113.
35. See Robin Prior, *Gallipoli, The End of the Myth* (New Haven: Yale University Press, 2009), pp. 44–59. Chapter 4 is particularly valuable in understanding the difficulties in and probabilities of hitting targets from the battleships available at the Dardanelles.
36. Ibid., p. 277.
37. Ibid., p. 242.
38. ATASE Archive 4618, Record 43, File 57, commander, 9th Division to commander, Çanakkale Fortress, 5 March 1915 reproduced in TCGB, *Askeri Tarih Belgeleri Dergisi 38/88*, pp. 11–14.
39. TCGB, *Çanakkale Cephesi Harekati Inci Kitap*, p. 316. The casualty figures following are drawn from ATASE Archives 4669, 5283, 5640 and 5675.
40. ATASE Archive 4701, Record H-1, File 1-181, Orders Number 129, Çanakkale Fortress Command, 19 March 1915 cited in TCGB, *Çanakkale Cephesi Harekati Inci Kitap*, p. 279.
41. TCGB, *Çanakkale Cephesi Harekati Inci Kitap*, pp. 250–251.

42. Winston S. Churchill, *The World Crisis*, pp. 414–416.

43. Ibid., p. 415.

44. C.F. Aspinall-Oglander, *Military Operations Gallipoli, vol. 1*, p. 99; Philip J. Haythornthwaite, *Gallipoli 1915* (London: Osprey, 1991), p. 33; Marder, *From The Dreadnought to Scapa Flow*, vol. 2, p. 248; Alan Moorehead, *Gallipoli* (New York: Harper, 1956), p. 75; Robert Rhodes James, *Gallipoli* (New York: Macmillan, 1965), p. 64.

45. Tim Travers, 'The Other Side of the Hill', 9. Based on Ottoman sources Professor Travers of the University of Calgary has concluded that the Ottoman defenses had more than enough shells left to continue the battle. Edward J. Erickson, *Ordered To Die, A History of the Ottoman Army in the First World War* (Westport, CT: Greenwood Press, 2000), p. 80. The author noted that about a sixth of the heavy ammunition had been expended.

46. Sir Julian S. Corbett, *History of the Great War Based On Official Documents, Naval Operations, vol. 2* (London: Longmans, Green and Co., 1921).

47. Ibid., p. 224.

48. Martin Gilbert, *Winston S. Churchill, Volume V, The Prophet of Truth, 1922–1939* (Boston: Houghton Mifflin Company, 1977).

49. Ibid., p. 14.

50. Winston S. Churchill, *The World Crisis 1915* (London: Thornton Butterworth Limited, 1923), p. 257.

51. Ibid., pp. 267–268.

52. Ibid., pp. 263–269.

53. Winston Churchill, *The World Crisis* (London: Thornton Butterworth Limited, 1930 abridgement), p. vii.

54. Ibid., p. 415.

55. Major Dr Carl Mühlmann, *Der Kampf um die Dardanellen 1915* (Berlin: Drud und Berlag von Gerhard Stalling, 1927), p. 74.

56. Moorehead, *Gallipoli*, p. 75. Moorehead did not state the source of his figures.

57. James, *Gallipoli*, p. 64. James did not note the source of this account.

58. Haythornthwaite, *Gallipoli 1915*, p. 33. Haythornthwaite did not note the source of this information.

59. TCGB, *Çanakkale Cephesi Harekati Inci Kitap*, pp. 106–140.

60. Ibid., pp. 148–165.

61. Ibid., pp. 148–154.

62. Expending their heavy shells at the same rate of the 18 March engagement, the Ottomans had enough shells for five more days of battle, without even firing their 20/22 caliber heavy guns.

63. TCGB, *Çanakkale Cephesi Harekati Inci Kitap*, pp. 211–212.

64. Ibid., p. 211. Additionally three Germans were killed and fifteen were wounded.

65. Ibid., p. 296.

66. Marder, *From The Dreadnought to Scapa Flow*, vol. 2.

67. Ibid., p. 263. Professor Marder's account of the conception, planning, execution and post-mortem of the naval attack is the finest in print and stands the test of time after thirty-five years.

68. Corbett, *Naval Operations, vol. 2*, p. 224.

69. TCGB, *Çanakkale Cephesi Harekati Inci Kitap*, Map 1. Some western histories show the numerical serials erroneously numbered from north to south, an example is Corbett, *Naval Operations, vol. 2*, map facing p. 230.

70. TCGB, *Çanakkale Cephesi Harekati Inci Kitap*, pp. 38–40.

71. Marder, *From The Dreadnought to Scapa Flow*, pp. 248–250, 254–255. Professor Marder noted that reinforcements were dispatched immediately to replace losses. His analysis of the reorganized minesweeping arrangements using faster ships and better techniques planned for a subsequent assault is noteworthy and indicates the intellectual energy the navy was expending to solve the tactical problems involving the enemy defenses.

72. ATASE Archives 4669, Record H-12, File 1-85, 1914, Ottoman General Hqs Orders, 9 March 1915, cited in TCGB, *Çanakkale Cephesi Harekati Inci Kitap*, p. 171.

73. This perception also began with German memoirs and was perpetuated by later western authors.

74. ATASE Archive, Cabinet 91, Record 29, Shelf 2, File 169, 26nci Piyade Alay Tarihçesi, p. 7.

75. ATASE Archive 5025, Record 27, File 1/86-88, 9 Division Orders, 19 August 1914, Ek (Document) 1.

76. ATASE Archive, Cabinet 91, Record 29, Shelf 2, File 169, 26nci Piyade Alay Tarihçesi, p. 8.

77. ATASE Archive, Cabinet 91, Record 29, Shelf 2, File 170, 27ncu Piyade Alay Tarihçesi, p. 7.

78. Ibid., p. 8.

79. 27 Regt Order No. 5, 10 September 1914, reprinted in Binbaşı Halis Bey (Ataksor), *Çanakkale Raporu* (Istanbul: Arma Yayınları, n.d.; reprint of 1975 edition), pp. 42–43.

80. ATASE Archive 91/2, 27ncu Piyade Alay Tarihçesi, p. 7.

81. Detachment Orders Nos 8, 10, and 18, 1914, reprinted in Halis Bey (Ataksor), *Çanakkale Raporu*, pp. 46–58.

82. ATASE Archive 91/2, 27ncu Piyade Alay Tarihçesi, p. 7.

83 ATASE Library, Record 26-485, 25nci Piyade Alay Tarihçesi, unpublished staff study (Lütfi Doğanci), 1977, p. 7.

84. ATASE Library, Record 26-346, 9ncu Topçu Alay Tarihçesi, unpublished staff study (Mete Şefik), 1970.

85. ATASE Library, Record 26-834, 19ncu Tümen Tarihçesi, unpublished staff study, p. 9.

86. See Aspinall-Oglander, Bean, Hickey, James, Moorehead and Travers for statements to this effect.

87. ATASE Library, Record 26-466, 57nci Piyade Alay Tarihçesi, unpublished staff study, p. 19.

88. ATASE Archive, Cabinet 91, Record 29, Shelf 1, File 159, 19ncu Piyade Alay Tarihçesi, p. 4.

89. *Mümtaz subaylar* were officers who had graduated from the staff college but had not scored well enough on the examinations to qualify for the general staff corps. If they performed well in units or scored well on subsequent examinations, they were admitted as staff officers (*Erkan-ı Harp*). The assignment of Distinguished Captains Zeki, Hayri and Ata gave the new regiment an unusual number of highly trained officers. Fahrettin Altay, *Çanakkale Hatırları*, (Istanbul: Arma Yayınları, 2002), p. 12.

90. ATASE Archive 91/1, 19ncu Piyade Alay Tarihçesi, p. 19.

91. ATASE Library, Record 26-336, 77nci Piyade Alay Tarihçesi, unpublished staff study, p. 2.

92. Ibid., p. 3.

93. Ibid., p. 3.

94. ATASE Archive 497, Record 36, File 23, 19th Division Daily Orders, Maidos, 25/26 February 1915, p. 3.

95. ATASE Archive 91/1, 19ncu Piyade Alay Tarihçesi, p. 4.

96. ATASE Library, Record 26-326, 20nci Piyade Alay Tarihçesi, unpublished staff study, n.d., p. 4 and ATASE Library, Record 26-327, 21nci Piyade Alay Tarihçesi, unpublished staff study (Mekki Erertem), n.d., p. 20.

97. ATASE Archive, Cabinet 91, Record 1, Shelf 27, File 1549, 15nci Piyade Alay Tarihçesi, p. 5.

98. ATASE Archive, Cabinet 91, Record 34, Shelf 3, File 202, 46ncu Piyade Alay Tarihçesi, p. 6.

99. ATASE Archive, Cabinet 91, Record 29, Shelf 1, File 159, 47nci Piyade Alay Tarihçesi, p. 11.

100. Ibid., p. 12.

101. Ibid., p. 13.

102. Ibid., p. 14.

103. Liddle Collection (LC), Box Gall 216/1, Interview with General Askir Arkayan, undated.

104. LC, Box TU 01, item 4, tape 49, Interview with Lt Col Abil Savasman, July 1972.

105. ATASE Archive, Cabinet 6, Record 34, Shelf 9, File 1-14, 11nci Piyade Tumen Tarihçesi, p. 13.

106. Ibid., p. 14.

107. Travers and Erickson have recently examined certain aspects of Ottoman corps-level performance. However, their work is localized in time and space and a complete analysis of Ottoman corps-level operations remains incomplete.

108. TCGB, *Türk Silahlı Kuvvetleri Tarihi (1908–1920)* (Ankara: Genelkurmay Basımevi, 1971), pp. 140–141. See Erickson, *Defeat in Detail*, pp. 24–33 for detailed discussions of Ottoman army reorganization efforts.

109. See Erickson, *Defeat in Detail*, pp. 77–162 for an examination of the fighting record of Mahmut Muhtar's III Corps in the Balkan Wars.

110. Prime Minister Archives, Archive Number 6, Change of Command Directives, 6 January 1914, reprinted in TCGB, *Turk Silahli Kuvvetleri Tarihi (1908–1920)*, pp. 195–196.

111. The material for the following biographical information on Esat was assembled from İsmet Görgülü, *Türk Harp Tarıhı Derslerinde Adı Geçen Komutanlar*, (Istanbul: Harp Akademileri Yayını, 1983), pp. 298–300.

112. For a detailed discussion of Esat's defence of Yanya, see TCGB, *Türk Silahli Kuvvetleri Tarihi, Balkan Harbi (1912–1913), IIIncü Cilt, 2nci Kisim, Garp Ordusu Vardar Ordusu, Yunan Cephesi Harekati* (Ankara: Genelkurmay Basımevi, 1993), pp. 518–672 and Erickson, *Defeat in Detail*, pp. 293–316.

113. Liman von Sanders, *Five Years in Turkey* (London: Bailliere, Tindall & Cox, 1928), pp. 78–79.

114. TCGB, *Çanakkale Cephesi Harekati (Amfibi Harekat)* (Ankara: Genelkurmay Basımevi, 1978), pp. 61–62.

115. Cemal Akbay, *Birinci Dünya Harbinde Türk Harbi, 1nci Cilt, Osmanli Imparatorlugu'nun Siyası ve Askeri Hazırlıkları ve Harbe Girisi* (Ankara: Genelkurmay Basımevi, 1991), pp. 175–176.

116. TCGB, *Çanakkale Cephesi Harekati (Haziran 1914–Nisan 1915)*(Ankara: Genelkurmay Basımevi, 1993), pp. 96–101.

117. ATASE Archive 3964, Record H-5, File 1-10/11, III Corps Orders, 8 November 1914.

118. TCGB, *Çanakkale Cephesi Harekati (Haziran 1914–Nisan 1915)*, p. 228.

119. ATASE Archive 3475, Record H-4, File 2-20, Paragraphs 1-9, III Corps Orders, 7 April 1915.

120. ATASE Archive 3475, Record H-4, File 2-20, Paragraph 10, III Corps Orders, 7 April 1915.
121. TCGB, *Türk Silahli Kuvvetleri Tarihi, Balkan Harbi (1912–1913), II Cilt, 2nci Kisım, 1nci Kitap, Şark Ordusu, Ikinci Çatalca Muharebesi ve Şarkoy Çikmarması* (Ankara: Genelkurmay Basımevi, 1993), pp. 62–63 and Erickson, *Defeat in Detail*, p. 127.
122. NARA, RG 353, Roll 41, Report – Evacuation of Gallipoli, 3 May 1915, American Embassy, Constantinople.
123. David Jones, 'Imperial Russia's Forces at War', in Allan R. Millett and Williamson Murray (eds), *Military Effectiveness, Volume I: The First World War* (Boston: Unwin Hyman, 1988), p. 281.
124. David G. Herrmann, *The Arming of Europe and the Making of the First World War* (Princeton: Princeton University Press, 1996), p. 203.
125. TCGB, *Türk Silahlı Kuvvetleri Tarihi (1908–1920)*, Ek (Document) 4. See Table of Peacetime Organisational Cadres. Interestingly, thirteen NCOs were assigned to the infantry battalion headquarters.
126. Yücel Yanıkdağ, 'Educating the Peasants: The Ottoman Army and Enlisted Men in Uniform', *Middle Eastern Studies*, 40 (6), November 2004, 94. Yanıkdağ noted that the literacy rate of the Ottoman Empire in 1914 was about 5 to 7 percent.
127. Ibid., 99–101.

Chapter 2

1. TCGB, *Çanakkale Cephesi Harekati Inci Kitap*, p. 212.
2. ATASE Archive 4669, Record H-13, File 1-19, General Hqs message, 22 March 1915 and ATASE Archive 4669, Record H-13, File 1-2, General Hqs message, 23 March 1915 cited in TCGB, *Çanakkale Cephesi Harekati Inci Kitap*, pp. 213–214.
3. ATASE Archive 180, Record 774, File 1-5, Ottoman army headquarters Number 2793 to Ottoman general staff, 7.45 am, 25 March 1915 reproduced in TCGB, *Askeri Tarih Belgeleri Dergisi 38/88*, pp. 18–20.
4. ATASE Archive 180, Record 774, File 1-6, Orders (top secret), 26 March 1915 cited in TCGB, *Çanakkale Cephesi Harekati Inci Kitap*, p. 218.
5. ATASE Archive 3474, Folder H-1, File 1-21, Orders, Provisional Corps, 1 April 1915 cited in TCGB, *Çanakkale Cephesi Harekati Inci Kitap*, p. 226.
6. ATASE Archive 3474, Folder H-3, File 2-5 and 2-6, Orders, Provisional Corps, 5 April 1915 cited in TCGB, *Çanakkale Cephesi Harekati Inci Kitap*, p. 227.
7. ATASE Archive 3474, Folder H-3, File 2-14, Fifth Army orders, 19 April 1915 cited in TCGB, *Çanakkale Cephesi Harekati Inci Kitap*, pp. 234–235.
8. ATASE Archive 3474, Folder H-4, File 2-19, Orders, Fifth Army, 7 April

1915 reproduced in TCGB, *Çanakkale Cephesi Harekati Inci Kitap*, pp. 228–230.

9. Liman von Sanders, *Five Years in Turkey*, p. 61. This myth was perpetuated by all subsequent western writers, for example, Churchill, *The World Crisis*, p. 412, Moorehead, *Gallipoli*, p. 104, and James, *Gallipoli*, p. 71. For a more recent example see Travers, *Gallipoli 1915*, pp. 38–39. Travers stated that the Ottoman defensive structure scattered the troops too widely for an effective defense.

10. Liman von Sanders, *Five Years in Turkey*, p. 61.

11. TCGB, *Çanakkale Cephesi Harekati Inci Kitap*, Kroki (Overlay) 14.

12. Ibid., Kroki (Overlay) 15.

13. C.E.W. Bean, *Official History of Australia in the War of 1914–1918* and Nigel Steel and Peter Hart, *Defeat at Gallipoli*.

14. Robert Rhodes James, *Gallipoli*, and Michael Hickey, *Gallipoli* (London: John Murray, 1995). James, for example, erroneously maintained that the southern sector was divided between Kemal and Sami until about 7.30 am, when Liman von Sanders ordered Esat to take command, p. 112. Alan Moorehead's *Gallipoli* created the lasting impression that a single regiment (the 57 Regt) stopped the Australians, pp. 138–140.

15. Travers, *Gallipoli 1915*, *passim*.

16. Ibid., p. 82. However, Travers does credit the Turks with very effective shrapnel fire and sniper fire.

17. Haluk Oral, *Gallipoli Through Turkish Eyes 1915*, translated by Amy Spangler (Istanbul: Türkiye Iş Bankası Kültür Yayınları, 2007), p. 316.

18. Halis Bey (Ataksor), *Çanakkale Raporu*, p. 15. Major Halis published the *Canakkale Report* in 1933 as a serial in the Turkish magazine *Küçük Mecmua*. Halis' report contains several hundred regimental and battalion orders from period May 1914 through August 1915 that he had retained as personal copies.

19. Ibid., p. 105. See copy of 27 Regt Order No. 25, 22 April 1915, Paragraph 8.

20. ATASE Archive 91/2, 27ncu Piyade Alay Tarihçesi, p. 10.

21. Australian historian Frank Cain has noted that the landing on the narrow Anzac beach 'could not have been as unintentional as first thought.' Cain quoted Captain C.G. Dix of the Beach Party, who thought that the intended beach was so heavily mined, wired and covered by guns that landing there 'must have been nearly impossible.' Frank Cain, 'A Colonial Army in Ottoman Fields: Australia's Involvement in the Gallipoli Debacle', in Yigal Sheffy and Saul Shai, *The First World War: Middle Eastern Perspectives* (Tel Aviv: Tel Aviv University, 2000), p. 180.

22. ATASE Archive 180, Record 777, File 4-19, III Corps to Fifth Army.

23. Ibid.

24. National Defense University (NDU) Special Collections, Gallipoli Box, Log Entry, HMS *Bacchante*, 4.20 am, 25 April 1915.

25. Ibid., 4.43 am Log Entry.

26. ATASE Archive 4836, Record H-10, File 1-73, 9th Division Orders, 5.55 am, 25 April 1915.

27. Ibid. See distribution of orders.

28. TCGB, *Birinci Dünya Harbinde Türk Harbi Vnci Cilt, Çanakkale Cephesi Harekati (Amfibi Harekat)* (Ankara: Genelkurmay Basımevi, 1979), pp. 107–109.

29. ATASE Archive 4836, Record H-11, File 1-19, 9th Division Orders.

30. ATASE Archive 91/2, 27ncu Piyade Alay Tarihçesi.

31. Mustafa Kemal, *Ariburnu Muharebeleri Raporu*, reprinted in İhsan Ilgar and Nurer Uğurlu, *Esat Paşa'nın Çanakkale Savaşı Hatırları* (Istanbul: Örgün Yayınevi, 2003), pp. 393–394.

32. Oral, *Gallipoli Through Turkish Eyes 1915*, p. 58.

33. ATASE Archive 5026, Record 28, File 1-12, Combat Report, 27th Regt.

34. ATASE Archive 91/2, Regimental Attack Order, 12 noon, 25 April 1915, appendixed in 27ncu Piyade Alay Tarihçesi, p. 14.

35. Travers, *Gallipoli 1915*, pp. 72–77.

36. Message from Avni to Şefik, 3.05 pm, 25 April 1915 reproduced in Oral, *Gallipoli Through Turkish Eyes 1915*, p. 286.

37. Christopher Pugsley, 'Stories of Anzac', in Jenny Macleod, *Gallipoli. Making History* (London: Frank Cass, 2004), pp. 49–54.

38. Ibid.

39. TCGB, *Birinci Dünya Harbinde Türk Harbi Vncü, Çanakkale Cephesi Harekati, 1nci, 2nci, 3ncu Kitaplarin Özetlenmiş Tarihi* (Ankara: Genelkurmay Basımevi, 2002) p. 69.

40. Bean, *Official History of Australia in the War of 1914–1918*, pp. 450–454 and Travers, *Gallipoli 1915*, pp. 81–82. In particular, both authors erroneously state that the 77 Regt was fed into the fight between the 27 Regt and 57 Regt. However, the Turkish official history clearly states that it was ordered to the left flank of the 27 Regt and went into action there.

41. John Lee, *A Soldier's Life, General Sir Ian Hamilton 1853–1947* (London: Macmillan, 2000), pp. 161–162.

42. Bean, *Official History of Australia in the War of 1914–1918*, pp. 454–457.

43. Ibid., pp. 460–461.

44. İhsan Ilgar and Nurer Uğurlu (eds), *Esat Paşa'nın Çanakkale Savaşı Hatırları* (Istanbul: Örgün Yayınevi, 2003 reprint of 1975 edition), p. 509, Ek (Document) VI, Fahrettin's *Çanakkale Şavası*.

45. Ibid., pp 48–50.

46. Ibid., p. 426, Ek (Document) IV, Mustafa Kemal's *Arıburnu Muharebeleri Raporu*.
47. H.B. Danışman, *Gallipoli 1915, Day One Plus . . . 27th Ottoman Inf. Regt. Vs. ANZACS* (Istanbul: Denizler Kitabevi, 2007), pp. 42–46.
48. Mustafa Kemal, *Arıburnu Muharebeleri Raporu*, pp. 48, 508. These are tribes found in Northern Syria and Mesopotamia.
49. Interview with Dr Mesut Uyar, Captain, Turkish Army, Turkish Army Military Academy Archives Division, 12 April 2004. Uyar stated that the recruitment area of the 77 Regt was the city of Aleppo, which had 'a Turkish dominated population.' He is currently researching the Arab composition of the Ottoman army's officer corps in the First World War and finds the characterization of the 77 Regt as 'Arab' to be a mis-representation.
50. Message Saip to Şefik, 4 May 1915 reproduced in Oral, *Gallipoli Through Turkish Eyes 1915*, as Document 4, p. 286.
51. ATASE Archive 180, Record 776, File 4/4-1, Fifth Army Message to Ministry of War, 1.50 am, 26 April 1915.
52. TCGB, *Çanakkale Cephesi Harekati (Amfibi Harekat)*, p. 127.
53. The 1911 Ottoman army tables of organization for infantry divisions provided twenty-two officers (including the commander (a general officer) and chief of staff) and three NCOs as the entire division headquarters element. See TCGB, *Türk Silahli Kuvvetleri Tarihi,*, Ek (Document) 4. By way of comparison, British infantry divisions in 1914 had 71 personnel assigned to the divisional headquarters, including 5 general officers and 14 qualified staff officers. For discussion see Martin Middlebrook, *Your Country Needs You, From Six to Sixty-five Divisions* (Barnsley: Leo Cooper, 2000), pp. 2, 10–12.
54. TCGB, *Çanakkale Cephesi Harekati (Amfibi Harekat)*, pp. 132–133.
55. Ibid., p. 137.
56. ATASE Archive 2453, Record H-61, File 1-27, Ministry of War to III Corps Commander, morning of 28 April 1915.
57. TCGB, *Çanakkale Cephesi Harekati (Amfibi Harekat)*, p. 155.
58. Ibid., p. 157. The Ottoman attack was planned at divisional level using 1:25,000 scale maps that were known to be based on old and incomplete data. Therefore, commanders were directed to make checks physically and corrections as necessary.
59. Ibid., p. 157. This page contains a quote from an order in the Atatürk Archives, Archive 6-35, Record 10, File 1-7.
60. Ibid., p. 158.
61. Ibid., p. 160.
62. Ibid., p. 162.

63. ATASE Archive 91/1, 15nci Piyade Alay Tarihçesi, p. 5.
64. Message Saip to Şefik, 4 May 1915 reproduced in Oral, *Gallipoli Through Turkish Eyes 1915*, as Document 4, p. 75.
65. 19th Division Orders for 4 May 1915 reproduced in Oral, *Gallipoli Through Turkish Eyes 1915*, as Document 5, p. 83.
66. The historiography of the Cape Helles landings is largely the same as that of the ANZAC landings since the authors chose a wide-angle view of the entire pattern of landings.
67. ATASE Archive 91/2, 26nci Piyade Alay Tarihçesi, pp. 8–9.
68. Ibid., p. 12.
69. Ibid., p. 12.
70. ATASE Archive 5337, Record H-5, File 1-23, Combat Orders, 26 Regt.
71. TCGB, *Çanakkale Cephesi Harekati (Amfibi Harekat)*, Kroki (Map Overlays), pp. 28–29.
72. Ibid., p. 226.
73. Registration and shooting 'off the map' were gunnery concepts that would not be used in the Ottoman army until 1917.
74. TCGB, *Çanakkale Cephesi Harekati (Amfibi Harekat)*, p. 227.
75. ATASE Archive 5337, Record H-1, File 1-1, Combat Orders, 26 Regt.
76. ATASE Archive 180, Record 777, File 4-19, commander, III Corps to commander, Fifth Army, 4 am, 25 April 1915, reproduced in TCGB, *Askeri Tarih Belgeleri Dergisi 38/88*, pp. 25–26.
77. TCGB, *Çanakkale Cephesi Harekati (Amfibi Harekat)*, p. 232.
78. The Beaten Zone is a technical term in machine-gun employment that denotes the area into which most of the bullets fall. It is elliptically shaped along the gun-target line.
79. ATASE Archive 91/2, 26nci Piyade Alay Tarihçesi, p. 12.
80. TCGB, *Çanakkale Cephesi Harekati (Amfibi Harekat)*, p. 235.
81. Ibid., pp. 237–238.
82. Ibid., pp. 242–243.
83. ATASE Archive 5337, Record H-5, File 1-26, Combat Orders, 26th Infantry Regiment.
84. TCGB, *Çanakkale Cephesi Harekati (Amfibi Harekat)*, pp. 243–244.
85. ATASE Archive 5337, Record H-5, File 1-27, Situation Report, 26 Regt.
86. TCGB, *Çanakkale Cephesi Harekati (Amfibi Harekat)*, p. 265.
87. Ibid.
88. In fairness to Halil Sami, as the 9th Division commander, he remained technically responsible for all of the beaches until relieved of this responsibility in the ANZAC sector in the late afternoon by Esat.
89. Selahattın Adıl Paşa, *Çanakkale Hatırları, 1. Cilt* (Istanbul: Arma Yayınları, 2001), p. 144. Reprint of the memoirs of a participant.

90. ATASE Archive 180, Record 777, File 4-19, III Corps report to Fifth Army, 3.20 pm, 25 April 1915.

91. Ibid.

92. İsmet Görgülü, *Türk Harp Tarıhı Derslerinde Adı Geçen Komutanlar* (İstanbul: Harp Akademileri Basımevi, 1983), p. 437. Halil Sami's performance would continue to erode. Finally on 7 July 1915, he was relieved of command for being 'tired and weary' and sent to Constantinople.

93. See Edward J. Erickson, *Ordered To Die*, pp. 83–84, for the story in English of Sergeant Yahya and his determined defense of this position.

94. ATASE Library, Record 26-485, unpublished staff study (Doğanci), 25nci Piyade Alay Tarihçesi, p. 12.

95. TCGB, *Çanakkale Cephesi Harekati (Amfibi Harekat)*, pp. 261–262.

96. Ibid., pp. 270–271.

97. ATASE Archive 5337, Record H-1, File 1-3, Combat Orders, 3/26 Regt, 1 am, 26 April 1915.

98. TCGB, *Çanakkale Cephesi Harekati (Amfibi Harekat)*, pp. 278–279.

99. Ibid., p. 288.

100. Ibid., p. 292.

101. Travers, *Gallipoli 1915*, p. 92. Travers used British war diaries and a German letter, rather than Turkish sources, to support this idea.

102. ATASE Library, Record 26-326, unpublished staff study (Lütfi Doğanci 1977), 20nci Piyade Alay Tarihçesi, p. 23.

103. ATASE Archive 3459, Record 7, File 1-112, 9ncu Piyade Tumen Tarihçesi, p. 9.

104. ATASE Archive 4836, Record H-10, File 1-83, Combat Orders, 9th Division, 27 April 1915.

105. TCGB, *Çanakkale Cephesi Harekati (Amfibi Harekat)*, p. 299.

106. Ibid., p. 299.

107. The Turkish official history is especially critical of Halil Sami's failure to delay the attack until all preparations had been completed.

108. ATASE Archive 4836, Record H-11, File 1-27, Combat Orders, 9th Division, 28 April 1915.

109. Ibid.

110. TCGB, *Çanakkale Cephesi Harekati (Amfibi Harekat)*, p. 304.

111. Ibid., pp. 304–305.

112. Ibid., p. 305. Travers noted contemporary criticism by Captain Mühlmann that the Turkish fortress artillery did not support the fight at Cape Helles (Travers, *Gallipoli 1915*, p. 97). This would seem to be incorrect based on Turkish histories.

113. Ibid., p. 307.

114. ATASE Archive 4836, Record H-11, File 1-27, Combat Report, 9th Division, 28 April 1915.

115. Field Marshal Lord Carver, *The Turkish Front 1914–1918*, p. 36. Orders did not leave the 29th Division headquarters until 11 pm for an attack scheduled for 8 am on the following morning.

116. Ibid.

117. TCGB, *Çanakkale Cephesi Harekati (Amfibi Harekat)*, p. 309.

118. ATASE Archive 4836, Record H-10, File 1-85, Combat Report, 9th Division, 28 April 1915.

119. TCGB, *Çanakkale Cephesi Harekati (Amfibi Harekat)*, p. 311.

120. LC, GALL 216/1, item 1, Interview with General Askir Arkayan, July 1972, Observation Officer in 3rd Battery, 150mm Howitzer Demonstration Battalion.

121. Travers, *Gallipoli 1915*, p. 93.

122. TCGB, *Çanakkale Cephesi Harekati (Amfibi Harekat)*, Kroki (Map) 4 and 5.

123. Ibid., pp 51–52.

124. Ibid., pp. 53–55.

125. Ibid., p. 58.

126. Ibid., p. 63.

127. Ibid., p. 73.

128. Aspinall-Oglander, *Military Operations Gallipoli, vol. 1*, p. 261.

129. ATASE Archive 4775, Record H-2, File 1-8, Combat report, 39 Regt to commander, 3rd Division, 7.30 am, 26 April 1915, reproduced in TCGB, *Çanakkale Cephesi Harekati (Amfibi Harekat)*, p. 75.

130. ATASE Archive 4775, Record H-2, File 1-9, Combat report, 39 Regt to commander, 3rd Division, 2 pm, 26 April 1915, reproduced in TCGB, *Çanakkale Cephesi Harekati (Amfibi Harekat)*, pp. 76–77. Actually, the fortunate Lieutenant Colonel Nurettin survived to retire as a brigadier general, dying on 8 June 1937 in Istanbul.

131. TCGB, *Çanakkale Cephesi Harekati (Amfibi Harekat)*, p. 79.

132. Ibid., p. 85.

133. Ibid., p. 30.

134. Ibid., p. 32.

135. Liman von Sanders, *Five Years in Turkey*, p. 64.

136. III Corps Orders, 10.10 am, 25 April 1915, full text copy reprinted in TCGB, *Çanakkale Cephesi Harekati (Amfibi Harekat)*, p. 32.

137. Ibid., pp. 32–33.

138. ATASE Archive 3474, Record H-3, File 3-32, Fifth Army orders to XV Corps, 12 pm, 25 April 1915, reproduced in TCGB, *Çanakkale Cephesi Harekati (Amfibi Harekat)*, p. 65.

139. ATASE Archive 3474, Record H-3, File 3-32, Fifth Army report, 5 pm,

25 April 1915, reproduced in TCGB, *Çanakkale Cephesi Harekati (Amfibi Harekat)*, p. 65.

140. See for example ATASE Archive 180, Record 776, File 4/4-1, Message Number 3486, Fifth Army headquarters to Enver Pasha, 26 April 1915, reproduced in TCGB, *Askeri Tarih Belgeleri Dergisi 38/88*, pp. 32–34. This message, concerning the army's actions during the afternoon of 25 April, was sent at 1.50 am, acknowledgement was received at 3.35 am and it was passed to the duty officer at 4.50 am.

141. See for example ATASE Archive 180, Record 777, File 7-23, Intelligence Directorate, Ottoman general staff to commander, Fifth Army, 26 April 1915, reproduced in TCGB, *Askeri Tarih Belgeleri Dergisi 38/88*, pp. 34–36.

Chapter 3

1. ATASE Archive 4836, Record H-10, File 1-86, Fifth Army Orders to III Corps, 28/29 April 1915, cited in TCGB, *Çanakkale Cephesi Harekati (Amfibi Harekat)*, p. 327.
2. TCGB, *Çanakkale Cephesi Harekati (Amfibi Harekat)*, p. 328.
3. Ibid., pp. 333–334.
4. ATASE Archive 4836, Record H-11, File 1-33, Orders, 9th Division, 1 May 1915, reproduced in TCGB, *Çanakkale Cephesi Harekati (Amfibi Harekat)*, p. 342.
5. TCGB, *Çanakkale Cephesi Harekati (Amfibi Harekat)*, p. 346.
6. Ibid., pp. 348–349.
7. Ibid., p. 353.
8. Ibid.
9. Ibid., p. 360.
10. Ibid., pp. 393–395.
11. Ibid., pp. 368–369.
12. Attack Order, Southern Group, 3 May 1915, quoted from Remzi Yiğitgüden, *Çanakkale Cephesi* (Ankara: ATASE Dossier 51, n.d.), pp. 2336–2337 and reproduced in TCGB, *Çanakkale Cephesi Harekati (Amfibi Harekat)*, p. 366.
13. Ibid.
14. TCGB, *Çanakkale Cephesi Harekati (Amfibi Harekat)*, pp. 382–383.
15. Ibid., p. 389.
16. ATASE, 19ncu Piyade Alay Tarihçesi, 6, Archive 91/1.
17. TCGB, *Çanakkale Cephesi Harekati (Amfibi Harekat)*, pp. 394–395.
18. Ibid., Çizelge 1 (Table 1), Fifth Army Strength Reports 25 April 1915, p. 442.
19. Archive 3964, Record H-171, File 1-14, Ottoman General Staff to Fifth

Army, 4 May 1915, ATASE quoted in TCGB, *Çanakkale Cephesi Harekati (Amfibi Harekat)*, p. 395.

20. Ibid., p. 396.

21. ATASE Archive 3474, Record H-5, File 2-12, Southern Group to Fifth Army, 7 May 1915, quoted in TCGB, *Çanakkale Cephesi Harekati (Amfibi Harekat)*, p. 414.

22. Travers, *Gallipoli 1915*, pp. 125–128.

23. İsmet Görgülü, *On Yillik Harbin Kadrosu 1912–1913, Balkan–Birinci Dünya ve Istiklal Harbi* (Ankara: Türk Tarih Kurum Basımevi, 1993), pp. 70–71.

24. ATASE Archive 3474, Record H-5, File 2-30, General Headquarters to Commander, Fifth Army, 13 May 1915, reproduced in TCGB, *Çanakkale Cephesi Harekati (Amfibi Harekat)*, pp. 180–181.

25. Colonel Süleyman Askeri was a well-known guerilla commander of the Ottoman Teşkilat-ı Mahsusa, who led irregular forces in western Thrace after the Balkan Wars and who was then commanding in Mesopotamia against the British. He was also a member of the inner circle of the CUP (Young Turk) party. Badly wounded in action against the British, Süleyman Askeri committed suicide in mid-April 1915.

26. ATASE Archive 3474, Record H-6, File 3-16, 'Operations' Headquarters Northern Group to Fifth Army, 14 May 1915, reproduced in TCGB, *Çanakkale Cephesi Harekati (Amfibi Harekat)*, pp. 185–187.

27. ATASE Archive 3474, Record H-6, File 3-24, Fifth Army Orders, 1115, 17 May 1915, reproduced in TCGB, *Çanakkale Cephesi Harekati (Amfibi Harekat)*, p. 184.

28. ATASE Archive 3474, Record H-6, File 3-15, Report from Commander 19th Division to Northern Group, 17 May 1915, reproduced in TCGB, *Çanakkale Cephesi Harekati (Amfibi Harekat)*, pp. 187–188.

29. ATASE Archive 3474, Record H-6, File 3-30, Fifth Army Orders to Northern Group, 1350, 17 May 1915, reproduced in TCGB, *Çanakkale Cephesi Harekati (Amfibi Harekat)*, pp. 191–192.

30. ATASE Archive 3964, Record H-22, File 1-12, Corps Order No. 15, Northern Group, 2000, 18 May 1915, reproduced in TCGB, *Çanakkale Cephesi Harekati (Amfibi Harekat)*, pp. 193–194. Esat's Northern Group retained the numbered corps orders system of his III Corps headquarters.

31. TCGB, *Çanakkale Cephesi Harekati (Amfibi Harekat)*, pp. 196–197.

32. Ibid., pp. 197–198.

33. Ibid., pp. 198–199.

34. Ibid., pp. 201–203.

35. Ibid., p. 198.

36. ATASE Archive 3964, Record H-2, File 1-7, Combat Report from 2 Div to

Northern Group, 0510, 18 May 1915, reproduced in TCGB, *Çanakkale Cephesi Harekati (Amfibi Harekat)*, p. 201.

37. TCGB, *Çanakkale Cephesi Harekati (Amfibi Harekat)*, see pp. 205–209 for a complete discussion of these events.

38. ATASE Archive 3964, Record H-23, File 1-11, Report from Northern Group to Fifth Army, 1120, 19 May 1915, reproduced in TCGB, *Çanakkale Cephesi Harekati (Amfibi Harekat)*, pp. 210–211.

39. See Aspinall-Oglander, *Military Operations Gallipoli, vol. 2*, pp. 20–22 for a complete version of how the cease fire came into being. The Turkish official history treats the incident with a single paragraph but notes that the cease fire was welcomed because the constant sight of such a large number of Ottoman dead in front of their own trenches caused a severe morale problem for the Northern Group.

40. ATASE Archive 4836, Record H-17, File 1-4, Special Orders, 9th Division, 28 May 1915, reproduced in TCGB, *Türk Silahi Kuvvetleri Tarihi Osmanli Devri Birinci Dünya Harbinde Türk Harbi Vnci Cilt 3ncu Kitap, Çanakkale Cephesi Harekati (Haziran 1915–Ocak 1916)* (Ankara: Genelkurmay Basımevi, 1980), pp. 31–32.

41. Aspinall-Oglander, *Military Operations Gallipoli, vol. 2*, pp. 49–53. Aspinall-Oglander's assertion is based on comments by German Colonel Hans Kannengiesser, who was a 'trustworthy eye witness.' It is unclear what position Kannengiesser served in as he was neither a staff officer in the XV Corps headquarters nor did he command any tactical units at this time.

42. ATASE Archive 3474, Record H-8, File 1-4 and Record H-9, File 6, Combat Reports, Southern Group, 5 June 1915, reproduced in TCGB, *Çanakkale Cephesi Harekati (Haziran 1915–Ocak 1916)*, pp. 60–61.

43. ATASE Archive 4865, Record H-8, File 1-4 and Record H-6, File 1-5, Order Number 8, 12th Division, 6.30 pm, 5 June 1915, reproduced in TCGB, *Çanakkale Cephesi Harekati (Haziran 1915–Ocak 1916)*, p. 66.

44. ATASE Archive 3474, Record H-6, File 5-48 and Record H-9, Files 6-1 and 6-2, Losses, 3–6 June 1915, reproduced in TCGB, *Çanakkale Cephesi Harekati (Haziran 1915–Ocak 1916)*, p. 72.

45. ATASE Archive 3474, Record H-9, File 6-24, After Action Report from Colonel Weber to Fifth Army, 10 June 1915, reproduced in TCGB, *Çanakkale Cephesi Harekati (Haziran 1915–Ocak 1916)* as Ek (Document) 7, pp. 583–585. The discrepancy in reported Ottoman losses for Third Krithia is highlighted in the Turkish official history which estimated about 9,000 total casualties in 3 days of combat.

46. For a more complete understanding of how and why Ottoman divisions were able to maintain combat effectiveness readers may wish to refer to

the author's book *Ottoman Army Effectiveness in WW I: A Comparative Study* (London: Routledge, 2007).

47. ATASE Archive 3474, Record H-9, File 6-7, Army Order Number 40, Headquarters Fifth Army, 7 June 1915, reproduced in TCGB, *Çanakkale Cephesi Harekati (Haziran 1915–Ocak 1916)*, p. 82.
48. TCGB, *Çanakkale Cephesi Harekati (Haziran 1915–Ocak 1916)*, pp. 83–84.
49. ATASE Archive 4857, Record H-8, File 1-15, Weber to division commanders, 7.30 pm, 8 June 1915, cited in TCGB, *Çanakkale Cephesi Harekati (Haziran 1915–Ocak 1916)*, p. 88.
50. ATASE Archive 3474, Record H-10, File 1-9, Liman von Sanders to Enver, 17 June 1915, reproduced in TCGB, *Çanakkale Cephesi Harekati (Haziran 1915–Ocak 1916)*, p. 587.
51. ATASE Archive 3474, Record H-10, File 1-5, Enver to Liman von Sanders, 17 June 1915, reproduced in TCGB, *Çanakkale Cephesi Harekati (Haziran 1915–Ocak 1916)*, p. 589.
52. ATASE Archive 3474, Record H-10, File 1-47, Secret Cipher Southern Group to Fifth Army, 20 June 1915, reproduced in TCGB, *Çanakkale Cephesi Harekati (Haziran 1915–Ocak 1916)* as Ek (Document) 10, pp. 591–593.
53. TCGB, *Çanakkale Cephesi Harekati (Haziran 1915–Ocak 1916)*, pp. 122–124.
54. Ibid., pp. 126–128.
55. ATASE Archive 4761, Record H-6, File 1-11, Situation Report 2nd Division, 7.15 pm, 21 June 1915, reproduced in TCGB, *Çanakkale Cephesi Harekati (Haziran 1915–Ocak 1916)*, pp. 130–131.
56. Cemil Conk Paşa, *Çanakkale Hatırları* reprinted in *Çanakkale Hatırları, 2. Cilt,* (Istanbul: Arma Yayınları, 2002), pp. 42–143.
57. ATASE Archive 4761, Record H-6, File 1-13, 34th Regiment Situation Report to 2nd Division, 3.40 pm, 22 June 1915, reproduced in TCGB, *Çanakkale Cephesi Harekati (Haziran 1915–Ocak 1916)*, pp. 134–135.
58. Fifth Army report cited in TCGB, *Çanakkale Cephesi Harekati (Haziran 1915–Ocak 1916)*, p. 143.
59. TCGB, *Çanakkale Cephesi Harekati (Haziran 1915–Ocak 1916)*, p. 152.
60. Süleyman Şakir, *Cepheden Hatırlar, Altıncı Fırka Çanakkale Harbi'nde* (Ankara: Vadi Yayınları, 2006), translated by Servet Avşar and Hasan Babacan from *Donanma Mecmuası, No. 158–159* (18 March 1918), pp. 32–33.
61. ATASE Archive 4857, Record H-12, File 1, Southern Group orders 12.00 pm, 28 June 1915, quoted in TCGB, *Çanakkale Cephesi Harekati (Haziran 1915–Ocak 1916)*, p. 154.
62. ATASE Archive 4857, Record H-12, File 1-4, Lüftü to commander 11th Division, 4.25 pm, 28 June 1915, quoted in TCGB, *Çanakkale Cephesi Harekati (Haziran 1915–Ocak 1916)*, p. 155.
63. ATASE Archive 4857, Record H-12, File 1-11, Weber to Faik, 8.30 am,

29 June 1915, quoted in TCGB, *Çanakkale Cephesi Harekati (Haziran 1915–Ocak 1916)*, p. 161.

64. Şakir, *Cepheden Hatırlar*, pp. 50–55. While his battalions were being sent in penny packets into the unfolding fight, Staff Colonel Sakir was ordered by telephone to continue onward with his remaining units to reinforce the 4th Division on the left flank.

65. ATASE Archive 4857, Record H-12, File 1-13, II Corps Orders, Attack order for 29 June, 143 Rakımlı Tepe, 6 pm, 29 June 1915, reproduced in TCGB, *Çanakkale Cephesi Harekati (Haziran 1915–Ocak 1916)*, pp. 165–167.

66. TCGB, *Çanakkale Cephesi Harekati (Haziran 1915–Ocak 1916)*, p. 168.

67. ATASE Archive 4763, Record H-7, File 1-42, II Corps Orders, 11.20 am, 1 July 1915, reproduced in TCGB, *Çanakkale Cephesi Harekati (Haziran 1915–Ocak 1916)*, pp. 178–179.

68. ATASE Archive 4763, Record H-7, File 1-52, After Action Report from Major Reşat, 21 August 1915, reproduced in TCGB, *Çanakkale Cephesi Harekati (Haziran 1915–Ocak 1916)*, p. 181.

69. TCGB, *Çanakkale Cephesi Harekati (Haziran 1915–Ocak 1916)*, pp. 186–188.

70. Ibid., pp. 193–194.

71. See Erickson, *Defeat in Detail*, pp. 131–136 for a thorough description of the artillery command arrangements and dispositions during the Çatalca battles in 1912/13.

72. Ibid., p. 195.

73. Ibid., pp. 195–196.

74. ATASE Archive 4775, Record H-4, File 1-18, Situation report from Lieutenant Colonel Nurettin, 5.30 am, 5 July 1915, reproduced in TCGB, *Çanakkale Cephesi Harekati (Haziran 1915–Ocak 1916)*, p. 196.

75. ATASE Archive 4775, Record H-4, File 1-18, Situation report from Lieutenant Colonel Ismail Hakkı, 5.25 am, 5 July 1915, reproduced in TCGB, *Çanakkale Cephesi Harekati (Haziran 1915–Ocak 1916)*, p. 196.

76. ATASE Archive 4763, Record H-7, File 1-68, Situation report from Lieutenant Colonel Cafer Tayyar, 11.45 am, 5 July 1915, reproduced in TCGB, *Çanakkale Cephesi Harekati (Haziran 1915–Ocak 1916)*, p. 200.

77. ATASE Archive 3849, Record H-22, Files 1-35, 1-37, 3rd Division strength returns 5 July 1915 and 3rd Division casualty reports 6 July 1915, reproduced in TCGB, *Çanakkale Cephesi Harekati (Haziran 1915–Ocak 1916)*, p. 205.

78. ATASE Archive 3849, Record H-22, Files 1-37, 1-40, 5th Division strength returns 5 July 1915 and 5th Division casualty reports 6 July 1915, reproduced in TCGB, *Çanakkale Cephesi Harekati (Haziran 1915–Ocak 1916)*, p. 206.

79. Şakir, *Cepheden Hatırlar*, p. 34.

80. Report from Staff Captain Nihat to Çanakkale Group Commander, 20 March 1918 (no archival citation), reproduced in TCGB, *Çanakkale Cephesi Harekati (Haziran 1915–Ocak 1916)*, pp. 209–210.

81. ATASE Archive 181, Record H-779, File 4, Ciphered Report from Commander, Fifth Army to Enver Pasha, 4 am, 22 June 1915, reproduced in TCGB, *Askeri Tarih Belgeleri Dergisi 38/88*, pp. 72–73.

82. ATASE Archive 181, Record H-779, File 4-1, Ciphered Report from Commander, Fifth Army to Enver Pasha, 5.10 am, 25 June 1915, reproduced in TCGB, *Askeri Tarih Belgeleri Dergisi 38/88*, pp. 79–80.

83. ATASE Archive 181, Record H-778, File 105-1, Ciphered Report from Commander, Fifth Army to Ottoman general staff, 22 June 1915, reproduced in TCGB, *Askeri Tarih Belgeleri Dergisi 38/88*, pp. 76–77.

84. ATASE Archive 3474, Record H-12, File 8-25, Enver Pasha to Commander, Fifth Army, 6 July 1915, reproduced in TCGB, *Çanakkale Cephesi Harekati (Haziran 1915–Ocak 1916)*, p. 211.

85. ATASE Archive 181, Record H-779, File 31, Ciphered Telegram from Ahmet Fevzi, Saros Group to Enver, 2 July 1915, reproduced in TCGB, *Askeri Tarih Belgeleri Dergisi 38/88*, p. 87.

86. ATASE Archive 3474, Record H-12, File 8-24, Liman von Sanders to Commander, Northern Group, 7.50 pm, 6 July 1915, reproduced in TCGB, *Çanakkale Cephesi Harekati (Haziran 1915–Ocak 1916)*, p. 219.

87. Liman von Sanders, *Five Years in Turkey*, pp. 79–82.

88. ATASE Archive 4763, Record H-7, File 1-104, Southern Group Orders, 11 July 1915 reproduced in TCGB, *Çanakkale Cephesi Harekati (Haziran 1915–Ocak 1916)*, pp. 228–229.

89. Aspinall-Oglander, *Military Operations Gallipoli, vol. 2*, p. 100.

90. ATASE Archive 4821, Record H-22, File 1-29, Mehmet Vehip to commander, 6th Division, 9.15 am, 12 July 1915, reproduced in TCGB, *Çanakkale Cephesi Harekati (Haziran 1915–Ocak 1916)*, p. 245.

91. Southern Group orders, 10 pm, 12 July 1915, reproduced in Şakir, *Cepheden Hatırlar*, pp. 82–83.

92. TCGB, *Çanakkale Cephesi Harekati (Haziran 1915–Ocak 1916)*, p. 249.

93. Copy of 6th Division orders sent to commander, Southern Group, 8 pm, 13 July 1915, reproduced in Şakir, *Cepheden Hatırlar*, pp. 83–84. Şakir's memoirs for the period 12–14 July 1915 contain dozens of group, area, division and regimental orders and messages, making the period one of the most fully documented wartime episodes available in secondary sources.

94. See TCGB, *Çanakkale Cephesi Harekati (Haziran 1915–Ocak 1916)*, p. 251 for the entire report.

95. Ibid., p. 263.

96. ATASE Archive 3474, Record H-13, File 9-45, Enver Pasha to commander, Fifth Army, 17 July 1915, reproduced in TCGB, *Çanakkale Cephesi Harekati (Haziran 1915–Ocak 1916)*, p. 264.

97. ATASE Archive 3474, Record H-14, File 10-7, Liman von Sanders to Straits Fortress Command, 26 July 1915, reproduced in TCGB, *Çanakkale Cephesi Harekati (Haziran 1915–Ocak 1916)*, p. 267.

98. TCGB, *Çanakkale Cephesi Harekati (Haziran 1915–Ocak 1916)*, p. 269.

99. Andrew Mango, *Atatürk, The Biography of the Founder of Modern Turkey* (Woodstock, NY: Overlook Press, 1999), p. 151. Other than his assertion to this effect there is little evidence to support Mustafa Kemal's claim. See also Mustafa Kemal, *Anafarta Hatırları* (Ankara: 1962) reprinted in Esat Paşa, *Çanakkale Savaşı Hatırları* (Istanbul: Örgün Yayınevi, 2003), pp. 507–508.

Chapter 4

1. Aspinall-Oglander, *Military Operations Gallipoli, Vol. 2*, p. 182.

2. SATASE Archive 4846, Record H-8, File 4-32, Mehmet Vehip to Fifth Army, 4.30 pm, 6 August 1915, reproduced in TCGB, *Çanakkale Cephesi Harekati (Haziran 1915–Ocak 1916)*, pp. 314–315.

3. ATASE Archive 4350, Record H-5, File 4-38, Mehmet Vehip to Fifth Army, 6.55 pm, 7 August 1915, reproduced in TCGB, *Çanakkale Cephesi Harekati (Haziran 1915–Ocak 1916)*, pp. 321–322.

4. ATASE Archive 4350, Record H-5, File 4-35, Fifth Army to Southern Group, 11.30 am, 7 August 1915, quoted in TCGB, *Çanakkale Cephesi Harekati (Haziran 1915–Ocak 1916)*, p. 323.

5. ATASE Archive 4350, Record H-5, File 4-36, Liman von Sanders to Southern Group, 2.25 pm, 7 August 1915, reproduced in TCGB, *Çanakkale Cephesi Harekati (Haziran 1915–Ocak 1916)*, p. 324.

6. Casualty returns, 1st, 10th, 13th and 14th Divisions, ATASE Archive 217, Record 5, File 54-108, tabular listing in TCGB, *Çanakkale Cephesi Harekati (Haziran 1915–Ocak 1916)*, p. 325.

7. TCGB, *Çanakkale Cephesi Harekati (Haziran 1915–Ocak 1916)*, p. 380.

8. Esat Paşa,*Çanakkale Savaşı Hatırları* (Istanbul: Örgün Yayınevi, 2003), pp. 187–189.

9. ATASE Archive 3474, Record H-14, File 1-17, Fifth Army to von Usedom, 26 July 1915, quoted in TCGB, *Çanakkale Cephesi Harekati (Haziran 1915–Ocak 1916)*, p. 330.

10. Görgülü, *On Yıllık Harbin Kadrosu*, p. 88.

11. TCGB, *Çanakkale Cephesi Harekati (Haziran 1915–Ocak 1916)*, pp. 335–337.

12. Ibid., p. 337. This conflicts with what Major Zeki told C.E.W. Bean in 1919, which was that Tevfik's death occurred 'on the second night of fighting or

third morning.' See C.E.W. Bean, *Gallipoli Mission* (Canberra: Australian War Memorial, 1952), p. 191.

13. ATASE Archive 3402, Record H-72, File 10-25, Report by Colonel Rüştü forwarded by Commander Northern Group to Commander Fifth Army, 7 August 1915, reproduced in TCGB, *Askeri Tarih Belgeleri Dergisi 38/88*, pp. 100–101.

14. ATASE Archive 3474, Record H-15, File 11-1, Liman von Sanders to Enver, 7 August 1915, quoted in TCGB, *Çanakkale Cephesi Harekati (Haziran 1915–Ocak 1916)*, pp. 337–338.

15. ATASE Archive 4883, Record H-8, File 1-7, Commander 16th Division to Northern Group, 6 am, 7 August 1915, quoted in TCGB, *Çanakkale Cephesi Harekati (Haziran 1915–Ocak 1916)*, p. 338.

16. TCGB, *Çanakkale Cephesi Harekati (Haziran 1915–Ocak 1916)*, p. 340. This number significantly exceeds Aspinall-Oglander's estimate of 5,000 Ottoman casualties (*Military Operations Gallipoli, Vol. 2*, p. 181).

17. See also H.B. Danışman (ed.), *Gallipoli 1915, Bloody Ridge (Lone Pine) Diary of Lt. Mehmed Fasih* (Istanbul: Denizler Kitabevi, 2003) for information on and photographs of Lone Pine during the period 11 October–19 December 1915.

18. ATASE Archive 4936, Record H-25, File 1-3, Combat report from Commander, 1st Battalion, 72nd Regiment, 1.30 am, 7 August 1915, quoted in TCGB, *Çanakkale Cephesi Harekati (Haziran 1915–Ocak 1916)*, p. 346.

19. TCGB, *Çanakkale Cephesi Harekati (Haziran 1915–Ocak 1916)*, Kroki (map) 39.

20. ATASE Archive 4936, Record H-25, File 1-3, Commander 19th Division to Commander Northern Group, 5.05 am, 7 August 1915, reproduced in TCGB, *Çanakkale Cephesi Harekati (Haziran 1915–Ocak 1916)*, p. 348.

21. TCGB, *Çanakkale Cephesi Harekati (Haziran 1915–Ocak 1916)*, p. 350.

22. Travers, *Gallipoli 1915*, p. 165.

23. TCGB, *Çanakkale Cephesi Harekati (Haziran 1915–Ocak 1916)*, p. 350.

24. See ATASE Archive 3402, Record H-72, File 10-17, Esat Pasha to Commander Fifth Army, 9.50 am, 7 August 1915, reproduced in TCGB, *Askeri Tarih Belgeleri Dergisi 38/88*, pp. 98–99, in which Esat explicitly outlines the enemy attacks on Chunuk Bair and Hill 971 as well as his response with the 9th and 19th Divisions.

25. Cemil Conk Paşa, *Çanakkale Hatırları*, p. 199.

26. Northern Group Orders, Kemalyeri, 11.10 am, 7 August 1915, reproduced in Cemil Conk Paşa, *Çanakkale Hatırları*, pp. 200–201.

27. ATASE Archive 4798, Record H-4, File 1-137, Commander 4th Division to Commander Northern Group, 3.30 pm, 7 August 1915 quoted in TCGB, *Çanakkale Cephesi Harekati (Haziran 1915–Ocak 1916)*, p. 353.

28. TCGB, *Çanakkale Cephesi Harekati (Haziran 1915–Ocak 1916)*, p. 354.

29. Ibid., p. 355.
30. ATASE Archive 4798, Record H-2, File 1-103, Commander Fifth Army to Commander Northern Group, 10.10 pm, 7 August 1915, quoted in TCGB, *Çanakkale Cephesi Harekati (Haziran 1915–Ocak 1916)*, p. 356.
31. Although Liman von Sanders had issued this order at 10.10 pm the previous evening, copies did not make it through to Cemil until 9 am, 8 August 1915.
32. TCGB, *Çanakkale Cephesi Harekati (Haziran 1915–Ocak 1916)*, p. 360.
33. Travers, *Gallipoli 1915*, pp. 166–167.
34. Liman von Sanders, *Five Years in Turkey*, pp. 84–85.
35. Professor Travers asserted that the 7th and 12th Divisions 'certainly arrived late on 7 August.' See Travers, *Gallipoli 1915*, p. 199. However, Ahmet Fevzi's orders of 3.40 am, 8 August place the lead elements of the 12th Division arriving just west of Turşunköyü and the 7th Division just east of Kücük Anafarta. Moreover, Ahmet Fevzi ordered them to send a battalion forward to secure their assembly areas. It is clear from these orders that the main bodies of the divisions could not have closed on their assembly areas until midday, 8 August. See ATASE Archive 4863, Record H-12, File 1-15, Group Orders, Anafarta Group, 3.40 am, 8 August 1915, reproduced in TCGB, *Çanakkale Cephesi Harekati (Haziran 1915–Ocak 1916)*, pp. 403–404.
36. İsmail Hakkı Sunata, *Gelibolu'dan Kafkaslara, Birinci Dünya Şavası Anılarım* (Istanbul: Kultur Yayınlari, 2003), pp. 126–129.
37. ATASE Archive 4936, Record H-34, File 1-3, Record of telephone conversation (Secret) between Liman von Sanders and the Northern Group, 7 pm, 8 August 1915, reproduced in TCGB, *Çanakkale Cephesi Harekati (Haziran 1915–Ocak 1916)*, p. 361.
38. Oral, *Gallipoli Through Turkish Eyes 1915*, pp. 338–339.
39. Ibid., p. 327.
40. Izzettin Çalışlar, *On Yıllık Savaşın Günlüğü*, edited by Dr İsmet Görgülü (Ankara: KYK, 1999), p. 104, cited in Oral, *Gallipoli Through Turkish Eyes 1915*, p. 327.
41. TCGB, *Çanakkale Cephesi Harekati (Haziran 1915–Ocak 1916)*, p. 391.
42. See Aspinall-Oglander, *Military Operations Gallipoli, vol. 2*, p. 266 for Willmer's report to Fifth Army, 7 pm, 7 August 1915.
43. ATASE Archive 4863, Record H-12, File 1-15, Group Orders, Anafarta Group, 3.40 am, 8 August 1915, reproduced in TCGB, *Çanakkale Cephesi Harekati (Haziran 1915–Ocak 1916)*, pp. 403–404.
44. TCGB, *Çanakkale Cephesi Harekati (Haziran 1915–Ocak 1916)*, p. 413.
45. These two officers were buried side by side and are remembered with a fine memorial monument in the Büyük Anafarta cemetery. See Gürsel

Göncü and Şahin Aldoğan, *Çanakkale Muharebe Alanları Gezi Rehberi (Gallipoli Battlefield Guide)* (Istanbul: M.B. Yayınevi, 2004), p. 129.

46. Ibid., p. 416.
47. Ibid., p. 366.
48. Ibid., p. 368.
49. ATASE Archive 4835, Record H-9, File 1-195, Telephonic orders from Fifth Army to Northern Group commander, 3.14 pm, 9 August 1915, reproduced in TCGB, *Çanakkale Cephesi Harekati (Haziran 1915–Ocak 1916)*, p. 369.
50. TCGB, *Çanakkale Cephesi Harekati (Haziran 1915–Ocak 1916)*, pp. 416–417.
51. Ibid., p. 417.
52. ATASE Archive 4835, Record H-9, File 1-195, Orders to 8th Division commander from Anafarta Group commander, 10.20 pm, 9 August 1915, reproduced in TCGB, *Çanakkale Cephesi Harekati (Haziran 1915–Ocak 1916)*, p. 374.
53. Mango, *Atatürk*, p. 152.
54. TCGB, *Çanakkale Cephesi Harekati (Haziran 1915–Ocak 1916)*, p. 374.
55. Aspinall-Oglander, *Military Operations Gallipoli, vol. 2*, p. 307.
56. James, *Gallipoli*, pp. 299–300. James asserted that over a thousand men died at the Pinnacle and another thousand died in the debacle at the Farm within a matter of minutes.
57. Göncü and Aldoğan, *Çanakkale Muharebe Alanları Gezi Rehberi*, p. 73.
58. Oral, *Gallipoli Through Turkish Eyes 1915*, p. 338.
59. TCGB, *Çanakkale Cephesi Harekati (Haziran 1915–Ocak 1916)*, p. 422.
60. Ibid, pp. 426–427.
61. Ibid., p. 428.
62. Ibid., p. 432.
63. ATASE Archive 3474, Record H-16, File 2-23, Telegraph message from Liman von Sanders to Enver Pasha, 16 August 1915, quoted in TCGB, *Çanakkale Cephesi Harekati (Haziran 1915–Ocak 1916)*, p. 437.
64. Aspinall-Oglander, *Military Operations Gallipoli, vol. 2*, p. 344.
65. TCGB, *Çanakkale Cephesi Harekati (Haziran 1915–Ocak 1916)*, p. 438.
66. ATASE Archive 3474, Record H-16, File 2-25, Saros Group orders, 7.40 pm, 17 August 1915, quoted in TCGB, *Çanakkale Cephesi Harekati (Haziran 1915–Ocak 1916)*, p. 439.
67. TCGB, *Çanakkale Cephesi Harekati (Haziran 1915–Ocak 1916)*, p. 450.
68. Ibid., p. 452.
69. Ibid. p. 453.
70. Ibid., p. 457.
71. Ibid., p. 453.
72. Ibid., p. 454.

73. ATASE Archive 3474, Record H-17, File 3-3, Mustafa Kemal to Liman von Sanders, 9 pm, 22 August 1915, reproduced in TCGB, *Çanakkale Cephesi Harekati (Haziran 1915–Ocak 1916)*, pp. 455–456.

74. ATASE Archive 3474, Record H-17, File 3-25, Liman von Sanders to commander, Anafarta Group, 29 August 1915, reproduced in TCGB, *Çanakkale Cephesi Harekati (Haziran 1915–Ocak 1916)* as Ek (Document) 15, pp. 612–613.

75. Ibid.

76. Fahri Belen, *Birinci Cihan Harbinde Türk Harbi, 1918 Yılı Hareketleri, Vnci Cilt* (Ankara: Genelkurmay Basımevi, 1967), Ek (Document) 1 after p. 250. This table contains a complete list of all sixty-two Ottoman infantry divisions (as well as the five Caucasian infantry divisions) mobilized during the First World War. Belen's table also contains activation and deactivation dates as well as the location of activation or home garrison.

77. TCGB, *Çanakkale Cephesi Harekati (Haziran 1915–Ocak 1916)*, p. 467.

78. Ibid., p. 472.

79. Ibid., p. 471.

80. Ibid., p. 473.

81. Ibid., p. 474.

82. Ibid., p. 472.

83. Ibid., p. 475.

84. Ibid., p. 477.

85. Ibid., p. 494.

86. The Turkish official history makes the point that Mustafa Kemal's active command style, had he been healthy enough to lead, would have made the British and ANZAC evacuation much more problematic. See TCGB, *Çanakkale Cephesi Harekati (Haziran 1915–Ocak 1916)*, pp. 493–494 for commentary.

87. TCGB, *Çanakkale Cephesi Harekati (Haziran 1915–Ocak 1916)*, p. 494.

88. Aspinall-Oglander, *Military Operations Gallipoli, vol. 2*, pp. 472–473.

89. ATASE Archive 3474, Record H-56, File 1-9, Liman von Sanders to Enver Pasha, 8.45 am, 9 January 1916, reproduced in TCGB, *Çanakkale Cephesi Harekati (Haziran 1915–Ocak 1916)*, p. 499.

90. ATASE Archive 3474, Record H-17, File 1-7, Orders Number 107, Fifth Army headquarters, 9 January 1916, reproduced in TCGB, *Çanakkale Cephesi Harekati (Haziran 1915–Ocak 1916)*, p. 501.

Chapter 5

1. TCGB, *Turk Silahli Kuvvetleri Tarihi (1908–1920)*, p. 265.

2. TCGB, *Türk Istiklal Harbi'ne Kalilan Tümen ve Daha Ust Kademelerdeki Komutanların Biyografileri* (Ankara: Genelkurmay Basımevi, 1989),

pp. 124–126. The biographical material for Lieutenant Colonel Kazım comes from this source.

3. TCGB, *Türk Silahlı Kuvvetleri Tarihi (1908–1920)*, pp. 296–300. See Erickson, *Defeat in Detail*, pp. 55–59 for a thorough discussion in English of Ottoman staff procedures and the use of German publications and doctrines by the Turks.

4. General Orders (*Ordu Emirnamesi*), No. 1, reprinted in TCGB, *Türk Silahlı Kuvvetleri Tarihi (1908–1920)*, pp. 405–411.

5. TCGB, *Türk Silahlı Kuvvetleri Tarihi (1908–1920)*, p. 405 and, in English, Erickson, *Defeat in Detail*, p. 336.

6. General Orders No. 9, 24 May 1914, reprinted in TCGB, *Türk Silahlı Kuvvetleri Tarihi (1908–1920)*, pp. 327–328.

7. The modern Turkish General Staff archives in Ankara contain thousands of sequential war diaries from regiment through army group level, attesting to the thoroughness and integrity of the Ottoman Army's war-diary system.

8. TCGB, *Türk Silahlı Kuvvetleri Tarihi (1908–1920)*, pp. 329–330.

9. Oral, *Gallipoli Through Turkish Eyes 1915*, p. 224.

10. Orders regarding map distribution, Commander, 19th Division to Right Flank Units, 14 May 1915, reproduced in Oral, *Gallipoli Through Turkish Eyes 1915*, p. 224.

11. Oral, *Gallipoli Through Turkish Eyes 1915*, p. 229.

12. For a detailed explanation of the Ottoman army's reorganization into triangular corps and divisions, see Erickson, *Defeat in Detail*, Chapter 1.

13. Ibid., pp. 459–463.

14. Herman Cron, *The Imperial German Army, 1914–1918: Organisation, Structure, Orders-of-Battle* (Solihull: Helion and Company Ltd, 2002), p. 237.

15. TCGB, *Türk Silahli Kuvvetleri Tarihi Osmanli Devri Birinci Dünya Harbi Idari Faaliyetler ve Lojistik, Xncu Cilt* (Ankara: Genelkurmay Basımevi, 1985), p. 115.

16. Ibid., p. 102.

17. TCGB, *Çanakkale Cephesi Harekati (Haziran 1915–Ocak 1916)*, pp. 524–525.

18. Ibid., Çizelge (Table) 3.

19. Ibid., p. 529.

20. TCGB, *Türk Silahlı Kuvvetleri Tarihi (1908–1920)*, p. 358.

21. Ibid., pp. 360–361.

22. TCGB, *Çanakkale Cephesi Harekati (Haziran 1915–Ocak 1916)*, pp. 538–540.

23. NARA, M 1145, Dispatch 503, General Information of military troops and events in Constantinople, Captain R.H. Taylor, Constantinople Embassy, 14 February 1916.

24. Ibid.

25. NARA, M 1147, Dispatch 518, General military conditions in

Constantinople, Captain R.H. Taylor, Constantinople Embassy, 21 March 1916.

26. TCGB, *Türk Silahlı Kuvvetleri Tarihi (1908–1920)*, pp. 391–394. Ottoman soldiers fired only about 20–30 rifle bullets in training (p. 393).

27. ATASE Archive Cabinet 91, Record 34, Shelf 3, File 202, 48nci Piyade Alay Tarihçesi, p. 8. There were five officers killed and nine officers wounded in this attack as well.

28. Ibid., p. 8.

29. LC, Box TU 01, tape 69, Interview with Lt Gen Fahrettin Altay, July 1972.

30. TCGB, *Çanakkale Cephesi Harekati (Haziran 1915–Ocak 1916)*, Kroki (Map) 8 and 9.

31. ATASE Archive 3849, Record H-22, File 1-35, 3rd Infantry Division Strength Returns, 5 July 1915, reprinted in TCGB, *Çanakkale Cephesi Harekati (Haziran 1915–Ocak 1916)*, p. 205.

32. ATASE Archive 3849, Record H-22, File 1-37, 5th Infantry Division Strength Returns, 5 July 1915, reprinted in TCGB, *Çanakkale Cephesi Harekati (Haziran 1915–Ocak 1916)*, p. 206.

33. Ibid., pp. 205–206.

34. Ibid., p. 207. These additional casualties came from the following infantry divisions: 1st (2,853), 4th (963), 6th (2,932), 7th (265), 11th (3,311) and 12th (534).

35. Ibid., pp. 545–552.

36. Ibid., pp. 547–548.

37. NARA, M 1147, File 6368-13, Report on Turkey – the Dardanelles, Captain R.H. Williams, Constantinople Embassy, 3 May 1915.

38. Cemil Conk Paşa, *Çanakkale Hatırları*, pp. 146–151. The material in the paragraphs following are taken from these pages.

39. Although the Ottoman army's regular medical corps was made up of mostly Muslim professionals, the army relied on reserve Jewish and Armenian doctors to fill out its wartime establishments.

40. LC, Box TU 01, item 4, tape 49, Interview with Lt Col Abil Savaşman, July 1972.

41. TCGB, *Çanakkale Cephesi Harekati (Haziran 1915–Ocak 1916)*, p. 549.

42. Ibid., p. 538.

43. Ibid., p. 549.

44. Hikmet Özdemir, *The Ottoman Army 1914–1918, Disease and Death on the Battlefield* (Salt Lake City: University of Utah Press, 2008), p. 127, Table 6.20.

45. See Erickson, *Ordered To Die*, Appendix F, pp. 237–243 for tabular data on annual Ottoman army casualties.

46. Ibid., p. 555.

47. LC, Box TU 01, tape 67, Interview with Gen Fahri Belen, July 1972.

48. Danışman (ed.), *Gallipoli 1915, Bloody Ridge (Lone Pine) Diary of Lt. Mehmed Fasih*, pp. 33–35. See diary entries for 28 and 29 October 1915.

49. Ibid. See also LC, Box TU 01, tape 69, Interview with Capt A. Ozgan, 27th Infantry Regiment, July 1972 and LC, Box TU 01, tape 46, Interview with S. Artum, aide-de-camp, July 1972.

50. LC, Box TU 01, Letter to father, 7 May 1915 and letter to wife, 16 June 1915, Fahrettin Altay, July 1972. Altay requested that his father send him pastries, fruit, cologne, acid drops and new shirts.

51. Danışman (ed.), *Gallipoli 1915, Bloody Ridge (Lone Pine) Diary of Lt. Mehmed Fasih*, p. 44. See, for example, diary entry for 31 October 1915.

52. TCGB, *Çanakkale Cephesi Harekati (Haziran 1915–Ocak 1916)*, p. 555.

53. LC, Box TU 01, tape 69, Interview with Lt Gen Fahrettin Altay, July 1972.

54. Ibid.

55. Danışman (ed.), *Gallipoli 1915, Bloody Ridge (Lone Pine) Diary of Lt. Mehmed Fasih*, pp. 160–161.

56. Murat Çulcu, *Ikdam Gazetesi'nde Çanakkale Cephesi, 3 Kasım 1914–3 Şubat 1916 (Cilt 1 & 2)* (Istanbul: Denizler Kitabevi, 2004), pp. 266–267. This book contains the entire collection of official communiqués relating to the Gallipoli campaign from 3 November 1914 through 3 February 1916.

57. Oral, *Gallipoli Through Turkish Eyes 1915*, p. 201.

58. Ibid. See photograph of the delegation on p. 203.

Select Bibliography

Archival sources

Ankara: Askeri Tarıhı ve Stratejik Etut Başkanlığı (ATASE) – Turkish General
  Staff
    TGS Archives – archives
    TGS Archives – unpublished staff studies
Ankara: Askeri Tarıhı ve Stratejik Etut Başkanlığı Kutuphane (ATASE Library)
    TGS Library Archives – unpublished staff studies
Leeds: Brotherton Library, Liddle Collection (LC)
    Gall 216 - Gallipoli Interviews
    TU 01 – Turkish Interviews
Kew: United Kingdom National Archives (TNA)
Washington, D.C.: National Archives and Records Administration (NARA)
    RG 120, Boxes 5828, 5836 – GHQ, AEF
    RG 353 – US State Department, Internal Affairs, Turkey
    RG 1271, Files 6368, 844, 8759 – War College Division, General Staff
Washington, D.C.: National Defense University (NDU) Library
    Gallipoli Collection

Printed document collections

T.C. Genelkurmay Başkanlığı. *Askeri Tarih Belgeleri Dergisi*, Auğustos 1989, Yıl
  38, Sayı 88. Ankara: Genelkurmay Basımevi, 1989

Ottoman and German army training manuals

Hidemati Seferiye Nizamnamesi (Felddienst Ordnung (1908))
Piyade Talimnamesi (Exerzier-Reglement für die Infanterie (1906))
Takimin Muharebe Talimi and Bölügün Muharebe Talimi (Beifrage zur
  Taktischen Ausbildung unser Offiziere (1904))

Official histories based on official records

Akbay, Cemal. *Birinci Dünya Harbinde Türk Harbi, 1nci Cilt, Osmanli
  Imparatorlugu'nun Siyası ve Askeri Hazırlıkları ve Harbe Girisi*. ('Ottoman
  Empire Military Mobilisation and Entry into the War') Ankara: Genelkurmay
  Basımevi, 1991
Ari, Kemal. *Birinci Dünya Savası Kronolojisi*. ('First World War Chronology')
  Ankara: Genelkurmay Basımevi, 1997
Aspinall-Oglander, C.F. *History of the Great War, based on Official Documents:
  Military Operations Gallipoli, vol. 1 and 2*. London: HMSO, 1924–1930
Bean, C.E.W. *Official History of Australia in the War of 1914–1918: The Story of
  ANZAC, vol. 1–2*. Queensland: University of Queensland Press, 1981 (reprint
  of 1942 edition)
Belen, Fahri. *Birinci Cihan Harbinde Türk Harbi 1914, 1915 Yili Hareketleri, I–V Cilt*.
  ('The Turkish Front in the First World War, Years 1914–1915') Ankara:

258

Genelkurmay Basımevi, 1965–67 (five-volume series)

British General Staff. *Armies of the Balkan States, 1914–1916*. Nashville, TN: Battery Press, 1997 (reprint)

Intelligence Section, Cairo, British Army. *Handbook of the Turkish Army*, 8th Provisional edition, February 1916. Nashville, TN: Battery Press, n.d. (reprint)

Iskora, Emekli Orgeneral Muharrem Mazlum. *Harp Akademileri Tarihçesi, 1846–1965, Cilt I (2nci Baskı)* . ('History of the Staff College, 1846–1965') Ankara: Genelkurmay Basımevi, 1966

Thomazi, Albay A. *Canakkale Deniz Savası*. ('Gallipoli Naval Campaign') Ankara: Genelkurmay Basımevi, 1997

T.C. Genelkurmay Başkanlığı. *Birinci Dünya Harbi IXncü Cilt, Türk Hava Harekatı*. ('First World War, Turkish Air Operations') Ankara: Genelkurmay Basımevi, 1969

T.C. Genelkurmay Başkanlığı. *Birinci Dünya Harbinde Türk Harbi Vnci Cilt, Çanakkale Cephesi Harekati (Amfibi Harekat)*. ('First World War, Turkish War, Gallipoli Front Operations, Amphibious Operations') Ankara: Genelkurmay Basımevi, 1979

T.C. Genelkurmay Başkanlığı. *Birinci Dünya Harbinde Türk Harbi Vnci Cilt, Çanakkale Cephesi Harekati Inci Kitap (Haziran 1914–25 Nisan 1915)*. ('First World War, Turkish War, Gallipoli Front Operations, June 1914–April 1915') Ankara: Genelkurmay Basımevi, 1993

T.C. Genelkurmay Başkanlığı. *Birinci Dünya Harbinde Türk Harbi Vncü, Çanakkale Cephesi Harekati, 1nci, 2nci, 3ncü Kitapların Özetlenmiş Tarihi*. ('First World War, Turkish War, Gallipoli Front Operations, Condensed History of vol. 1–3') Ankara: Genelkurmay Basımevi, 2002

T.C. Genelkurmay Başkanlığı. *Türk Istiklal Harbi'ne Kalilan Tümen ve Daha Ust Kademelerdeki Komutanların Biyografileri*. ('Turkish War of Independence, Biographies of Divisional-level Commanders and Above') Ankara: Genelkurmay Basımevi, 1989

T.C. Genelkurmay Başkanlığı. *Türk Silahli Kuvvetleri Tarihi, IIIncü Cilt 5nci Kısım (1793–1908)1nci Kitap*. ('Turkish Armed Forces History, 1793–1908') Ankara: Genelkurmay Basımevi, 1978

T.C. Genelkurmay Başkanlığı. *Türk Silahli Kuvvetleri Tarihi, IIIncu Cilt 6ncü Kisim (1908–1920) 1nci Kitap*. ('Turkish Armed Forces History, 1908–1920') Ankara: Genelkurmay Basımevi, 1971

T.C. Genelkurmay Başkanlığı. *Türk Silahi Kuvvetleri Tarihi Osmanli Devri Birinci Dünya Harbinde Türk Harbi Vnci Cilt 3ncu Kitap, Çanakkale Cephesi Harekati (Haziran 1915–Ocak 1916)*. ('Turkish Armed Forces History, Ottoman State in the First World War, Turkish War, Gallipoli Front Operations, June 1915–January 1916') Ankara: Genelkurmay Basımevi, 1980

T.C. Genelkurmay Başkanlığı. *Türk Silahli Kuvvetleri Tarihi Osmanli Devri Birinci Dünya Harbi İdari Faaliyetler ve Lojistik, Xncu Cilt*. ('Turkish Armed Forces History, Ottoman State in the First World War, Administration and Logistics') Ankara: Genelkurmay Basımevi, 1985

T.C. Genelkurmay Başkanlığı. *Türk Silahli Kuvvetleri Tarihi, Balkan Harbi (1912–1913), II Cilt, Edirne Kalesi Etrafindaki Muharebeler*. ('Turkish Armed Forces History, Balkan War, Battles around the Edirne Fortress') Ankara: Genelkurmay Basımevi, 1993

T.C. Genelkurmay Başkanlığı, *Türk Silahli Kuvvetleri Tarihi, Balkan Harbi (1912–1913), IIIncü Cilt, 2nci Kisim, Garp Ordusu Vardar Ordusu, Yunan Cephesi Harekati*. ('Turkish Armed Forces History, Balkan War, Western Army,

Vardar Army and Greek Front Operations') Ankara: Genelkurmay Basımevi, 1993

T.C. Genelkurmay Başkanlığı. *Türk Silahli Kuvvetleri Tarihi, Balkan Harbi (1912–1913), II Cilt, 2nci Kısım, 1nci Kitap, Şark Ordusu, Ikinci Çatalca Muharebesi ve Şarkoy Çikmarması*. ('Turkish Armed Forces History, Balkan War, Battle of Second Catalca and the Sarkoy Amphibious Invasion') Ankara: Genelkurmay Basımevi, 1993

Türk Hava Kuvvetleri. *Türk Havacilik Tarihi 1914–1916 (Ikinci Kitap)*. ('Turkish Air Force History, 1914–1916') Eskisehir: Ucus Okkulları Basımevi, 1951

Memoirs

Adil, Selahattin. *Çanakkale Hatırları (1982)* in *Çanakkale Hatırları, 1. Cilt*. Istanbul: Arma Yayınları, 2001

Ahmad Izzet Pascha. *Denkwurdigkeiten Des Marschalls Izzet Pascha*. Leipzig: Verlag von K.F. Koehler, 1927

Aker, Şefik. *Çanakkale-Arıburnu Savaşları ve 27. Alay (1935)* in *Çanakkale Hatırları, 1. Cilt*. Istanbul: Arma Yayınları, 2001

Altay, Fahrettin. *Çanakkale Hatırları (n.d.)* in *Çanakkale Hatırları, 2. Cilt*. Istanbul: Arma Yayınları, 2002

Atatürk, Mustafa Kemal. *Anafartaları Hatırları (1955)* in *Çanakkale Hatırları, 1. Cilt*. Istanbul: Arma Yayınları, 2001

Conk, Cemil. *Çanakkale Hatırları ve Conkbayırı Savaşları (1955)* in *Çanakkale Hatırları, 2. Cilt*. Istanbul: Arma Yayınları, 2002

Danişman, H.B. (ed.). *Gallipoli 1915, Bloody Ridge (Lone Pine) Diary of Lt. Mehmed Fasih*. Istanbul: Denizler Kitabevi, 2003

Eşref, Ruşen. *Anafartalar Kumandanı Mustafa Kemal ile Mülakak (1930)* in *Çanakkale Hatırları, 3. Cilt*. Istanbul: Arma Yayınları, 2003

Gücüyener, Şükrğ Fuad. *Çanakkale'de Kumkale Muharebesi Çanakkale'de Intepe Topçuları (1932)* (Binbaşı Şevki Bey, Taşköprülü Aloş, Bursalı Mehmet Onbası, Çerkeşli Ömer, Aydınlı Ethem Çavuş) in *Çanakkale Hatırları, 3. Cilt*. Istanbul: Arma Yayınları, 2003

Güralp, Şerif. *Çanakkale Cephesinden Filistin'e*. Istanbul: Güncel Yayıncılık, 2003

Halis Bey (Ataksor), Binbaşı. *Çanakkale Raporu*. Istanbul: Arma Yayınları, n.d. (reprint of 1975 edition)

Ilgar, İhsan and Uğurlu, Nurer (eds). *Esat Paşa'nın Çanakkale Savaşı Hatırları*. Istanbul: Örgün Yayınevi, 2003 (reprint of 1975 edition)

İncescu, Sokrat. *Birinci Dünya Savaşinda, Çanakkale-Arıburnu Hatırlarım* in *Çanakkale Hatırları, 1. Cilt*. Istanbul: Arma Yayınları, 2001

Kannengiesser, Hans. *The Campaign in Gallipoli*. London: Hutchinson & Co., n.d.

Kemalyeri, Mucip. *Çanakkale Ruhu Nasıl Doğu? (1972)* in *Çanakkale Hatırları, 3.Cilt*. Istanbul: Arma Yayınları, 2003

Liman von Sanders, General of Cavalry. *Five Years in Turkey*. London: Bailliere, Tindall & Cox, 1928

Mühlmann, Carl. *Der Kampf um die Dardanellen 1915*. Berlin: Drud und Berlag von Gerhard Stalling, 1927

Münim, Mustafa. *Cepheden Cepheye, Çanakkale ve Kanal Seferi Hatırları*. Istanbul: Arma Yayınları, 1998 (reprint of 1940 edition)

Sabri, Mahmut. *Seddülbahir Muharebeleri ve 26. Alay 3. Tabur Harekatı (1933)* in *Çanakkale Hatırları, 3. Cilt*. Istanbul: Arma Yayınları, 2003

Şakir, Süleyman. *Cepheden Hatırlar, Altıncı Fırka Çanakkale Harbi'nde.* Ankara: Vadi Yayınları, 2006

Sunata, İsmail Hakkı. *Gelibolu'dan Kafkaslara, Birinci Dünya Şavası Anılarım.* Istanbul: Kultur Yayınlari, 2003

Tunççapa, M. Şakir. *Çanakkale Muharebeleri Hatırlarım (1958)* in *Çanakkale Hatırları, 3. Cilt.* Istanbul: Arma Yayınları, 2003

Secondary works

Abadan, Yavuz. *Mustafa Kemal ve Ceteçilik.* Istanbul: Varlık Kitabevi, 1972

Atatürk, Mustafa Kemal. *Zabit ve Kumandan ile Hasbihal.* Ankara: Türk Tarih Kurumu Basımevi, 1956

Bean, C.E.W. *Gallipoli Mission.* Canberra: Australian War Memorial, 1952

Bond, Brian (ed.). *The First World War and British Military History.* Oxford: Clarendon Press, 1991

Carver, Field Marshal Lord. *The Turkish Front 1914–1918, The Campaigns at Gallipoli, in Mesopotamia and in Palestine.* London: Sidgwick & Jackson, 2003

Cassar, George H. *Kitchener's War, British Strategy from 1914 to 1916.* Washington, D.C.: Brassey's Inc., 2004

Cebesoy, Ali Fuat. *Sınıf Arkadaşım Atatürk.* Istanbul: Kanaat, 1996

Cecil, Hugh and Peter Liddle (eds). *Facing Armageddon, The First World War Experienced.* London: Leo Cooper, 1996

Chaussaud, Peter and Peter Doyle. *Grasping Gallipoli: Terrain, Maps and the Failure at the Dardanelles 1915.* Staplehurst: Spellmount, 2005

Cohen, Eliot A. and John Gooch. *Military Misfortunes, The Anatomy of Failure in War.* New York: The Free Press, 1990

Churchill, Winston S. *The World Crisis.* New York: Charles Scribner's Sons, 1931

Corbett, Sir Julian S. *History of the Great War Based On Official Documents, Naval Operations, vol. 2.* London: Longmans, Green and Co., 1921

Cron, Herman. *The Imperial German Army, 1914–1918: Organisation, Structure, Orders-of-Battle.* Solihull: Helion and Company Ltd, 2002

Çulcu, Murat. *Ikdam, Gazetesi'nde Çanakkale Cephesi, 3 Kasım 1914–3 Şubat 1916 (Cilt 1 & 2).* Istanbul: Denizler Kitabevi, 2004

Danışman, H.B. *Gallipoli 1915, Day One Plus . . . 27th Ottoman Inf. Regt. Vs. ANZACS.* Istanbul: Denizler Kitabevi, 2007

Erickson, Edward J. *Ordered To Die, A History of the Ottoman Army in the First World War.* Westport, CT: Greenwood Press, 2000

Erickson, Edward J. *Defeat in Detail, The Ottoman Army in the Balkans 1912–1913.* Westport, CT: Praeger, 2003

Erickson, Edward J. *Ottoman Army Effectiveness in WW1: A Comparative Study* (London: Routledge, 2007)

Falls, Cyril. *The Great War.* New York, NY: G.P. Putnam's Sons, 1959

Falls, Cyril. *Armageddon: 1918.* Philadelphia, PA: J.B. Lippincott Company, 1964

Ferguson, Niall. *The Pity of War.* New York, NY: Basic Books, 1999

Fewster, Kevin, Vecihi Başarın and Hatice Başarın. *Gallipoli, The Turkish Story.* Crows Nest, Australia: Allen and Unwin, 1985

Fosten, D.S.V. and R.J. Marrion. *The British Army 1914–18.* London: Osprey Publishing Ltd, 1978

Gilbert, Martin. *Winston S. Churchill, Volume V, The Prophet of Truth, 1922–1939.* Boston, MA: Houghton Mifflin Company, 1977

Gillon, Captain Stair. *The Story of the 29th Division, A Record of Gallant Deeds.* London: Thomas Nelson and Sons Ltd, 1925

Godwin-Austin, A.R. *The Staff and the Staff College*. London: Constable and Company Ltd, 1927

Göncü, Gürsel and Şahin Aldoğan. *Çanakkale Muharebe Alanları Gezi Rehberi (Gallipoli Battlefield Guide)*. Istanbul: M.B. Yayınevi, 2004

Gooch, John. *The Plans of War, The General Staff and British Military Strategy c.1900–1916*. New York, NY: John Wiley & Sons, 1974

Görgülü, İsmet, *Türk Harp Tarıhı Derslerinde Adı Geçen Komutanlar*. Istanbul: Harp Akademileri Basımevi, 1983

Görgülü, İsmet. *On Yillik Harbin Kadrosu 1912–1913, Balkan–Birinci Dünya ve Istiklal Harbi*. Ankara: Türk Tarih Kurum Basımevi, 1993

Gudmundsson, Bruce I. *On Artillery*. Westport, CT: Praeger, 1993

Hall, Richard C. *The Balkan Wars 1912–1913, Prelude to the First World War*. London: Routledge, 2000

Haythornthwaite, Philip J. *Gallipoli 1915*. London: Osprey Press, 1991

Heller, Joseph. *British Policy Towards The Ottoman Empire*. London: Frank Cass and Company, 1983

Herrmann, David G. *The Arming of Europe and the Making of the First World War*. Princeton, NJ: Princeton University Press, 1996

Hickey, Michael. *Gallipoli*. London: John Murray, 1995

Hickey, Michael. *The First World War, The Mediterranean Front 1914–1923*. Oxford: Osprey Publishing, 2002

Holt, Tonie and Valmai. *Major and Mrs Holt's Battlefield Guide Gallipoli*. Barnsley: Leo Cooper, 2000

James, Robert Rhodes. *Gallipoli*, New York, NY: Macmillan, 1965

Johnstone, Tom. *Orange, Green and Khaki, The Story of the Irish Regiments in the Great War, 1914–18*. Dublin: Gill and Macmillan Ltd, 1992

Keegan, John. *The First World War*. New York, NY: Alfred A. Knopf, 1999

Kent, Marian (ed.). *The Great Powers and the End of the Ottoman Empire*. London: George Allen & Unwin, 1984

Langensiepen, Bernd and Ahmet Güleryuz. *The Ottoman Steam Navy*. Annapolis, MD: Naval Institute Press, 1995

Larcher, Commandant M. *La Guerre Turque Dans La Guerre Mondiale*. Paris: Chiron & Berger-Levrault, 1926

Latter, Major General J.C. *The History of the Lancashire Fusiliers 1914–1918*. Aldershot: Gale & Polden Ltd, 1949

Lee, John. *A Soldier's Life, General Sir Ian Hamilton 1853–1947*. London: Macmillan, 2000

Liddle, Peter. *Men of Gallipoli, The Dardanelles and Gallipoli Experience August 1914 to January 1916*. London: Allen Lane, 1976

Macleod, Jenny. *Gallipoli, Making History*. London: Frank Cass, 2004

Mango, Andrew. *Atatürk, The Biography of the Founder of Modern Turkey*. Woodstock, NY: Overlook Press, 1999

Marder, Arthur, J. *From The Dreadnought to Scapa Flow*, vol. 2. London: Oxford University Press, 1965

Middlebrook, Martin. *Your Country Needs You, From Six to Sixty-five Divisions*. Barnsley: Leo Cooper, 2000

Miller, Geoffrey. *Straits: British Policy Towards the Ottoman Empire and the Origins of the Dardanelles Campaign*. Hull: University of Hull Press, 1997

Millett, Allan R. and Williamson Murray (eds). *Military Effectiveness, Volume I: The First World War*. Boston, MA: Unwin Hyman, 1988

Moorehead, Alan. *Gallipoli*. New York, NY: Harper & Row, 1956

Moorhouse, Geoffrey. *Hell's Foundations, A Town, Its Myths & Gallipoli*. Sevenoaks: Hodder and Stoughton Ltd, 1992

Mortlock, Michael J. *The Landings at Suvla Bay, 1915*. Jefferson, NC: McFarland & Company Inc., 2007

Mühlmann, Carl. *Das Deutsch-Türkische Waffenbundnis im Weltkriege*. Leipzig: Verlag Koehler & Amelang, 1940

Newman, Steve. *Gallipoli Then and Now*. London: Battle of Britain International Ltd, 2000

Nicolle, David. *The Ottoman Army 1914–1918*. London: Reed International Books, 1996

Oral, Haluk. *Gallipoli Through Turkish Eyes 1915*, translated by Amy Spangler. Istanbul: Türkiye İş Bankası Kültür Yayınları, 2007

Örses, Tunca and Necmettin Özçelik. *I. Dünya Savaşı'nda, Türk Askeri Kıyafetleri*. Istanbul: Denizler Kitabevi, n.d.

Özdemir, Hikmet. *The Ottoman Army 1914–1918, Disease and Death on the Battlefield*. Salt Lake City: University of Utah Press, 2008

Pakenham, Thomas. *The Boer War*. New York, NY: Random House, 1979

Paşa, Esat. *Çanakkale Savaşı Hatırları*. Istanbul: Örgün Yayınevi, 2003

Prior, Robin. *Gallipoli, The End of the Myth*. New Haven, CT: Yale University Press, 2009

Robertson, John. *Anzac and Empire, The Tragedy & Glory of Gallipoli*. London: Leo Cooper, 1990

Samuels, Martin. *Command or Control? Command, Training and Tactics in the British and German Armies, 1888–1918*. London: Frank Cass, 1995

Schulte, Bernd F. *Vor dem Kriegsausbruch 1914, Deutschland, die Türkei und der Balkan*. Düsseldorf: Drost Verlag, 1980

Shaw, Stanford. *The Ottoman Empire in World War I, Volumes 1 and 2*. Ankara: Türk Tarih Kurumu, 2007

Shaw, Stanford J. and Ezel Kural Shaw. *History of the Ottoman Empire, Volume 2: Reform, Revolution, and Republic: The Rise of Modern Turkey, 1808–1975*. Cambridge: Cambridge University Press, 1977

Sixsmith, E.K.G. *British Generalship in the Twentieth Century*. London: Arms and Armour Press, 1970

Steel, Nigel and Peter Hart. *Defeat at Gallipoli*. London: Macmillan, 1994

Stevenson, David. *Armaments and the Coming of War: Europe, 1904–1914*. Oxford: Clarendon Press, 1996

Strachan, Hew. *The First World War, Volume I, To Arms*. Oxford: Oxford University Press, 2001

Taylor, Phil and Pam Cupper. *Gallipoli A Battlefield Guide*. Kenthurst: Kangaroo Press, 1989

Toker, Feza and Tolga Örnek. *Çanakkale Savaşı Gerçeği, Gelibolu*. Istanbul: Ekip Film Yayınları, n.d.

Travers, Tim. *The Killing Ground*. London: Allen & Unwin, 1987

Travers, Tim, *Gallipoli 1915*. Charleston, SC: Tempus Publishing, 2001

Trumpener, Ulrich. *Germany and the Ottoman Empire*. Princeton, NJ: Princeton University Press, 1968

Tuncoku, Mete. *Çanakkale 1915 Buzdağının Altı*. Ankara: Türk Tarih Kurumu, 2007

Turfan, M. Naim. *Rise of the Young Turks*. London: I.B. Tauris & Co. Ltd, 2000

Van Creveld, Martin. *Command in War*. Cambridge: Harvard University Press, 1985

Wallach, Jehuda L. *Anatomie Einer Militärhilfe, Die preussisch-deutschen*

Militärmissionen in der Türkei 1835–1919. Düsseldorf: Droste Verlag, 1976
Weber, Frank G. *Eagles on the Crescent: Germany Austria, and the Diplomacy of the Turkish Alliance, 1914–1918*. Ithaca, NY: Cornell University Press, 1970
Woodward, David. *Armies of the World 1854–1914*. New York, NY: G.P. Putnam's Sons, 1978
Yalman, Ahmed Emin. *Turkey in the World War*. New Haven, CT: Yale University Press, 1930
Yilmaz, Veli. *Birinci Dünya Harbinde Türk-Alman Ittifaki ve Askeri Yardımları*. Istanbul: Gem Offset, 1993

Articles and chapters

Cain, Frank. 'A Colonial Army in Ottoman Fields: Australia's Involvement in the Gallipoli Debacle' in Sheffy, Yigal and Saul Shai, *The First World War: Middle Eastern Perspectives*. Tel Aviv: Tel Aviv University, 2000
Doyle, Peter and Matthew R. Bennett. 'Military Geography: the influence of terrain in the outcome of the Gallipoli Campaign 1915', *The Geographical Journal* 165 (1), (March 1999): 12–36
Erickson, Edward J. 'One More Push: Forcing the Dardanelles in March 1915', *The Journal of Strategic Studies*, 24 (3) (September 2001): 158–176
Erickson, Edward J. 'Strength Against Weakness: Ottoman Military Effectiveness at Gallipoli, 1915', *The Journal of Military History*, 65 (October 2001): 981–1012
Erickson, Edward J. 'The Turkish Official Military Histories of the First World War, A Bibliographic Essay', *Middle Eastern Studies*, 39 (3) (July 2003): 190–198
Erickson, Edward J. 'Ottoman Encirclement Operations, 1912–1922', *Middle Eastern Studies*, 40 (1) (January 2004): 45–64
Jones, David. 'Imperial Russia's Forces at War' in Millett, Allan R. and Williamson Murray (eds), *Military Effectiveness, Volume I: The First World War*. Boston, MA: Unwin Hyman, 1988
Travers, T.H.E. 'Command and Leadership Styles in the British Army: The 1915 Gallipoli Model', *Journal of Contemporary History*, 29 (July 1994): 403–442
Travers, Timothy H.E. 'When Technology and Tactics Fail: Gallipoli 1915' in Chiabotti, Stephen D. (ed.), *Tooling for War, Military Transformation in the Industrial Age*. Chicago, IL: Imprint Publications, 1996
Travers, Tim. 'The Other Side of the Hill', *Military History Quarterly*, 12 (3) (Spring 2000): 2–20
Trumpener, Ulrich. 'Suez, Baku, Gallipoli: The Military Dimensions of the German-Ottoman Coalition, 1914–1918' in Kiraly, Bela K. and Nandor F. Dreisziger (eds), *East Central European Society in World War I*. New York, NY: Columbia University Press, 1985
Yanıkdağ, Yücel. 'Educating the Peasants: The Ottoman Army and Enlisted Men in Uniform', *Middle Eastern Studies*, 40 (6) (November 2004): 92–108
Yasamee, F.A.K. 'Abdülhamid II and the Ottoman Defence Problem', *Diplomacy & Statecraft*, 4 (1) (March 1993): 20–36
Yasamee, F.A.K. 'Some Military Problems faced by the Ottoman Empire at the beginning of the 20th Century', *KÖK Sosyal ve Stratejik Araştirmalar, Osmanlı Özel Sayısı*, 2000: 71–79
Zürcher, Erik-Jan. 'The Ottoman Conscription System In Theory And Practice, 1844–1918', *International Review of Social History*, 43 (3) (1988): 437–449

Index